A SORT OF CLOWNING

A SORT OF CLOWNING

(Life and Times, Volume II: 1940–59)

RICHARD HOGGART

Chatto & Windus
LONDON

Published in 1990 by
Chatto & Windus Ltd
20 Vauxhall Bridge Road
London SW1V 2SA

A CIP catalogue record for this book is
available from the British Library.

ISBN 0 7011 3607 3

Printed in Great Britain by
Mackays of Chatham, PLC
Chatham, Kent.

CONTENTS

Acknowledgments   viii

Preface   x

PART ONE: THE WAR YEARS

1   Oswestry to the *Otranto*   1940–2   3

2   North Africa and Pantelleria 1942–3   29

3   Naples   1943–6   48

PART TWO: WANDERING TEACHER

4   Redcar and Marske   1946–9   73

5   Hull: Settings and Settling In 1949–59   97

6   Teaching-and-Writing   The 1950s   122

7   Interlude – USA   1956–7   148

PART THREE: TAKING STOCK

8   'There's no Vocabulary': on Family Life   175

9   A Shape Proper to Itself?:
    On Writing a 'Life and Times'   204

Index   223

For Gwen and Roy Shaw

ACKNOWLEDGMENTS

For much help of many kinds I am deeply grateful to the following friends: Muriel Crane, Stephen Hearst, Graham Martin, John Miller, Michael Orrom, Bernard Schilling, Gwen Shaw and Roy Shaw.

My warm thanks also to Jeremy Lewis, Jenny Uglow, Jane Turner and the supporting services at Chatto & Windus.

As always, Catharine Carver has given unstintingly her uniquely gifted editing.

Once more also, I am glad to acknowledge my great debt to members of my family: my brother Tom, our children and, above all, my wife.

The author and publishers would like to thank the following for permission to include copyright material: Faber and Faber Ltd for quotations from *Collected Poems of W. H. Auden* and *The Dyer's Hand and Other Essays* by W. H. Auden, *The Elder Statesman* by T. S. Eliot and *High Windows* by Philip Larkin; Oxford University Press for a quotation from *The Complete Poems of Keith Douglas* edited by Desmond Graham (OUP 1978); Routledge and Kegan Paul Ltd for a passage from I. A. Richards; and the Society of Authors for a passage from G. B. Shaw.

PREFACE

A Sort of Clowning continues the story of my life and times which began with *A Local Habitation*. It is, though, self-contained in the sense that you need not have read the first volume to follow the second.

The way I am telling the story is unusual, and I thought at first that an introduction explaining what I am about might be useful. But who reads explanatory introductions? And the explanation I prepared grew to the length of a full chapter, became not so much an explanation as a discussion of autobiographical writing in Britain and an analysis of the difficulties and benefits of trying to do something different.

Another discursive or reflective chapter forced itself on me: on the nature of family life, especially as it strikes someone who had not known the usual kind of family life before.

So after several other notions these two chapters have been put at the end, in their own 'Taking Stock' part, after the slightly more chronological first two parts. The hope is that they will not only sum up but will throw a particular light on those earlier chapters.

RICHARD HOGGART

                    If the worst
Of flawless weather is our falling short,
It may be that through habit these do best,
Coming to water clumsily undressed
Yearly; teaching their children by a sort
Of clowning; helping the old, too, as they ought.

                    Philip Larkin, 'To the Sea'

PART ONE

❧

THE WAR YEARS

The soldier . . . of today is not a romantic animal, full of fancies as to a love-lady or a sovereign . . . but busied in charts, exact in sums . . . thinking, as the Duke of Wellington was said to do, *most* of the shoes of his soldiers . . .

W. Bagehot, *The English Constitution: Checks and Balances*

CHAPTER I

OSWESTRY TO THE OTRANTO
1940–2

Each day after an early tea-cum-supper, and after the officers had retired for their pre-dinner drink with the commandant, the thirty or so new recruits in each hut at the Initial Training Camp in Oswestry were required to sit on the ends of their beds, blanco'ing webbing and polishing boots – whilst being read to.

Our reader was an old sweat just promoted to lance-bombardier. He was in his late twenties and so still young enough for combat service. Probably his superiors had decided he wasn't, even after all his service, bright enough for the real thing.

So there he was, reading by order from the history of the regiment. This had to mean the history of the Royal Artillery as a whole, since we had not yet been assigned to particular kinds of gunner unit. The brush had to be very broad and the story amorphous. It was as though a very minor clerk had been ordered to read each night on the history of municipal housing to the drafted tenants of a bunch of anonymous estates. Probably the print had to be large too, since the lance-bombardier was barely literate.

The ceremony seemed to recall something similar. After two days the echo was recognisable. This was a bizarre simulacrum of a situation one had met in Victorian domestic novels: the nursemaid reading each night to the children before they settle for bed, whilst the adults dress for dinner. Oswestry was like that: anachronistic but amiable, all in all.

I

I arrived there in early autumn 1940 after scrambling through an

M A thesis at Leeds University, labouring for a few weeks on the building of blast walls and spending a last few days of freedom at Stalybridge near Manchester, the home of my girl-friend Mary. We felt bad enough as the train for the Welsh Marches moved away. But we could have no conception that it would be almost six years before the khaki came off.

The indeterminate, bucolic, slow-moving Shropshire–Welsh market town was just realising that the phoney war was over; Dunkirk and the Battle of Britain had galvanised similar camps and towns all over the country. The corridorless trains regularly disgorged young men, most of us nervous, to do basic square-bashing, arms drill (the Naming of Parts and the rest), personal-hygiene training, some startling antics with fixed bayonets and grenade lobbing. As we arrived, to be greeted with an edible hot meal before being kitted-out – for Oswestry, though full of featureless huts round a huge parade ground, did not make you feel agoraphobic and anonymous, and decent food always reduces that risk – we took over the barracks and beds of others who, now ready to be taught their precise specialisms, had left that morning for camps devoted to twenty-five-pounder field guns, light ack-ack or heavy ack-ack, or other branches of the artillery. But at that point heavy ack-ack had most of the attention, since German raids were regular and increasing.

People like me had read so much, heard so much on the radio, seen so much in the cinema about the rituals of the army, many of them comical, from the strangulated-magpie shrieks of sergeant-majors on parade to the elaborate other ranks/non-commissioned officers/commissioned officers dance of rules and manners, that to experience them at last in real life seemed at first not truly real and slightly comic, even though menacing. These people could, after all, do nasty things to you, such as stopping your leave.

We knew about militarism as a powerful part of British culture, a long-continuing, historic part; but at bottom it remained an aspect of the country we had not known or wanted to know or ever expected to know except in emergencies such as the present – about which we had thought little before early 1939 anyway. We had, even before we put on the khaki, encased ourselves in our own protective cover, an ambiguous mixture of responses, slightly detached and snide, nervous but in parts verging on the rebellious.

The men in the group of barrack-huts which housed our platoon came from all over the country; their social backgrounds were as diverse as could be, as were their levels of ability. There may have been a tendency for the recruiting boards not to put those judged really dim into the artillery, where they might have had to read figures on dials accurately; but on the whole we were a widely-based demographic and cultural sample. There were working-class lads from all over Britain who had left school at fourteen; some had landed in and stayed in dead-end jobs, others had been apprenticed to a craft and been now pulled away just as they knew their trades; there were ranges of middle-class boys of the sort who used to go, and whose grandchildren now go again, to fee-paying day-schools; there were public-school boys (one who became a friend had been to that artistic public school, Bedales); and there was a small group of graduates. We became the hut scribes and decipherers of documents.

One saw again, and from a new angle, how a wealthy and in many respects civilised country did shamefully and smugly little for most of its people. Pulling up and away from Hunslet, that working-class swathe of south Leeds, and Jack Lane elementary school, had shown me something of the stringent selective processes by which only the very gifted among the poor were given much educational opportunity. That was a vertical, single city, vision. Oswestry showed that this process was repeated horizontally right across the country, that there was a huge layer spread over all the counties who, whatever their differences in accents and geographical settings, were brothers of the Hunslet boys because they all shared this lack of opportunity. Above them, and better treated, was the thinner horizontal layer of the various ranks of the middling-classes, and above again the wafer-thin and privileged ranks of the upper group. A basic training camp was a microcosm of British society in both its decencies and its gross imperfections; and its meaning was not lost, emotionally, even on many of those who would have been unable to identify that meaning analytically. The Services reinforced, repeated, set in their own amber, the class-determined, three-tiered definition of British life. There has been much discussion of the levelling nature of war service. That is a flattering unction; the levelling is temporary and marginal (though by 1945 we had, mistakenly, begun to hope and almost believe not).

To describe the Services without recognising their class nature would be like describing a vehicle without reference to its main frame.

Within those civilian social groupings there was a temporary, army-defined group: the PO's, or potential officers. Our basic training was no different from that of the others, but we were put together in part of one of the huts and tended to sit together at meals. Our cards were, literally, marked and an instructor was likely to say by way of admonishment: 'We don't expect that from a PO.' (The army's use of the first person plural is almost regal.) This defined group had to be socially mixed, if the army was to get enough junior officers quickly. There were public-school boys who had been in their schools' Cadet Corps, and that ensured immediate PO status; there were the few graduates and some small-town professionals in their early years on the ladders – solicitors' clerks, insurance assessors, teachers, people with a few HSC's (A Levels) or Teacher's Certificates. The most insecure were those who had left the lower rungs of very particular ladders – banking, estate agencies, salesmen in some narrow specialisms – and had at first only a shaky confidence in their own general adaptability.

In some respects we felt like a coherent group, but the feeling ran shallow. The ex-Cadet Corps public-school boys had their own mores, interests, styles of recreation and ways of speaking; and, usually, money from home to allow them to practise those habits. The group within a group to which I belonged did include the Bedales youth and a single non-PO; the rest were PO's with some intellectual and artistic interests, devoted to spotting and tagging any higher military lunacy, and managing on their army pay, which meant spending most spare time in the camp canteen not in the local bars.

Beds were soon exchanged so that the main groups were together. At the far end from the door, and that gave a little time to hide gambling or secret drinking, was the rougher and mainly urban group: getting drunk too often, vomiting on the floor now and again, smoking furtively after lights out, fiddling booze or rations with bent storekeepers, boasting endlessly about 'bints' they had had or proposed to have, refusing to get under the shower more often than every week or two, now and again brawling with similar groups from other huts or within themselves.

It is surprising, given all these differences, that the atmosphere of the platoon was in general equable and live-as-let-live. Partly but not altogether that was the prisoners' or pressed men's sense of sticking together, against the decisions of the power which overarched us and defined so minutely our days. We ganged up to scorn the symbolic indicators of that status, and not only the more obvious ones such as the occasional bullying sergeant. Our own platoon's first indicator was the regular army lance-corporal assigned to our hut, whose job was rather like that of the prefect in charge of a school dormitory. He was not bad-tempered, but by long habit kept his nose clean, especially with duty officers on their rounds of inspection, even if that meant making a sacrifice of some fairly harmless recruit. He could tell instantly when an officer was in a bad mood or simply out to teach us a lesson, justly or not. One heavily-moustached, red-faced, regular lieutenant, also clearly marked-down as not-advanceable, practised that weak routine. On the day we were due to be let out of camp for the first time since we had arrived, and were desperate to see our waiting girl-friends again, he kept us in on the grounds that one of our number had not blanco'ed a belt properly. It was a trick, like hitting a puppy early on, just to show it who's master. Any one of us would gladly have offered to cosh him if it could have been a fair fight. Of all the other training NCOs and officers only one remains in the memory, a tall, fresh-faced sergeant of exceptional kindness; he bullied no one, yet no one thought him soft.

We had all expected the food to be awful but it was, as our first meal had indicated, good. Tasty, that is, as can be achieved by some people where others would make the same army issue into inedible dishes; and many did. After PT the hot rissoles for breakfast, with slabs of bread and butter and mugs of tea, were as good as most breakfasts I and most of us had regularly known.

We were finally let out, in our prickly rough khaki and with short-back-and-sides, after we had learned to 'walk like soldiers'. By that time we had shaken down to the routines and made our first friendships. I found a kind elderly lady living alone in a little terrace house, who was glad to let a room to Mary, for whom the school half-term break coincided with our first release. Our girl-friends did their best not to appear too startled by the way we looked; and at least we were fitter than we had probably ever been. Mary and I went on walks in the lanes not far outside the town; the countryside of the Marches rolled as gently as drawings in a child's book; the horizons were near, and the air fresher than any I had lived in before.

We left Oswestry in early 1941, trained to its simple level, like colts taught to perform the first few elementary but essential movements before the more complex training was added. 'You won't learn much at that first place,' my professor at Leeds, Bonamy Dobrée, had said, in his more patrician, First World War regular officer's manner. 'Just how to obey orders. That's all the private soldier needs.' We had been given a little more than that, but not much.

I was assigned to one of the heavy ack-ack officer cadet training units; not their regular, peacetime centre, but a new one at Llandrindod Wells, a good distance south and just inside Wales. The recruitment board, sitting near the University to pick up fresh graduates, had had no doubts about where I should serve. It should be the artillery, where officers had to have 'more brains than the infantry'. That became anti-aircraft artillery and then heavy ack-ack – huge 3.7 guns deployed in fours in an arc of about 120 degrees, with the command post at the centre of their part-circle.

I went back to Llandrindod almost thirty years later to see if the place still had the haunting, enclosed atmosphere we knew – though no doubt the memory had by then been well tailored by time – like a faded set from an Edwardian operetta in a provincial theatre, a tatty, once elegant emptiness. That feeling had almost but not quite gone, in spite of the usual cluster of chain-stores.

It was a small town tucked in the hills, devoted before the war to caring for the elderly well-to-do (clever children would simply have had to get out of that geriatric spa), and now preoccupied with servicing the officers' training camp. There were some new, *ad hoc* enterprises, such as outfitters for officers and gentlemen. The big hotels were all requisitioned. That for our troop was in the Gwalia which had a triangular corner-site in the centre of town gazing on a bit of a square, usually damp and chilly during our time there. In the evening the square nevertheless looked imitation Italianate, as though it were hesitantly expecting the chorus of the Carl Rosa Company to burst into it in full voice. The Gwalia had a large central lobby with the upper rooms opening onto a landing which ran in an oval all round the interior and looked over railings onto the lobby. Again, one could imagine that chorus strung round there, backing-up the principals in their full-throated quartet on the ground floor.

The group was, as at Oswestry, drawn from all over Britain, but this particular group brought out three main odd thoughts: that sense of a much larger than previously known, but not very varied, Britain which Oswestry had first evoked; the sense of one's particular generation moving in line abreast to a limited set of destinations; and, yet once again, the intuition that that group from a larger Britain had been selected by much the same old rules, that the tramlines were still there, the opening-out only partial.

Socially, our central or most common point of origin was lower-middle- to slightly middle-class with a very few from the upper middle-class at one end and a very few from the cleverer among the respectable working-class at the other; there were graduates and among them a few who had come up entirely by scholarships from poor homes, still academic rarities. The social spread was not great, nor the spread of brains. The average level of intelligence was respectable but not impressive; if it had not been at least that, then the weeding-out machinery would have been incompetent even for those days.

On the other hand, the general level of intellectual interest, interest in ideas or in the arts, was too low to have shown on any scale. Not more than one in twenty or thirty had, or had been taught to think it would be worthwhile to have, those sorts of interest. People of that minority discovered each other by the usual half-conscious, oblique processes: catching an ironic grin across the lecture hut in response to one of the more silly muscular injunctions by the officer introducing us to the elements of 'the killer-instinct', seeing a copy of *Penguin New Writing* sticking out of a back trouser-pocket, or overhearing a remark about a film or play due to appear in town. This wasn't separatist snobbery. I do not recall any airs of cultural or intellectual superiority in the members of that group, or very few.

The range of evening recreations was much like Oswestry's, but with a slightly middle-class overlay. We soon had our own selective maps superimposed on the tiny town and used them almost instinctively. Sitting in a favourite tea-shop one Sunday morning, Mary and I heard a booming-bittern voice and there was Sybil Thorndike with her husband, Lewis Casson. They were in town to play to the troops under the auspices of CEMA (the Council for the Encouragement of Music and the Arts – out of which wartime creation there eventually emerged the Arts Council). Whether they were performing *Saint Joan*, which the gallant lady had been playing since 1924 and which I had seen in Leeds in the mid-Thirties, I am not sure; it may have been *Macbeth*. The fluting voice asking for a scone as though for the documents of accession was unmistakable. The two had the air of faces and presences which expect to be looked at, which are always on public duty, for whom there is no easily apparent separation between the public and the private personalities.

Naturally, our lot exchanged books; in particular, Penguins, Penguin Specials, Pelicans and *Penguin New Writing*. Our girl-friends or families made sure we missed nothing of importance so long as it could be afforded. I still have the original paperback editions of *Four Quartets*, sent roughly as they appeared. 'East Coker' is inscribed 'Oswestry, Nov. 1940, Love from Mollie', so that was sent by a university friend of Mary's; 'Burnt Norton' has 'Newport, Sept, 1941' (a staging post on the way to our regiment's 'going mobile'); the front of 'The Dry Salvages' says 'Newport, Autumn, 1941'; and that of 'Little Gidding' reads 'Tunisia, Feb. 1943', which was just before the breakthrough on that front.

Best of all the memories from Llandrindod, like those from Oswestry, are of the times when Mary was able to get there for a day or two and we walked up and over the hills and valleys. The main mountains had not begun, so the landscape was hilly but not rough, and the rivers had a good broad sweep and flow to them. The farmers and land-girls went about their steady work but there was hardly any civilian traffic; instead, an embalmed quiet broken only by an occasional farm waggon or deliverer's van or a military lorry on the slightly more important roads, and hardly anything on the minor. If we could afford it we would stop at Rhayader where a local pub could still produce, for a couple of bob, gammon, egg and chips at most times of the day. With Mary teaching and me getting army pay – little but not much called upon – we were better off than we had ever been at university.

The training at Llandrindod was better than at Oswestry, but that was a small claim. The technical side was at the least competent; by the end we knew roughly how to look after a troop of guns and their ancillary gear. And their men? Not really. We had lectures on a subject known as 'man management', an alarming title which the War Office had picked up from I know not where – horse training? The circus? Early time-and-motion studies? Bonamy Dobrée would have been likely to describe its essence as 'always making sure the men are all right before you look after yourself'. Not crisp, but human.

We had a few lectures on how to give lectures – short lectures or 'lecturettes' – so that we could from time to time advise the men on new drills, the battle situation, how to avoid malaria and VD. At the end of that tiny course we each had to deliver a lecturette to the prescribed time and in the prescribed fashion; that is, according to rules which sounded as though they had been provided by a second-rate correspondence college, probably as part of a course for after-dinner speakers. It was essential, we were told, always to begin with a joke. That breaks the ice, puts the men at their ease. Most such jokes, dragged from the depths of memory and running from old-style *Punch* wit through schoolboy scatology to the fairly but guardedly obscene, were quite irrelevant to the speakers' subjects.

One cadet in a room near mine was the youngest of us all, innocent and very nervous. For his lecturette he had been assigned the subject 'You are in charge of the command post by day. Dive bombers head straight for you. What do you do?' The answer is simple. Since your command post instruments, built for tracking bombers high up in the sky and moving steadily towards their targets rather than for coping with dive-bombers, are now useless, you hand over to the sergeant in charge of each individual gun, with the loud command 'Gun control'; the sergeants then try to use them as peashooters aimed directly at the Stukas. You stay where you are, on the temporarily useless command post, though you may bend down so that only your tin-hatted head now shows above the few sandbags; you resume control as soon as each wave of dive-bombers has passed. For months, even years, afterwards most of us hoped it would be our good fortune one day to shout 'Gun control', clearly the pinnacle of the otherwise rather dull life of a heavy ack-ack officer.

In North Africa, that happened only once in our troop, and the junior lieutenant with me at the command post cracked and ran. We managed to spirit him away a few days later as a sick man and so avoided a court martial. The rest of us stayed at the instruments, as the teams did on other days, and followed the book of rules with a sense of detachment to which a word such as 'courage' would have seemed then, and seems now, quite inapplicable; just as the word 'cowardice' to describe the young lieutenant's action would have been an irrelevant and misleading label.

It was a macabre echo of the nervous cadet's worries about his lecturette at Llandrindod. He came to me for advice on how to plan the talk and, most desperately, was looking for an opening joke. I suggested he aim for one at least relevant to his theme but patently ironic, the theme itself being not comic. I failed to warn him that since irony was not a tone much recognised or used by army instructors, even if they were commissioned officers as ours was, he would have to leave his hearers in no doubt both that he was being ironic and that his basic seriousness was unimpaired. He began, on my prompting: 'Seeing dive-bombers coming straight at us, I would yell "Gun control", dive straight into the nearest slit-trench and from there calmly . . .' A feeble joke but no more feeble than most that had been offered, and not easily mistakable for a serious proposal. The instructor might have had a fundamental conviction that the subject was, like the monarchy or the Church, simply not the sort about which jokes should ever be made. And the nervous young man delivered his bit of irony in a voice of such flat and despairing solemnity that those of his colleagues not in the know did momentarily wonder if he was serious; the instructor was convinced, and delivered a rebuke so massive that it might have led to his failing the course as a whole. But Llandrindod Wells was, though often insensitive, rarely punitive; the nineteen-year-old got through. That misfired joke was acted out, in reality, two years later and a thousand miles away.

The rules of 'man management' seemed to have been drawn from a similar correspondence course to those on the giving of talks. They were almost useless because they were abstract, culturally rootless, inhuman or – more accurately – non-human, amateurishly and mildly Pavlovian, not connected to any social or geographic sense of the sorts of men we would have charge of. Such rules could not make much impact on most of the units we eventually joined or on any similar group; they wholly ignored class differences and all the indicators of those differences which divide – accent, poise, forms of speech, gestures – so only those officers-to-be who were wholly encased in the ways and rules of a fairly privileged level of class could accept them at face value. They were too obviously simple, at a disconnectedly low level, for the more intelligent to take seriously.

When you started working within a troop, and most of us stayed with the one troop almost throughout our service, you soon saw what kinds of officer most affected the men and in what ways. A charmer, hail-fellow-well-met, one of the boys, was always liked so long as he wasn't an out-and-out skiver or a social snob; cheerful-ness made up for a lot. The men's attitude here was like that of some Leeds brickies with whom I had built hospital blast-shelters during the Phoney War towards the boss's lazy, philandering but cheerful son. Yet the Other Ranks were shrewd enough, since so much in the comfort and due regulation of their lives now depended on these young men above them, to respect more an officer who was conscientious and hard-working, who could be told about prob-lems at home and relied on to give thoughtful advice. We had a solicitor from a small town who filled that role best of all of us. He also had a courageous but unflamboyant sense of responsibility when he made difficult decisions.

At one point, in Italy, I served for a short spell as an Intelligence officer at brigade HQ, and had yet another solicitor as my immediate superior. A soldier had committed murder and fled. The Military Police found him weeks later, running a brothel very efficiently. He was sentenced to death. The rules still required that an officer attend the execution, ready with his pistol to ensure, if need be, that the man was quite dead. That officer had to come from brigade HQ, which arranged the execution; and the junior Intelligence officer was the usual choice. The thought was horrible, but I expect I would have gone through with it. Then the gentle solicitor came to me and said it seemed 'rather hard' that, because of the accident of my being seconded for a few weeks to Brigade HQ at that time, I should have to assume such a duty; he would do it himself.

Those were two kinds of officers who, in very different ways, were most liked or admired or both by the men. Others, not particularly hail-fellow-well-met nor conspicuously brave nor markedly decent, were tolerated because, though it was obvious that they were unusually fortunate in being on the more comfortable side of the fence, they were not swine. And there were the swine: lazy, at least marginally unscrupulous, exploiters of their excessive temporary powers, ready to push anyone else over the edge to save their own skins. There were not many of those; they could occur at all levels, but flourished best above the level where there had to be daily contact with the men in a body – starting at battery HQ level.

The responses by the gunners cut across class-based reactions. Observing them, one could see the outline of a possible course on relationships in the army which had a texture, a truth to the often contradictory grain of English life, which the course we had been given almost entirely lacked. The most striking indication of the inadequacy of that course was that it found time, when so much else was missing, to advise us on how to 'handle' our batmen or 'body-servants'.

Once in our regiments, we soon knew, behind the faces we kept up, that many a sergeant was more valuable at his work than we were at ours; some could easily have done our work but did not have even Higher School Certificate, and their accents weren't right. There was a quiet gunner, a private, who had run his own shop in East Anglia and was clearly more intelligent, and more competent at paperwork, than most of the officers – so he was made a corporal, as the troop clerk, and did a great deal of necessary work which a second-lieutenant would have thought slightly beneath him. He had a wry, taking-it-all-in smile when young officers asked him to assume duties which were their responsibility but which fazed them – while at the same time they patronised him. As our landing-craft was dive-bombed on the approach to the Mediterranean island of Pantelleria he stayed at the Bofors light ack-ack gun, firing throughout. 'Officer material' – who would never be asked to become an officer and would almost certainly have refused if asked, being happier without all the social concomitants of that role.

Towards the end of the Llandrindod course we were given practical hints on how to comport ourselves as officers, how to acknowledge a salute from lower ranks and such considerations;

and were enjoined to be fair with the men without stepping over the line into over-friendliness and so destroying the necessary distance between us. But fairness was insisted upon: in such matters the course was, though intellectually and imaginatively feeble, not brutal or harsh in the injunctions it offered; there was a humaneness behind it, but a humaneness not sufficiently self-aware to be able to express itself in the complex ways the situations we would later confront warranted.

All this led to the grand passing-out parade at which a visiting general would take the salute and declare almost every one of us, for few failed, commissioned officers of His Majesty. In the last couple of weeks there was much visiting of those 'outfitters to officers and gentlemen' who had set up their stalls in town. There was a pecking-order there too. Those who did not have to worry about keeping within their uniform allowance, probably because their families would pay extra, went to a rather special one; a few others sought out the cheapest, and the majority went to a reliable middle-ranking firm. Its name was, I think, Alkit and it had, until recently, a shop on Cambridge Circus in London, from which generations destined for India and other points east and south had no doubt been kitted-out. It offered a respectable barathea suit and a range of accoutrements, from the little stick or cane to less symbolic objects such as a canvas washbasin on a collapsible wooden stand which had obviously been designed, many decades before, for colonial service. One could imagine generations of Indian Army officers taking a good wash and then turning to their body-servants for the outstretched towels. The folding canvas toilet-bag was most useful and service-able, though.

Before the great day we had a fullscale rehearsal on the parade ground in front of the camp commandant, a shadowy figure of whom we had had until then scarcely a sight. I was on the wing nearside to the saluting stand. Just after we had gone past the base on which he was standing-in for the general, the colonel stopped the parade and said, imperiously but also in wonder and regret, as he pointed towards someone in our troop: 'That man is congenitally incapable of walking in step. Lose him in the middle somewhere.' It was indeed I, and I had a moment of mild embarrassment. My friends thought it rather a fitting judgment both actually and symbolically and I, as we finally marched off, decided I couldn't object to it.

Before our first posting, we were all given a few days leave which Mary and I spent together, though I cannot now remember whether first at her parents' home in Stalybridge or at Leeds. We certainly visited both places and I was admired in my barathea – the first officer in our two extended families and probably the only one, or one of very few, native to the streets of Hunslet, though I expect Hunslet had a good share of NCOs. It had been odd to sit on a Leeds tram in a Cockburn High School cap; it was odder to do so in an officer's outfit . . . feeling like a budgie on display after it had successfully mounted the little ladders in its cage.

We saw my sister Molly and brother Tom, of course. Molly had been working in a mill in Pudsey but was now in the ATS. Tom had had a rum time. When the war broke out, he had a job in the offices of a Sheffield steelworks, as a stock clerk, and was doing very well. He was a member of the Peace Pledge Union; I suppose hardly anyone around him, including those in the large family at Petre Street in Sheffield (the home of the aunt and uncle who had taken him in when we three were orphaned round about 1926), knew what that meant or took it seriously. His application to be registered as a conscientious objector failed. This must have been, at the earliest, in late 1940 because I gave evidence on his behalf, in uniform, hoping that might help. It didn't; they used the 'brave' brother to denigrate the 'cowardly'. His application being refused, he expected an early call-up. But a bomber raid on Manchester destroyed his papers for quite a long time, so he had to find work. Since only shifty firms would employ a CO, there began a sequence of hard and sometimes hilarious spells with dubious Sheffield outfits of various kinds; makers of cheap and nasty biscuits, for example.

Tom had told the tribunal that he was willing to be a front-line stretcher-bearer, a more hazardous occupation than a heavy ack-ack officer's and as hazardous as a foot soldier's at the front, but they were unmoved. When his papers finally came to light, however, Tom was posted to the Army Medical Corps, took part in the Normandy landings, was a front-line stretcher-bearer, was made a sergeant but refused officer-training, and saw much more danger than I saw in my longer service.

2

When I joined it in early 1941, the 58th HAA (heavy anti-aircraft)
Regiment had its 3.7″ guns on fixed sites in Kent, but was soon to start
retraining for mobile duties abroad. It had had a distinguished record
during the Battle of Britain, won some decorations and was proud –
an unusual characteristic in HAA Regiments, which tended to be
workaday and slightly subfusc. The 58th's officers had even begun to
wear their hats slightly tilted, as though to suggest a raffish gallantry.
I reported to a battery at Green Street Green, near Orpington. It was
then, its natural quietness emphasised by the war, truly part of Kent
rather than of outer London.

The regiment had been a Kentish Territorial Army unit and
when I and a couple of other newly-commissioned officers arrived
some of its pre-war weekend officers remained, most upgraded by
now, without much regard to competence. New second-lieuten-
ants were being fed in as they left their training camps. So were
other ranks, though they tended to be from a quadrant running
from the east to the south of London; the regiment was sometimes
erroneously said to be largely composed of cockney gunners. In
the spring of 1941, many of the NCOs too were, like the officers,
still from the old Territorial Army days. But month by month new
people came in at all levels, so that the regiment was in a constant
state of shift and change. By the end of my first year there the
regiment had substantially lost its TA character and, as to officers
and NCOs, had been moulded into a geographically unidenti-
fiable unit – like many another as forces were built up for the first
real push forward since the retreat from Dunkirk. No one felt it
necessary to introduce us to 'the history of the regiment'. Kent
weekend fun-and-games had yielded by a powerful demographic
and geographic kneading process to a regiment of conscripts who
were not bloody-minded but also were not, most of them, disposed to adopt local unit patriotisms either. Yet virtually none of
us had any doubt that the war had to be fought. We took it as
axiomatic that Hitler's was an evil regime and Mussolini's comically vile, and were not in that influenced merely by the stridencies
of the popular or other press. From the early Thirties there had
been available a reasonably accurate picture of what Nazism

meant, and at several intellectual levels a reasonably well-inform-
ed debate. Compared with most of the popular press of today,
that of the late Thirties could be sober and educative as it felt the
need.

The gunners were, all in all, respectable men taken from the
workshops, the commercial concerns, the roads of Britain. I say
'roads' because mobile HAA regiments needed above all, in their
Other Ranks, men capable of driving huge high-sided waggons,
loaded with the heavy 3.7 shells in their steel boxes, attached by a
steel tow bar to the gun itself which was even longer than the lorry
and higher, since it had great metal legs with circular iron corner-
pads for standing on the ground, folded up on each side for
movement on the road or across country. The great lumbering outfits
looked as if a monstrous four-legged insect, travelling upside-down
and with a huge rear-pointing proboscis, had been captured by or
attached itself to a rhinoceros's behind. In convoy the junior officers
on motorbikes, Matchless 350s or BSA 500s, wove in and out of the
big stuff, fussily like sheepdogs or smoothly like pilot fish if things
were going well.

The men who drove these behemoths had virtually all been heavy
goods vehicle drivers in civvy street, long-distance hauliers. I had
met long-distance drivers before, working in the university vacation
for a firm which did the Newcastle to London and reverse run daily,
with stops at Leeds. Those men tended to be fly, fiddlers, the light-
fingered, light-vehicle cowboys of the profession. They carried
mixed goods, much of each load portable, so they found ways of
knocking some of it off. The regimental gun-towing drivers
belonged to a different guild. They had been used to driving great
loads of material too heavy to be lifted except by crane at each end
of the run; and to passing hour after hour in their cabs by day and
night as they pulled up and down the trunk-roads of Britain – the
A1 to east Scotland, the A5 for North Wales and Ireland, the A6 for
Shap and Carlisle and Glasgow. They tended to be fairly short and
squat with huge shoulders but precise hands, physically like a very
common type among the coal-miners of Yorkshire I knew and, like
them, more often mild than aggressive, manifestly good-natured –
cousins also of those mainline railway-engine drivers you sometimes see sitting opposite in a train, men who look fatherly and
husbandly, rooted and reliable men. They sit comfortably within

their own bodies and have that steadiness, in repose, which comes from practising a craft and being quietly proud of it without ever taking its risks for granted.

Thirty-five years after I first came to know these men, two of them, Londoners who had kept in touch with each other, sought me out at my work in London, having seen my name and address somewhere. We sat in a pub in Lewisham and reminisced; they hadn't a cynical bone in their bodies, but their judgments on the personalities we had known were shrewder than we, the officers, would have suspected or been happy to acknowledge at the time. These two men recalled an incident in which, they said, I had 'done well' by refusing to obey an order from a bullying senior officer because it would have in some way damaged our troop and was unjustified. I still have no memory of such an incident.

The four or five officers in the troop changed hardly at all for months on end, so you had to get on with one another; and in spite of all your natural and social differences you did. There wasn't very much you could do about changing your circumstances if you did fall out, but still the tolerance of differences was high. Together day after day, month after month, sleeping in the same or adjoining huts or tents and sharing all mealtimes, doing the same repetitive drills and sharing the collective round of responsibilities, you soon know one another better than you are likely to know any other group of people with whom your contact is fortuitous, not brought about by blood or family or neighbourhood links, or professional congeniality or intellectual similarities.

Above all, you learn not to stress differences; you converge to the tolerant, undivisive middle. For a short period we had a fellow-officer, a commercial solicitor from North London working for his family firm somewhere in the City. As his week's copy of the *Tatler* arrived, he would remark, only half jokingly, that it was so nice to keep in touch with one's friends. His solipsist ambition soon got its reward and he was given a sort of pen-pushing promotion. Trained by family, tribe and school in all the habits of his commercial-professional and metropolitan middle class, he had incuriously taken those habits as the very norm and centre of civilised life. That assurance contained its own kind of insensitivity to the reality of others' lives; his jokes about money or with sexual overtones had a crudeness which would not have done for the people of provincial suburbia or respectable working-class Huns-let; and they would have been right.

There was, too, an extrovert publican-in-the-making, good-natured, used to assuming that every night was party night. There was an insurance assessor, not long married and very homesick; again, good-natured; and unmalicious. There was a relaxed and witty Irishman in some form of selling; and, most intriguing of all, there was a plump man in an undemanding and moderately successful line of business who, more than any of us, took the world as he found it. He had a rather lazy, that's-the-way-the-world-wags, grin which is like a badge or Masonic signal in such people. I have always found them fascinating; and at last I know why. His blood wasn't hot enough to demand a succession of parties or other excitements; he wasn't worried, anxious, striving; he didn't see the point of that; he was a bit of an axolotl though he could move fast on occasion and had his own brand of dry, frictionless wit. Like the rest of us, he wasn't spiteful and he belonged to the secret, unarticulated club of those who were not going to climb over anyone else's back to early promotion. I sometimes found myself thinking solemnly: you and I are able to take life so much as we find it and so comfortably because for centuries a few others have refused to take the terms of life which were offered them and those around them. That was a mistaken reaction. There have always been such relaxed people when other men were dying in the fight against the worst of injustices; and it is right there should be.

Since the 58th was due to be re-trained for its mobile role, another regiment was assigned to its Kentish bases; and we were on the loose for months at a time, often doing locums round sizeable industrial areas – an intensive course in the seediness of so much of pre-war, provincial, industrial Britain, and in the kindnesses its people almost hectically assumed they had to offer 'the lads'. At this distance I cannot remember where we went first: I recall a spell in Newport, protecting the docks, and one in an exceptionally friendly Barnsley protecting nothing I can now name, and a little time in Leeds and near Gloucester; there were probably other camps and places. A bare, wind-ridden camp in the depths of Dorset, during the winter of 1941–2, became the base for our first serious mobile training and that was like a long winter at Flintcomb-Ash – so cold that one morning, helping to herd a convoy, I fainted off the Matchless motor-bike and fell into a ditch; but came to and caught them up.

This succession of moves and halts introduced us, as few peacetime professions could have, to the landscapes and people of the United Kingdom; and, for some of us, to the freshness of countryside sleep. For month after month we crossed and recrossed a deceptively quiet – apparently marking-time, but in the industrial areas increasingly productive – England, Scotland and Wales, the countryside deep in intensive work, almost no tourists even at weekends (except for our own girl-friends, who came whenever they could, battling with successions of blacked-out train journeys to places they had to look up on maps), but with increasing numbers of people directed to labour on the land, or servicemen in new camps. The towns, on whose football pitches and parks we squatted, hummed but did not seem greatly strained. There was tight rationing of most foodstuffs but, most important of all for immediate adult satisfaction, no shortage of tea or beer.

Villages, towns and cities were hospitable beyond what we had expected; we had after a while to fend off well-meant invitations, usually for a nice cup of tea and a sit-down. I remember best a bonhomous family on one of the hills just outside Glasgow; they seemed to have been keeping open house for months to groups of servicemen of whatever nationality who passed through. Without any appearance of subterfuge or guilt, the father displayed a garage stacked high not so much with food – though that was there – as with 'things that might come in', or be useful as barter; dozens of shooting-sticks, perhaps fallen off the back of a particularly large estate-waggon, space-heaters, cartons of the large size of Pears transparent soap and, much trickier, some of the first nylons we had seen.

More than one battery major and regimental lieutenant-colonel came and went, and occasionally a brigadier. Gloucester-way we had a short, eyebrow-raising period with a rather elderly senior officer from, I think, brigade H Q – perhaps the brigadier himself – who had a name like Bandersnatch; at any rate, his name fitted his slightly-cracked character. On arrival, he issued to the troops on their various sites a histrionic first order of the day in the manner of Wellington before Waterloo: 'I have no friends in the army', it began, 'and I do not intend to make any'. Word went through the units just before his first visit to our camp that his obsession of the week was fire-buckets, the fresh painting thereof, the clean sand therein, the white-washing of their stands and, even more, the shininess of the bases (which were rounded like eggs so that one was forced to hang them on their stands not rest them on the ground). Bandersnatch, the word went, picked up the buckets, lifted them high to ensure that the bases were shiny and then forgetfully put them on the ground. So someone had to follow him to put the sand back in, ripple it on top so it didn't show the earth it had just picked up, and hang the buckets once again on their hooks. Otherwise, Bandersnatch on his way back would see them and accuse the unit of leaving spilled fire-buckets lying around. All passed well with his visit to us until he came to the sentry at the back gate, an unassuming, shy lad whose feet were at odd angles. 'Put your feet together, man,' snapped Bandersnatch. His snapping was not hurtful – more like a large, hairy family dog going through the motions. 'Can't, sir. Sorry, sir'. 'Why not, man?' ''Ammer toes, sir'. 'Have 'em off, man, have 'em off'; and so he swept to his Humber Snipe staff car or battle waggon. We were sorry not to see him again.

There was a major who had been something in the City, portly and fortyish: he ran his unit office as though he expected at all times to be stabbed in the back by colleagues seeking his job. He spent the whole of his first week with us minutely combing the details of every set of regulations appertaining to a battery in camp. There were many, each on hardboard and varnished over: on theft, insubordination, suicide, civilians found on site, damage to property. I asked him why, one day as he pored over the fire regulations and made a minute amendment. 'Ah well, Hoggart,' he said, tolerantly but helpfully, as to one unused to the ways of a shifty world, and pointing to one bit of the small print, 'I could be liable under that clause. Ignorance would be no excuse and it would be too late then to say it's an excessive requirement.'

At least he had a sense of humour. He both believed in his tricks and methods and saw the funny side of them, and it all showed in his comically-foxy face. After his week with the regulations, he turned his attention to more interesting matters and offered to teach me how, as you stand facing someone seated at his desk, you can read his papers upside down: 'Keeps you ahead. Takes him by surprise.' It would have been interesting to try that on a Vice-Chancellor, but their desks were always too large.

He also went, quite soon. Most of these transients were odd rather than blatantly unpleasant and there were few bullies in our environment. But some there were, from colonels through sergeant-majors to lance-bombardiers. War pulls them out just as surely as it pulls out the brave. 'Now thrive the armourers' – and the petty dictators, the mean-minded and the sadistic, the congenital exploiters; for once, everything is justified on the grounds that the war must be won. And all that applies not only to the services and to men; they have their civilian sisters.

A touching brief interlude to life in that succession of camps started one day when a bitch basset hound wandered into camp and stopped at my feet. I raised my hand to pat her and she pee'd, as if involuntarily. Gradually she gained confidence and the wetting stopped, but only with me. Clearly, she had been abominably treated by some human. Our short and – for her – intense unique attachment couldn't last long; fairly soon we were set to move to where she could not be taken. A vet said she was incurable, not likely to be able to extend her new-found confidence to anyone else, and would have to be put down.

Other interludes were more comical. Army life, in war as in peace, is punctuated by requirements to send officers, in particular, on courses for upgrading in old skills or introducing to new. These were received in the regimental adjutant's office with a mixture of exasperation and slight worry. Who can we spare this time? Once it was clearly in people's minds that I was a graduate (there were others, but I was twice a graduate and probably looked unathletic and bookish), the problem was solved. I was first ordered to go on a catering course for officers, near Chester. Something had to be done to improve the reputation and the reality of army food; Mr Salmon, or perhaps it was Mr Gluckstein, from Lyons, agreed to direct a course on making mass catering edible.

I remember three things from that course, apart from the fascination of Mr Salmon's or Mr Gluckstein's gleaming-spectacled account of how Lyons fed tens of thousands palatably each day. One was how to cook a hedgehog in clay (my effort came out charred); the other was related to charring generally, being the army cooks' basic guiding-lines: 'When it's brown it's done/When it's black it's buggered.' The third piece of knowledge, which must have been meant to bring a touch of home comfort to the troops, was a simple recipe for jam doughnuts. My attempt to brighten life at Stalybridge with these, when Mary and I had a weekend there immediately after the course, produced a spectacularly moving mountain of dough since I had confused ounces with pounds in adding the yeast.

Another course in those early days caused greater and more public embarrassment. I was ordered by regimental HQ to report to Tunbridge Wells for a course in planning, logistics, tactics, and the like. Hoggart can do that, they must have said, he's used to writing things down at length. But they hadn't read the rubric which said that the course was for very experienced, promising and fairly senior officers who seemed fit for promotion to field rank; captains who could be given accelerated promotion to major, at the least. It was a splendidly well-endowed course, in a comfortable private mansion with food up to the standard of a very good hotel. The work was interesting, the company agreeable and the setting delightful; I had never before been among the elegancies of a southern spa and retirement town devoted in peacetime to the care and pleasure of the middle classes. When we had all sat our final examinations, with much writing and plotting and planning on graph paper, I was found to have come first. Which amused everyone in the group. I expect they cooked the books so as to hide the fact that a second lieutenant of a few months' service appeared to merit quick promotion to major. The regiment enjoyed it, though HQ was tender for a while.

All this phase – the winter of 1942–3 – of what often seemed like aimless movements began to find a focus as we moved around Scotland . . . the Isle of Whithorn, St Andrews, the Kyle of Lochalsh and somewhere not far from Edinburgh. We were getting near the time and place of our specific commando-type (it was no more than that, like British port-type wine) training and toughening. Tottering along tree trunks over man-made ponds, climbing up netting, we were again made moderately fit after the soft life of the temporary camps. We might therefore, it was planned, have fought off more effectively anyone who made a hand-to-hand attack on our gunsite, though it would have been much easier for them and more effective to attack us from a distance with mortars. But that was almost the end and limit of our sub-commando training. Except for the lecture.

For the lecture the officers of the whole regiment were gathered in a large hut with a makeshift platform. Suddenly a keen-eyed and clearly quite humourless man in his mid-thirties, brought up for the occasion from some boffins' dirty-tricks unit down south, bounced up there. Public school, one would have said, certainly, though not a major one. Rimless glasses, thin lips and thin moustache. He had found his exact niche: devising almost undetectable and usually murderous ways of escaping from your captors in the first minutes or, if you failed, from the prison camp. In full flow he spoke with a tight, passionate conviction about the micro-tools we would, once in the field, be given. He seemed entirely oblivious to the horrible nature of some of those tools and of the other do-it-yourself procedures he described. I remember especially hints on how exactly to disable a man by, in effect, manually castrating him; plus lethal chopper-blows to the neck, and a minute needle which could be concealed in the lapel of the battledress jacket and, applied in the right way, kill in seconds. Our favourite, which we all coveted but were not given, was the magnetic fly-button – once you had escaped, leaving your captors with broken necks or useless genitalia or poison in the veins, you opened your trousers, balanced the button on the end of your thumb and so found the way back to unit.

What would such a man do in civilian life: Join MI5 or MI6? Run a tough security outfit? Go up to the City each day and see how many of his competitors his sharp mind could financially castrate or otherwise disable? Take up teaching in a public school and keep a special eye on the Cadet Corps? I saw a psychological cousin of this man – in precision of mind and unshakeable zest for his craft, though not in screwballery – also jump on to a platform to lecture, this time in the summer of 1945. Now that hostilities in Europe were over, officers from all over that theatre had been called to London for a short course which would allow them the better to advise the men of their regiments on what civilian life promised to be like. Since we had been away from Britain for years, most of us had little practical idea of what was in store, even though our wives and families had tried to keep us in touch. This young man – for by then he seemed young to us but already, we could tell, destined for a shining career in the administrative class of the Civil Service or, now, in advanced computing – had been one of the inventors of the demobilisation booklet, a complex and brilliant creation, and he took us painlessly through the coupons for food, for demobilisation clothing and for everything else the returning warrior would need.

Such exponents of technocratic skills, with total conviction and no sense of the bizarre or the comical, are like entirely interchangeable parts at the service of any authority which calls on them for 'presentations'. They must exist in every kind of society, democratic or authoritarian; cleverly-tooled instruments for and to the needs of their societies, functionally no more than that. But I have never seen them mentioned in books on education and teaching. They are the anonymous, value-free underside.

3

We all guessed by then that only a few weeks separated us from going off to a new major front, not in Europe but perhaps in Africa, well west of where Montgomery's army was building up for a decisive campaign. We did not actually know that, but knew it wasn't a bad guess. We were ordered to give no hint to our nearest and dearest and, my impression was, most of us obeyed, painful though that was. Mary and I parted, with no word about the regiment's likely future, after a few days' honeymoon in a guest-house in the Cotswolds – if you chose your walks carefully you could miss most of the military encamped around.

That was mid-July, 1942. A few weeks before, we had bought a 'utility' wedding-ring, for a pound, in Paisley towards the end of what we easily guessed would be our final training before going overseas. It survives. We bought an engagement ring, to mark Mary's birthday and our forty-sixth wedding anniversary, in 1988.

It was a classic wartime wedding: Mary in a serviceable, light worsted two-piece costume, me in the barathea uniform; only eight or nine at lunch afterwards; some boiled fresh salmon Mary's mother had spirited from somewhere and cream cakes from the shop next door; then the train to a badly-battered Manchester Station and so south to the countryside.

The start of that honeymoon gave warning of a capacity for

sudden and total absent-mindedness, when caught up in moments-out-of-time or at least in happy dislocations of routine, which can still seem alarming. En route to be married, I queued at Glasgow railway station, cashed a travel warrant for a first-class return from there to Cheltenham, turned away from the booking office and simply let the ticket fall to the floor, as though it had no connection with me. In that crowd there was no finding it. Almost four years to the day later, embarking at Calais on the demobil-isation boat for Dover, I took from the hands of a military transport sergeant the tag without which no one was allowed to board – and at once let it fall. That time I was luckier. Much scrambling under others' boots finally revealed it. Both these incidents were caused by being disconnected from day-by-day life because some more powerful, and happy, experience had obliquely broken in; with having escaped from time.

Then, one day in the early autumn of 1942, we came yet again to Glasgow and headed for Greenock docks with our guns, through the damp grey streets, through the deadness which more than any other part of the week the mid-afternoon of Sunday in big British cities used to embody – and to some extent still does: the pubs shut and not opening for four or five hours; the cinemas shut too in those days, and all the shops; most working-class children shunted off to Sunday school and many of the parents in bed having their only unfatigued love-making of the week; miles of streets between you and any fields and hardly any trams or buses; city life no more than ticking over, at its lowest daylight ebb, like a half-animated old and tired animal with a stale, gassy smell; a farewell to Britain much truer than the wavings from sunny village greens or suburban lanes in the usual war films.

As we slowly circumnavigated a tight corner between tenements we passed a cluster, two young women and two youths, obviously working-class, the girls stocky and bold-looking. They knew we were off to embark. The girls then shouted at us so that we all turned in their direction, and at the same time lifted their skirts right up to their waists. No knickers. Even we could translate their Glasgow twang: 'Have a good look, lads; it'll be the last cunt you'll see for a long time.' We did not feel they were taunting us; they were being generous, animal and spontaneous, offering a bit of some-thing which was a little better than nothing.

Once, in the middle-Sixties, I sat with a Polish art critic at a pavement café in Paris. He remarked that he had been an airman during the war and had a spell in Glasgow. We fell to talking about the harsh raucousness and unabashed vitality which could still be found in the Gorbals then, by comparison with which Primitive Methodist Hunslet seemed genteel. His eyes began to focus on a distant memory he clearly treasured. A whole bunch of them, he said, used to pick up girls and take them under the railway arches. The girls didn't mess around. They put their backs to the walls on each side of the arch and lifted their skirts straightaway, four or five of them in each row. And as the Poles poked them, he remembered, the girls chattered in their incomprehensible dialect and laughed to each other 'like birds', with the sound being echoed off and round the arches. 'I think of them now,' he said, 'whenever I hear a group of starlings gathering in the evening. It is one of the happiest memories of the war, of my life.' Not just because of the free sex, he added, 'but because they were so relaxed, as though giving you a piece of sweet cake out of simple kindness. Gauguin's Tahitian girls couldn't have been more easy with themselves or with us.' Memory had filtered those scenes and given them an abstracted glow; but he was not a fool and knew he was reacting to an experience of unusual vigour, and one with its own kind of honesty.

CHAPTER 2

ॐ

NORTH AFRICA AND PANTELLERIA
1942–3

We came to the docks and a great passenger boat – the *Otranto*, something over 20,000 tons – and were at once formally separated into classes, the men into lower areas where they slung hammocks wherever they could and were fed mush – cottage pie, shepherd's pie, mince and peas, meat and vegetable stew – from huge rectangular trays, in successive groups, out of central serving-hatches; the officers, in cabins, were served by waiters in the ship's dining-room. Even after a year and a half's experience of the army's caste system, this was a shock; the physical divisions were in themselves so marked – and to retain waiters in a ship heading for a beach assault!

Not that we headed quickly. We were on that boat five or six weeks. The convoy had to be assembled and the enemy put off the scent. This required us to join other big and loaded ships in a huge and well-hidden loch. Except in one particular, we had no individual contact with those on other ships; we sat like non-communicating packages waiting to be despatched. Our one contact was through the intermingling of our shit. As each day the thousands of men in each ship relieved themselves, the ordure went straight into the water. We began to notice this after a day or two and it gradually became more obvious, so that after a week or two the whole loch was visibly spattered with floating turds, most much larger than I was used to, turds every yard or so, through which the little rubber dinghies which some of the troops used for exercises from their own ships picked their way gingerly.

Our ship held also No. 1 Commando, very much a tough, 'élite' unit going to what was I suppose their first large-scale direct assault.

We gave our men some daily exercise but not in the way the commandos did. They were a rough bunch and brutally trained. One of their senior officers was said to have remarked that he pitied the police when his lads got back on the streets of the big cities. Their colonel was a Scots laird with a nickname like Mad Mac. I watched him one day making them jump at dangerous speed over a huge, thick ship's rope which was being spun in great arcs. One missed his footing, was hit fully in the small of the back by the rope and fell in agony; clearly due for a long spell in hospital and not likely again to be fit for commando service. The men swinging the rope hesitated for a fraction until Mad Mac shouted violently: 'Keep it moving! Get him away!' It is easy to see the justification which would have been made for the colonel's action: even if his best friend falls a commando must keep moving or their advantage may be lost. But they were not in action, the man was badly hurt, thirty seconds of comfort would not have weakened the men's resolve.

The founding father of the commandos was the Chief of Combined Operations, Mountbatten; just before we finally left the loch, he appeared as if from nowhere to inspire his men. He was a magnificent figure, tall, handsome, resplendent in senior naval officer's uniform, covered with gold braid and medals, bursting with confidence. He jumped on to a bollard and the commandos were ordered to gather round him; all other troops were ignored. I cannot remember exactly what he said, but it was to the effect that they were to spearhead the first large Allied invasion since the start of the war, the first turning of the tide; that they were the crack men who would do it. The voice of this aristocrat of German stock – this man of great brilliance and great beauty and great bravery, this exceptionally hard and inventive worker, this high liver, this friend if not by then relative of English royalty – his voice and his whole bearing marked him out as exactly all those things. Not one in fifty of the commandos would have been able to identify or interpret much of this; they would never have met that style in their lives. There was a touch of Harry at Agincourt and a foreshadowing of Montgomery at El Alamein. The commandos loved it because they knew at least that they were being told they were great lads. But it was not uplifting or civilised or dignified; it was not Harry at Agincourt. In all its aspects it encapsulated too much in the divided

British class system and the divisive peacockery of monarchy and near-monarchy for that; it was, for all its glitter, demeaning.

And thus we left Britain.

I

We sailed far west and then south in a great arc for many days, then turned east and headed towards the worst danger point, the Straits of Gibraltar. The spies in Portugal and Spain, and the Italians, had to be given as little warning as possible. Once we were inside the Mediterranean, it became clear from the ceaseless rivulets of gossip between crew and troops that before long we were going to turn sharp right, south for the Algerian coast. The morning of the turn, when the officer and I who shared a cabin had just finished shaving and were about to set off for breakfast, there was an enormous booming whoosh. We looked out of the porthole and saw the liner next to us, which carried Poles, with her stern at almost ninety degrees out of the water, in the moment before she dived for the sea-bed. The Italian submarines had made one kill at least. Our accompanying destroyers did what they could to find survivors, but could not leave the main body unprotected for long. We sailed on until night fell and then hove to, totally blacked out, within landing-craft distance of the Algerian coast.

Zero hour for Operation Torch was just before dawn on 8 November 1942, and breakfast an hour or so before then. We had not expected sausage and mash with waiter service, for the officers, immediately before taking to the landing-craft. Then we sat on the still warm deck waiting our turn. The commandos were to be first off and sat around with blackened faces; their flamboyant colonel moved among them in a soft cap and twirled a stick – as though he was setting off for a day's beagling with his Highland servants, or stag-hunting with his gillies. Did he have a dog, or did he only look as though he should have had? Just before the moment of assault the radio began to crackle as a message was beamed to the coast. Roosevelt had recorded the announcement, which began 'Nous sommes arrivés parmi vous,' in an accent which made Churchill's French sound Parisian.

Word came back very quickly that, in a quite literal sense, our part of the coast was clear. As we took to our boats, dawn had just broken. The first dry white light of Africa, with even then the promise of early heat. That beach now comes into view whenever I read Camus's *The Outsider*. The bit our craft touched down on was deserted except for a small Arab boy, perhaps ten years old. He asked if we had any fags. We were seven or eight miles west of Algiers. We had motorbikes and light vehicles, but had to wait for the guns to be unloaded at a dock. We took such cover as there was, sat around waiting for orders, opened tins for a second breakfast and wondered when we would see the big city. By seven or eight o'clock I thought it time to have a look, so a sergeant and I got on a motorbike and headed for Algiers.

As we neared the town streets we could hear a growing roar of excitement. As soon as we were in those streets we were nearly lifted off the bike by cheering crowds, most of whom wanted to kiss us. It was exhilarating, funny and very queer. Where was everyone else? Where were the commandos? The top brass? The enemy, for that matter? Best to get back to our makeshift camp. Which was delighted to tell us that, just after we had set off, our own regimental HQ had come through on the radio to say that the French garrison in Algiers had agreed to surrender without a fight but wanted a proper surrender ceremony. So all Allied troops were to stay outside the town until the generals on each side had got their finery ready and could meet in full fig in the town centre later that day. Our entry passed into unrecorded history.

This news meant that the docks were available, so we were able very soon to get the guns and big waggons off the cargo boats and lead them to a hill on top of the town, set them in the earth and prepare to defend the port as the Allied build-up developed. All very easy, and the raids not heavy. Meanwhile the main body of troops, Anderson's British First Army (very small) with the US II Corps, began to move east as their arms and material were unloaded, along the sometimes difficult and often mountainous road towards Tunis, a good five hundred miles from Algiers. The British Eighth Army, after its early November victory at El Alamein, was to move westward to make the link. Not much west of Tunis, there were German and Italian troops on the First Army's route, beginning to build up against the American–British arrival. Our regiment remained for the time being in a static, port-protecting role, waiting in our turn to be called forward and become properly mobile.

Algiers itself had little to offer, given the restrictions on the troops; the *kasbah* was rightly out of bounds and the town itself, though beautiful, brilliantly white and shining in sunlight, was not unlike Glasgow on a Sunday afternoon in the few distractions it could provide for servicemen, at no matter how loose an end they might be; altogether too strange and foreign and slightly dangerous in more than one way (robbery, VD, murder). After the first weeks, air raids being infrequent, we lived the dull internal life of a mild visiting force. Our gunsite was in the grounds of an expensive hotel much frequented by the more prosperous and glossy *pieds-noirs*, who continued to meet there throughout our stay for their midday aperitifs and evening meals, their gossip and their affairs, as though nothing unusual had happened. One middle-aged widower was more thoughtful and, at his modest-sized farmstead, would talk over a glass of wine about what the end of the war would bring for the French there.

The move east by the First Army reached, during that autumn and early winter, to somewhere near Gafsa in the south and in the north to near Souk Ahras, which is itself near Medjez el Bab; and Medjez el Bab was the gateway to and communications point for the capture of Bizerta and Tunis. But little happened in those months until, in mid-February, the Germans attacked, aiming chiefly at the Americans who were not yet used to battle and were knocked back at first. What we heard most about in Algiers, since it concerned the road we would eventually go down towards Bizerta, was of the Germans waiting in strength near Medjez on a hill commanding that one usable road. Was it called Longstop Hill? It was finally captured after repeated assaults and great losses by a British Guards regiment.

One day, which must have been in mid- to late February, I was called to regimental HQ. A British 25-pounder field regiment, moving up to support the advance, had been caught not far from Souk Ahras as the road crossed a bridge. The Germans had the bridge pinpointed and within a few minutes inflicted very severe losses in men and guns. Replacement 25-pounders and their towing vehicles were on the dockside and had to be taken up to the regiment as soon as possible. I was to be in charge of the convoy, with a sergeant and drivers from our regiment; we also had a light lorry and a 250 cc Matchless motorbike. I was able to choose the sergeant and most of the drivers. We were to leave from the docks very early the next morning.

A new young driver took us down in one of the troop's larger lorries and was then to return to camp. It soon became clear that he was fresh from being given driving instruction in the UK, and knew little about how to behave on bad surfaces. The road was greasy-wet and quite soon, on a hill down to the docks, he put us in the ditch. No one was hurt; we got the truck out after a short time and arrived at the rendezvous six or seven minutes late – to find a small, moustached brigade major, pop-eyed with fury. He bellowed, in a brutal manner I'd not met in regular officers, that we were late and would be reported to the brigadier.

By the time we had cleared Algiers that incident was out of our minds. Thousands had gone up that four hundred or so miles of road in the past few months, so we were not breaking any new ground. It was beautiful ground, above all for the light and smells, the one of a clarity we had not met before, the other a range of smells – gummy, bluey, unfamiliarly herby – we had not known before; all as lovely and as strange as was, later, the dry shimmer of the desert. Not that we talked about these impressions; the apparent incuriousness, or verbal inhibitions about discussing even strong responses, of most Britishers are hard to break down.

It was in any case a preoccupyingly tricky road in itself, wet and often full of mud from tank tracks, one lane each way, the surface pitted and the verges hazardous, being below the level of the road surface and simply churned mud or clay. In the higher parts – and these hills, the foothills of the Atlas mountains, were like the wilder parts of Wales – a slip onto those verges could send your truck rolling over and over down the steep hillside unless it hit the trunk of a cork tree quite soon, and jammed. We saw several such written-off vehicles in the worst parts where we were ourselves moving at walking pace, with the drivers, on bad corners, cleverly letting their trucks slide sideways into and out of the curves. Our chief problem was that we were a solitary convoy with no support or emergency services; nor, as we reached the area where German dive-bombers were active, had we any protection except what a jump into the ditch would give. So, though it wasn't a brave or dangerous operation, it was tricky for the three days or so each way.

But we were alone and free of the unit's daily routine, and it soon became clear that we were all enjoying ourselves very much. I had to make the decisions about where to stop for meals and for the night or what to do in any unexpected emergency; that apart, there was no sense of differences in rank. Time out, again; unfretted; and a complete unspoken assumption on all sides that normal routines and styles would be resumed the moment we got back to camp.

In Setif we had to steer round a narrow corner in the town's huddled centre, much as we had done in Glasgow a few months before. Again, we came upon a cluster of locals: girls, most of whom looked about twelve years old, leaning against the peeling stuccoed wall of a double-fronted house, smoking, getting what shelter they could from the afternoon sun, which even in that month could be uncomfortable. As we looked, an Arab came up and spoke to one girl. She threw away her fag and led him into the house. That would be a five-minute job in a sweaty room on a dirty blanket. The other girls, no doubt long used to Arabs and French soldiers and now accepting the British and Americans, called out half-heartedly; we were obviously just passing through. After all these years, a shaft of light on a hot stuccoed wall still brings back that sad little scene.

After Constantine, which I remember only as a startlingly French-looking apartmented city seen across yellow space, the pace quickened, and strafing of the road became fairly frequent. We grew used to sounding our horns as soon as someone spotted the dots coming our way out of the glare of the sun, and dropping into the ditch; I recall no serious damage to us or our gear. But finding shelter at night became a problem. To be exposed at dawn was to invite attack.

Towards the end of one day we moved off the hills onto a largish plateau. Ahead we could see a farmstead, a few irregularly-placed buildings and some trees; ideal shelter for the night. As we began to move up the track leading from the road we saw that a small British unit had already taken cover there. They were electrical and mechanical engineers, on the way up to their unit after getting new stores at a depot back west. Their captain came running out of the farmhouse, his hands held up and out in a 'back, you dogs!' gesture. He was a large, florid fellow in his mid-thirties who had the air of one who back in Civvy Street ran his own medium-sized business. I got off the motorbike and went up to him. His eyes flickered quickly to my shoulders and registered only a lieutenant's pips. He told me briefly and grossly that I could not take cover there (there was room); he wasn't having those bloody guns attracting all the Stukas for miles around. I told him we were hungry and tired and this was the only cover on the extensive plateau. He repeated that I must move on – 'and that's a fucking order'. It was a bluff and he knew it. I had witnesses and you don't pull rank if that puts other soldiers at risk. So we stayed, sleeping in or under the trucks. He slammed the farmhouse door and did not appear again before we left early the following day. The most interesting aspect of the cameo event was the realisation that all the bluster was called out, and was almost beyond his control, because he was scared stiff.

We moved on until we were almost at the end of the journey. As we approached one town – I think Souk Ahras – we saw a group of Flying Fortresses going in the same direction. Just over the town, which was in Allied hands, they uninterruptedly, serenely and exactly – as if on a training exercise – released their bombs; we stood nonplussed on the approach road. We learned later that they had been given a wrong map coordinate. We passed through the town a few minutes later – a few newly-bombed buildings, a few dead Arabs on the street, silence except for the first wailing of ambulances.

We found the 25-pounder regiment in an olive grove a few miles back from where they had been ambushed. They were still shocked, grief-stricken, dignified, but busy putting the pieces together again. The contrast with the style evoked by the maintenance-captain of not many hours before could hardly have been greater. These people were text-book and copybook model soldiers.

In a tent under a little cover the adjutant was making his final report to the colonel on the extent of the losses, and the movements in train to make them up. They were formally polite to each other and at the same time friendly, like people who off-duty could show a liking for one another. It was as though a trusted housemaster in a public school was sorting out the aftermath of a bad accident with the headmaster. But they each obviously felt deeply and knew the other did; they were grieving, but an outsider would not greatly have noticed or been meant to notice unless he had paid particular attention to the slightly more restrained than usual gestures and slightly more clipped than usual tones. The colonel indicated those among the nearest and dearest to whom he would himself write; all the relatives of the dead, it seemed.

Then the colonel left and the adjutant turned to me – there was no small talk and no thanks. Why could there have been? I had – in comparison with their experiences – done a very small thing as ordered; that was all. He said, firmly and conclusively, 'I will have to take all your men. I need drivers. I'll leave one to drive the truck back to Algiers for you, the sergeant and him to sleep in.' Naturally I asked if he had to; other drivers could have been called up in a few days. But I knew he was right. He had to get his regiment up to strength by all reasonable means and as soon as possible. He responded, equably, 'I'd commandeer you if you knew officers' drill on 25-pounders. But we've no time to train you.'

I told the men, who looked sick but knew there was nothing to be done. They gave me notes for home and messages for their friends in the troop, and the other three of us left within an hour of arriving. Clean and unfussy. We got back to Algiers in a few days with no more incidents than an occasional dive-bomber raid in the early stages. The colonel complimented me and went so far, with some embarrassment, as to say he had drafted a recommendation that I be mentioned in despatches. But a major at brigade HQ had vetoed that, he added, on the grounds that we had arrived late at the starting rendezvous. That was a relief.

Later on, when we were very much further forward and waiting for the final push to Bizerta, I was sent on another isolated mission – to go in a light goods vehicle far back down the line to collect some extremely delicate radar equipment. Going down was another interlude of time out, through a spring more rapid and insistent, more changed with every day, than any we had known. Coming back was repeatedly hair-raising because the shallow and narrow macadamed strips on the mountain roads were heavily filmed with greasy clay. To have rolled down the mountainside would have set the regiment back a further week and cost thousands of pounds. The driver was another novice and knew nothing, at first, about steering into skids. We managed until, at about five in the morning on level land and about thirty miles short of regaining the regiment, he slid us into a shallow ditch and up against a tree. The impact was not severe enough to damage the equipment but the two of us were bleeding heavily from hitting the windscreen. We stood on the long, inhospitable, cheerless roadside waiting for the first military vehicle, watching the light quickly change from turquoise to duck-egg blue before the heat began to blot out delicate colours. After ten minutes an American jeep came rattling along. We moved out and waved; the jeep accelerated and swerved round us, the three men in it staring straight ahead. Obviously out of camp illegally. Half an hour later other Americans took us to their unit, bandaged and fed us, and arranged for our truck to be hauled back on to the road. We reached camp only two or three hours later than we had planned.

I remember these interludes particularly because the greater part of our lives in those weeks was dull. Not just because heavy ack-ack, even in its mobile form, does not fight forward battles and only goes into action at certain times which the enemy decides; you do not initiate. But these weeks were boring for all the troops; when you are getting ready for a big move forward life is bound to be repetitive, routine, marking time. I could always read: redis-covering Shakespeare – more accurately, truly discovering him for the first time – in a copy found at a deserted wayside stopping-place; a manuscript anthology of favourite poems which Mary had made up for me in a pocket-sized black notebook, and odd books as they now came more easily through the mail, notably 'Little Gidding'.

We had by now moved east along those same mountain roads and then down to a pale-khaki plateau for the final push. We practised drills, waited, wrote home, kicked balls in the sand and started cautious bartering with the local Arabs, whose rough settlements clustered on the flatter parts, just off the road. Scarcely anyone had an interest in the Arabs themselves, or in their ways of life. They were there, as odd roadside weeds were there. They were filthy in dress and body, and practised ridiculous forms of worship – that summed up the general view of their way of going on. They were despised, but without heat; it never occurred to the British to wonder what the Arabs thought of them. The bartering was carried out with bad faith on both sides. Our cooks gave them leaf-tea, which was in fact used tea-leaves dried out. They respon-ded with hard-boiled eggs which, as they knew, were rancid. A surprise, because many of the men assumed that since the Arabs did their morning evacuations along a ditch outside their village and facing our camp, so that we saw a line of bare bottoms each day, they must be too primitive to understand even simple fiddling.

Further up, at brigade or division or corps level, it was decided that things were for the time being quiet enough for the boredom to be relieved by visitors from outside. An ENSA troupe arrived, notching up one-night stands across the build-up area. We managed to rig up a sort of large marquee, though three sides were open; the evening heat was still hard to bear even for a few minutes, let alone an hour. If ENSA had grades for its troupes, this must have belonged to the lower end. There were two men, one obviously homosexual; he was received in silence except for a few hisses. There was a small, chunky girl in spangles, tights and bra. Whether ENSA defined the dimensions of such an outfit I do not know, though I expect they did, and cautiously. Apart from its glittery finish it in no way sought to be fetching let alone erotic, being too substantial. But the girl wasn't one to be satisfied with that. She was enjoying going through North Africa rousing sex-starved men to near-frenzy. She was determined to use her parts – sizeable breasts, pneumatic bum and quite evident pubic girdle – as her bait. Soon many of the audience were breathing heavily. For her finale she performed the Crab, which involved bending over backwards so that her body was totally arched, her legs and arms supporting her and her lower trunk jutting upwards. She then inched slowly around, which I suppose is all you can do if you are in the Crab position, until her widespread legs and so her pelvic region were facing full frontally her audience. She remained there undulating her pelvis so that it repeatedly moved up and out at her audience. The atmosphere thickened and we began to wonder if one of the rougher gunners, inflamed by this great thrusting pouch, would break ranks, jump on the makeshift platform and attempt to mount her. She heaved and pushed a couple of times more and the tension reached a climax. At that moment a soldier at the far end of the tent lowered the temperature with half-a-dozen words. As though viewing a marked-down joint of meat from the back of a market-stall crowd late on a Saturday night, he called out cheerfully, 'Wrap it up. I'll take it.'

As distinct from the crude jokers, such a troop wit – one who could deflate a nasty situation or the bumptiousness of authority with a quick crack – was not common; still, there often seemed to be one on hand. Soon after the ENSA visit, and this was a sign that now the 'big push' was getting near, we were ordered to parade the troop and issue each soldier with a French letter. An unreal event to men who had for months been restricted to following the prick-teasing antics of Jane in the Forces' newspaper, and knew every curve of the Petty and Varga pin-ups stuck up in their tents. A tongue-in-cheek sergeant followed me down the line with a cardboard box of the plastic priapic offerings. I almost wished they'd blown them up in unison and cast them into the desert air. But they pocketed them dutifully. No second helpings, though the more obvious comics pretended to plead for them. One or two of the younger men stared, as though they had not only never used one but had not seen one before. In the end one soldier broke the slightly incredulous silence and said, mock-innocently, 'What are these for then, sir?' No need to search for an answer. A voice from the back called out, dead on cue, 'They're for tossing yourself off on Sundays'.

We reached an irregular countryside, with grass and a few small trees, immediately behind what would be the point of advance. We could be on that rough road within minutes, once the guns had been struck to move. Meanwhile we hammered them into their anti-tank positions; as pea-shooters again, with the two officers in the command post having to leave almost all decisions to the sergeant in charge of each gun. They could not be moved in less than about a quarter of an hour; they sat like huge laying birds. They could destroy a tank with one shot, so long as the tank didn't see them first. If it did, the gun lost.

We waited a few days, checking and double checking; the slit-trench latrines were a favourite place for watching low-level aerial skirmishes in which we could not have played a part. One man lost control of the great spare wheel he was cleaning and it rolled down the hillside straight into the back of another gunner. He was spirited down the line and, we assumed, back to England. That was the second such disappearance. One simply heard no more from them. Serious casualties of any kind were caught up on a conveyor belt which worked silently, fast and effectively; especially just before action.

In the early hours of one fairly dark night we heard the sound of tanks clashing two or three fields away and stood to; we could only wait tensely until we could actually see the outline of a tank, hope that by then there was enough light to let us recognise it as German, and hope to fire before it did. They came no nearer and the sounds died away. As soon as possible I walked over there. On the sides of a very shallow valley there were dead tanks, British and German, five or six. And dead men, British and German, in the tanks or hanging from them or just clear. Even so early, the bodies had begun to bloat and the flies to get to work. The smell remains unforgettable; not only the beginnings of putrefaction but burnt fluids of several kinds and, overall, something like formaldehyde. The Arabs too had already been there, hurriedly stripping anything useful before the medics arrived. Photographs of wives and girl-friends, fallen from the emptied pockets, lay in the scuffed sand. 'But she would weep to see today/how on his skin the swart flies move, /the dust upon the paper eye/ and the burst stomach like a cave.' It was a tiny but precisely composed and deeply telling microcosm of one of the realities of war: the complex modern technology, the fragile broken bodies – looking about fifteen years old, beautiful, lost and torn apart – and the indifferent landscape and sky. Once again, too, a sense of one's whole generation caught up and carried along by forces we understood only sketchily.

The next morning or the one after that, at above five, the Allied barrage began – the biggest so far in that war, we were told. It was awe-inspiring, a relentless pounding which shook the earth and threw garish lights and acrid smells into the air all around. Thousands of men serving hot guns like automata. We waited at the side of the dusty road until the barrage lifted; all packed and ready, the HGV drivers at their wheels as relaxed and steady as if they were waiting to pull out on to the A1 with a load of iron girders for Newcastle.

Within minutes of the guns falling silent we were ordered onto the road. It was like leaving the vast car park of the baroque, dawn version of a county fair. From every side vehicles of all kinds, tracked and half-tracked and untracked, were joining us. Dawn was almost up, but the air remained dark with blown sand and dust and vehicle fumes. We came to the point where the direct main road east, such as it was, properly began. Out of that dark swirl and glare and teeth-wrenching clatter there emerged at head height a rough, arrow-shaped sign, scrawled 'To Tunis'; and beside it, waving huge, glowing torches towards Tunis with the no-nonsense insistence of policemen clearing a difficult football crowd, were large, red-eyed Military Policemen. 'Keep moving,' 'Get going,' 'Shift,' 'Go!': and the whole man-loaded lot thrust forward as if pushed from behind as well. And yet again the sense of our whole generation on the move, caught up, sharing a heightened sense of life, of the common and the public life, living for once in history and with meaning – though if you had asked what the meaning was we would have been unable to answer. But it was all a thousand miles and as many years of experience away from the lamp-posts of Ancoats, or the cosy centre streets of St Albans; or from being collected at the kindergarten door on crepuscular evenings by nice-looking, comforting-smelling, loving mums; or from going down to the boozer with the lads on Saturday nights.

We moved steadily along an uncontested road; whatever was happening was happening a long way ahead. By midday, as we sat eating, a long line of Italian soldiers, unarmed, cheerful, the easiest of prisoners, straggled past towards our base, and internment somewhere in Britain. One, with a little English, stopped to talk – about how glad they were to be freed from the pressures of the German concept of soldiering and, with even greater feeling, about how much he missed making love to his girl-friend. Have to toss ourselves off, he said and then, enlisting us in the club, but it's not the same, is it? And now I suppose you lot and the Americans will be screwing them when you get to Italy. He assumed that we too, unlike the Germans, were unabashed *hommes moyens sensuels*, and he spoke without resentment.

The Eighth and First Armies met, the German and Italian lines collapsed and we were soon, by May of 1943, in Bizerta, setting up our guns for the defence of the port so that the big cargo ships could come in. After that things were quiet except for occasional air raids. It was during a particularly hectic raid that the young officer I mentioned in the first chapter ran for cover. The others – officers, NCOs and gunners – just went on amid the noise and smoke and eerie lights; that was what you were expected to do, so you did. No heroics, but no turning away.

2

Presumably the Germans had already begun to write off North Africa and were falling back for the defence of Sicily and then Italy itself. Quite soon, and with no explanation, we were replaced by another regiment and pulled back to a holding area. That gave opportunities for a visit to Tunis, which had almost overnight geared itself to becoming a bazaar for the new occupants. Even the women's lingerie shops were well-stocked, and with what we thought of as French fashions; so we sent brassières back home, after optimistic guesses at sizes. Hardly anyone thought of Carthage and most did not know of it. Like most cities of transit for soldiers, Tunis was to most of them entirely unhistoric, without depth or texture or meaning other than the immediately present, as flatly there as a cheap watercolour for tourists.

Then, again without warning or explanation, we were given a week's holiday at a rest camp near Sousse, just down the coast. Something was obviously building up. Sousse was idyllic: sun, sand and sea, reasonable food, no drills and no distractions; we all relaxed and began to hope that the coming move might even be back to England and preparations for the Second Front.

But it was to be Pantelleria, a sea-girt volcanic pimple between us and Sicily, with a small air base which was making itself a nuisance and would be an even greater nuisance if it was still operating when the assault on Sicily began, in July. Not a soul had heard of the island; hardly any Britons had, or have today. The obscurity is well-merited; even the sharpest operator would not try to sell it as a tourist destination. It felt like an anchored, battered, unloved and very foreign little barque in a vast expanse of blue water; but some of us came to like that cut-offedness, as its older natives did. It had long lived a life stripped down to sun, sand and the all-surrounding sea.

We headed there, guns and all, on nine or ten US LCTs or Landing Crafts, Tank – shallow in the water, little more than high-sided open metal holds, with the engines high on the back and a diagonal front ramp. There was a narrow walkway along the top of the sides, except at the ramp end, but most men sat around in the hold among the guns. To the American crew we were like anonymous packages – or aliens, native to these parts of the world, this Africa and this Europe, they knew nothing of and did not wish to know, judging from their complete lack of attempts at communicating. A black seaman was in the galley, frying huge pans of what we realised was the American tinned meat we'd heard about from home, Spam. To people living on boxed combat rations, the smell was like bacon and eggs and sausage and mash and chips all in one. We didn't expect any, but would have liked a nod and a glance. The cook never looked up. He simply did not know how to bear himself with these strange, pale, wiry beings. One sensed again the incurious cultural isolation, the manipulated self-sufficiency and nationalistic self-satisfaction – and hence the extreme foreignness – which had been made, by all the forces of persuasion going in that direction, to enclose so many Americans and to typify so much in American life, below the intellectual and self-aware level. By comparison we then seemed to ourselves almost cosmopolitan, or at least and for the first time part of a diversified but historically related group of European societies.

The troop captain had gone on an earlier craft, to recce the ground, so I was in charge of the troop. All was bright and quiet; we might have been making a pleasure excursion. Until we came near the tiny harbour. Suddenly there was an ear-splitting whine. Out of the sun, heading straight for us and already very near, was a Stuka, its markings and the pilot's head quite clear. A bomb detached itself as if casually, uncertainly, from a lazy spring, and curled towards us. It fell just to the side and drenched us all. It was then that our grocer NCO, that quiet man we relied on for so much, stood his ground and fired the unfamiliar light anti-aircraft gun throughout. I think we put him in for a mention. I don't expect he ever referred to it, once back behind the counter in his shop. Seeing from the nearby shore the dive, the bomb, and our craft disappearing in a great wave of water, the colonel turned to the adjutant and said, 'Well, there goes Hoggart's lot.' Our only casualty was a broken ankle; a gunner sunbathing on the upper rim had made a dive for the well.

We reached the harbour and had our first sight of saturation bombing so complete that not a building or a wall was standing. What had been a township was a large yard of broken building materials. But level, so that we drove across this new surface, on top of what had been homes and shops for centuries, as though it had been prepared for us. And so to the road out, much of which still remained, and to our gunsite. The rim of the small airbase was cluttered with hurriedly-left hutments, littered with ammunition, food and the first tiny Fiat runabouts we had ever seen. At quiet times, we drove them happily round the rough roads until either the petrol ran out or HQ caught up with us; that took three or four days.

Routine now took a new and unexpected form. We had heard that the Germans tended to plan their movements with soon-predictable regularity, but had assumed this was propaganda. By the second day it became clear that they would bomb us and dive bomb us, and the airstrip, every daylight hour and on the hour. So we were ready: those on duty fired back and the rest watched from the slit trenches, uttering routine imprecations such as 'Bugger this for a lark'. I don't think we brought any down but we probably put them off their aim, which is two-thirds of the ack-ack gunner's purpose; they did us no serious damage. It became a kind of game. One day an officer, also from Leeds so we were rather closer than was usual, overstayed his time on some errand and was a hundred yards short of camp as the hour struck. Suddenly he appeared on the perimeter, calling my name, and covering his rear with both hands as he ran. A Stuka was peppering the ground just behind him, but made no effort to lift the sights and kill him. It veered away as he reached us.

In the intervals we did what we could to clear the place, especially since disease threatened; there were unburied bodies around. That tiny, poor island had been blasted for days, and its people did not understand what had hit them. Out on the lava meadows their homes had often been beehive huts of concrete with a single entrance and few if any windows. One afternoon a sergeant came to say that some of the men, making ever wider cleaning-up circles round the camp, had found such a hut stinking and fly-ridden. They had peered inside and seen on a high rough bed the bloated body of an old man. We set off with a two-gallon can of petrol, over getting on for a mile of rough ground.

There was little more than the bed in the beehive; he had been scrabbling a bare living. His body was crawling with maggots, and crowds of huge flies buzzed frantically around it; if you had passed more than a few seconds in that stench you would have vomited.

The sergeant and I had put on gas masks, turned our shirtsleeves right down, and rolled our socks up as near as possible to the bottoms of our shorts. This so as to reduce the area which might be infected by fly bites. In the event, the gas mask saved my life. There was nothing to do but burn the body and its bier. The two of us drenched the body and led a trail of petrol from there out of the entrance to a point about three yards directly to the front. A lunatic thing to do in a Mediterranean high summer, especially in front of a structure of that sort. I told the others to stand back and set a match to the far end of the trail, intending to jump to one side immediately. But by then all the petrol in the beehive had vaporised; the place had become a bomb, waiting to be ignited. Virtually simultaneously with my striking the match there was an enormous flash and roar as the flames rushed for the only way out, through that narrow door – and enveloped me.

The MO came running within minutes, morphine at the ready; they found an old door and carried me on that back to camp. The rim of the gas mask was welded to my head all the way round; my hands and knees were badly burned; I was in deep shock. The next six weeks remain a blur of pain. I was judged too ill to be taken back to North Africa, but an American field hospital had just set itself up on the island, chiefly to look after casualties among their airmen using the strip in an emergency. I lay under a mosquito net, sweating as the sun beat down on the tent, nourished through a nostril and discovering that flies soon know you can't move; they foraged up the other nostril. Everyone did very well for the strange solitary Englishman, except for a sadistic Italo–American doctor who made sure that the daily changing of bandages was as painful as possible. As I became more conscious I began to worry about not being able to write the daily letter to Mary. But deliveries were so erratic that the gap was not the full six weeks, and she put that down to transport difficulties. The first letter after the gap told her I was out and about again, so she was at least spared some worry.

Those weeks and the first few weeks after I rejoined the regiment remain hazy. I cannot remember the journey back to North Africa or the actual moment of reaching the troop again. Did we in fact go back to North Africa? Or did we sail direct from Pantelleria to Italy? It was as though memories too had been burned out, and for months after the event. But by now Sicily had been taken; there was no longer any point in protecting Pantelleria; and by early September the Allies on the eastern side had crossed to Calabria and then went in at Salerno. The first big port was Naples and we were told to be ready to move soon after it was taken, at the beginning of October 1943.

CHAPTER 3

❧

NAPLES
1943–6

In a jeep one morning, going very slowly down Naples' always-crowded Via Roma, I looked out at a crowd jostling at a bus stop. An altercation had just blown up, the crowd parted as if almost courteously and certainly matter-of-factly, to leave a small stage for the tragic characters to act out their parts. A knife flashed and a man fell stabbed, it seemed through the heart. We passed back that way a few minutes later. The crowd was going about its business as usual; the waves of day-by-day ordinariness, of the humdrum goings-on, had swallowed the incident as it had swallowed many before.

I

Naples was Leeds in technicolour. I first realised there that, whatever the attractions of small market towns, West Country villages, amiable middle-sized and well-behaved cities, it was the big, messy, rough and noisy cities which most pulled. Naples was Leeds with knobs on, much surer of its own right to wilfulness and bad behaviour, aggressively ungenteel, scornful of Rome and even more of Florence, a world away from Milan and Turin. Naples was also, for all its squalor, a place of magnificence, once the seat of a kingdom, with a fine musical tradition, some considerable scholars and a great archaeological museum. I came to know something of all these attributes, but its first impact did not fade.

The second lesson was that Italy was a land of provinces far more distinct than any we knew, just holding together by thin threads. The self-conscious, uplifting, nation-making of the USA and, in a different manner, of the USSR would have evoked a large raspberry. Operatic-sized heroes did better as national symbols and unifiers. Meanwhile, the fact that they had lost the war fazed few; cheerfulness would keep breaking in. Few were subservient or apologetic or morose. That's the way it went; and they now truly believed they liked us and the Americans much more than they did the Germans.

The harbour was very badly battered and there was bomb damage everywhere. But from the first days the air hummed and fizzed with a vitality most of us had never known in any city. Unceasing noise, movement and smells: wine and American fags, not beer and Woodbines; and oranges and black-market coffee and lasagne and sweat, and corruption of all kinds. And there was something new to most of us – open homosexuality; much rough and risky trade in that, as dangerous for servicemen as prostitution.

Except for the very old, the very young and the patriots in mourning, almost everyone thieved or fiddled. What else would you, could you, do? Like giant fungi, melodramatic anecdotes emerged every day: how a jeep left ten minutes in a busy street by daylight had all its wheels spirited off; how a truck going to a wholesale butcher's had been stopped by the Military Police looking for stolen military supplies – who discovered, among the offal, human genitalia; how an American supply depot in the south of the city had been comprehensively robbed between two and five a.m. by little boys coming up from the sewer manholes within the depot and manoeuvring the goods through to other manholes outside the walls and so to a stream of waiting lorries (the depot commander had said he'd like a few staff with that logistic ability).

We had months and months in the Vomero football stadium high above the city and port, with only intermittent action, mainly by night. We all lived under the grandstands, and that was a pleasant change after so much tent life. Medium-rank apartment blocks looked down on us, not very curiously. Late 1943 soon gave way to 1944. By early 1944 we expected to go up the line once it began to move, as we had done before. But a sister regiment nearby, which had shadowed us through North Africa and seen us selected for Pantelleria, was chosen to leap-frog over us up towards the front. We ground to a long halt.

One sign of the changed climate was the arrival of the Basutos, not to drive or man the instruments but to do the heavy work on the guns. They had a minor chief with them, a courteous man who paid proper attention to their cultural rights, beginning with the precise preparation of their food, which was chiefly a form of ground meal. They slept in separate tents. The English gunners said their body sweat made them smell like horses; their leader told us mildly that the English smelt like mouse droppings.

There were enough troops at any time in Naples, stuck there for a while in transit or, soon, on rest periods, for them to make a few different sets of rabbit-tracks. For the first time for months, friendships rather than cagey transactions were made outside the troop, battery or regiment – some with the locals over in the apartments; a cook was caught heading for his lady friend with a leg of lamb up his battledress blouse. But most stuck as always to the camp-NAAFI-camp circuit, and perhaps a known bar or two.

Among my own closest friends was Andrew Shonfield, a lieutenant in the sister regiment – bored also by now but more decisive than I was, so he soon moved to HQ at Caserta and Intelligence work; but that brought him often into Naples. The friendship survived until he died, very quickly and prematurely, in early 1981. I first met him on some muddy exercise outside Naples in early 1944. His immediate attraction came from his, to me unusual, combination of physical and intellectual energy. My old professor Bonamy Dobrée was a man of great intellectual sparkle, and great physical charm. But that charm had to express itself in the precise, restrained codes for physical gesture used by the English upper class. It belonged to a separate compartment from his lively intellect – the style of that had been picked up on his slightly eccentric road through parts of academic life and the literary-artistic circle he moved in (Eliot, Lawrence, Read, Moore). I had met intellectuals many of whom didn't seem to know they had bodies, and men obviously full of physical health but with undeveloped intellects. In Shonfield they ran together. His style was intellectual-physical, but not class-defined. A Hungarian, one of the numerous gifted children of a rabbi who had moved across Europe before finally settling in the East End of London, Andrew had, apparently effortlessly, moved on from Westminster School to Balliol; and there acquired a Balliol style, a voice and manner, so rich that it seemed like a consummate stage performance. It did not therefore weaken the classless, unpuritanical, ungenteel, mind-and-body energy he radiated. It was a very muscular mind. He would roar into an argument with a great combative laugh and set about destroying his opponents' case as if by physical blows.

He had an enthusiastically catholic mind and assumed like a good European Jewish intellectual that, though he was an economist, he should know a lot about music and should keep up with what was going on in literature. He could not rest until he had tried his hand at a novel, and published one in the Sixties. He visited India to give economic advice but wanted, when he came back, chiefly to talk about where he thought Forster had got things wrong in *A Passage to India*. He became one of the most articulate of British protagonists for Europe; when he entered his final illness he was a professor at the European University in Florence.

I also became friendly with Joe Dine, an American press officer at divisional or corps level in Mark Clark's Fifth Army. He went on, characteristically, to become many years later one of the early workers in Public Service Broadcasting in the USA. Most of the Americans in and around Naples seemed, to the very prejudiced British eyes, just bigger, louder and better paid. Like the British but more so – as we had first noticed on the American landing craft taking us from North Africa to Pantelleria – most Americans preferred to be cocooned in the creaturely signs and symbols they had come to associate with their own superior nationhood. They thrived on the *Stars and Stripes* newspaper and all the other ample provision of what was known to interest 'the boys now over there', the PX, Coke, Lucky Strikes; their cocooning was more effective because richer than ours, and more intensively and confidently pursued. Most Britishers would allow them nothing; they had come in late, and so their courage had to be suspect. Joe Dine was the first American I had talked to at length who could criticise his country far more effectively than we could whilst still being clear-sightedly glad to be an American; and he had the American journalist's tenacity and frankness in pursuit of a story, which was not to be put down or off by rank.

One day I found him deeply upset. The monastery at Cassino was still held by the Germans after massive bombings, including Freyberg's futile thousand bomber raid, and other attacks of several

kinds. Mark Clark had then issued orders for an infantry regiment
in Dine's division or corps to make a frontal attack in daylight
across the level ground which led to the slope up to the monastery. If
they could cross that they might get shelter under the hill from the
storm of German bullets, bombs and shells, and later move up the
mount from there. Dine's general objected, arguing that such a
move would take the lives of hundreds of men to no good purpose;
the Germans had that area too well covered. Clark insisted; the
general continued to plead until, Joe Dine told me, he had tears in
his eyes. In the end he conceded and gave the order. Hundreds of
men were lost in a short time that day and with no gain.

The remnants of the regiment were to be sent back to the States to
re-form. Before they went the general would have a march past,
somewhere between Cassino and Naples. Would I like to go? There
was a bare field, with a tank as a saluting base. The men marched
past. Then the general told them to stand at ease and made a speech
of heroic, histrionic simplicity. It was one of those moments when
the American love of the dramatic, the heightened life, was fully
justified; and typically the general knew how to rise to it, not by the
stiff upper lip but by a brave recognition of the great courage, the
useless sacrifice it had entailed and a full emotional recognition of
the appalling loss it represented. It was heroic without heroics,
simple, dignified, direct and brave in saying what had happened. I
remember only one sentence, and that near the beginning, for its
Lincoln-like simplicity and force: 'Things have been done which I
would wish had not been done.' I think he went back to the States at
that time, too; it would not have been easy thereafter for him to
work under Clark.

It had by then become clear that our regiment would not be going
forward; the defence of Naples harbour, now a relatively slight job,
would remain our lot. The accommodations, contacts, which some
men had made to meet their wider interests now became even more
important. Some of us found chamber concerts being held every few
weeks in small, decrepit palaces. The taste for the San Carlo Opera
Company affected only a minority but ran across all ranks. I met a
cockney private who had become an enthusiast. Whether he had
ever seen the Carl Rosa or any other opera company before, I do not
remember. The San Carlo Company was not greatly distinguished
at that time and suffered from chronic shortages of gear; Mimi died

on a brown blanket clearly marked 'US Forces'. But that didn't
matter; they had a vitality which made the Carl Rosa Company look
wan. The private had gone round to the back of the house to tell the
prima donna how much he admired her, and eventually became her
boy-friend. She was from the Neapolitan working class (potential
opera singers were winkled out of those huddled apartments as
effectively as potential footballers were winkled out of the back
streets of Manchester . . . each art ran with the grain of its city). He
explained that Sunday dinner with her family was just like Sunday
dinner back home. Not meat and two veg, of course, but pasta. But
the quantity and the family warmth were much the same. A few
others, again of all ranks, began trying to explore the historic districts
– Pompeii, Ischia, Capri, Herculaneum; above all, Vesuvius, whose
enormous eruption started on 19 March 1944. A great many of us
went to view it as closely as possible, but it was surprising how little
this fantastic natural phenomenon, far greater than any of us had
seen or were likely to see again, moved most of the troops.

2

I do not now remember just when and how the Three Arts Club was
conceived. I expect a few of us who had made contact (none from my
own regiment) were talking one night and realised for the first time
that there were many like us in Naples for different periods of time –
interested in the arts, trying to write or draw or even compose, and
with only occasional congenial acquaintances. I do not remember
how it was that I became the main organiser of it; I expect it was
because I was based in Naples and many others were some miles out,
and because I already knew a few people in the Army Education
Corps, which had by then set up shop. I went to see the Education
Corps' Major Baxter, a quiet, polite and civil man, to ask if he was
willing to let us have accommodation – the Club would have to be
called formally an Army Education Centre, and its costs shown on
their books – without any strings at all, except our promise not to let
it become a place of ill-repute. It was a cheeky prescription, but he
accepted it within the day and stuck throughout to his promise,
though we could not avoid giving him some tricky moments now and
again.

Major Baxter's risk-taking cutting of official corners was matched later. We were then at the point of preparing our third anthology of Forces writing. But the only paper we could get was very poor. One of our American members took me to an office near the docks. The major in charge, bald, fat, shirt-sleeved, smoking a large cigar, looked like a character in a B-movie about St Louis. He listened as carefully as Major Baxter. 'OK,' he said, 'a good idea. How much paper do you want and what quality?' We came away with a promise, which was honoured, of enough very fine paper indeed.

So, in Naples in 1944, we had accommodation, good accommodation, in a street immediately off the Via Roma; the Via S. Brigida, near the transept of the Galleria Umberto. On the first floor: a large salon, plus odd smaller rooms. I expect we advertised the Club's existence in the Forces' newspapers, and that word of mouth did the rest. Very quickly Allied soldiers, sailors and airmen began to arrive, made contact with those with common interests, formed small groups, and took to meeting there whenever they were in Naples. Virtually all men; few women in those Services appeared to have artistic interests. I can recall two who came into the Club, one with a commissioned officer, the other with a lively and relaxed corporal who wrote poetry.

The men – from all arms of the three services and all Allied countries, most of them conscripts – were, within the Club, classless and rankless. Privates and lance-corporals talked to lieutenants and captains if they wanted to; if not, not. There was a democracy of artistic interest and of degrees of artistic talent which obliterated class and rank once they came through the door. In that sense the chemistry of the place was immediate and extraordinary. I remember suggesting, after about six months, that we might have some sort of Club general meeting to talk about where we were, and what next. I started the meeting by suggesting that we seemed to have created the skeleton of the Club-that-might-be, but a skeleton which already had a strong heart. An image plucked from the air, but one which – and this was the first of the few occasions in which I have felt I had caught the sense of a group as its spokesman – obviously chimed with what the group felt. I do not think any other common range of interests could have produced so completely demotic an atmosphere at all, let alone so quickly.

It's surprising now to recall how catholic we were. The painter members were among the most active and exuberant. In the seventeen months from June 1944 to September 1945 there were seven exhibitions of Allied paintings and photographs. Peter Lanyon produced a swirling, batty mural across the whole width and height of the salon's back wall. We met again in the early Sixties when he was at work on an even larger mural for the new Arts Building of the University of Birmingham. The Club also mounted five exhibitions of Italian art and held regular concerts and recitals with Italian, and some Allied, performers. Neapolitan intellectuals, artists and academics began to look in, relieved to find they did not have to regard the Allies simply as indeterminate khaki or olive-green figures who wandered their streets looking lost, or getting drunk, or trying to find women, or flogging PX or NAAFI goods. Without Italian help the exhibitions and recitals would hardly have started. Readings by poets and makeshift dramatic productions we could handle ourselves; but Italians looked in on those too and we encouraged them – not in an earnest and self-conscious spirit but because we could, here at last, even if in only a small way, ignore Services' rules and codes and follow our open-minded instincts.

The Club's most consistent work was in publications. Material poured in from as far afield as Casablanca and Florence; and from Americans, Australians, New Zealanders, Canadians and British. Our publisher, Gaspari Casella, printed the first two publications on what looked like toilet paper, slightly brown, coarse and thin. Perhaps it was. A story was going the rounds that a cargo ship had been seized in Naples docks, and contained among much else destined for the Italian troops in North Africa a very large consignment of toilet paper.

Verses from Italy appeared in September 1944. We had decided not to accept work from any poets who had been published before the war, though of course some sent in good material; we thought work from young men who had been inspired by the experience of war, and were writing for the first time, should have space if it showed what seemed like an honest response to those experiences and some talent to express them. Looking after four and a half decades over those eighteen poems by ten poets, I still think them well worth their places. It was incidental, but good to see after we had done the sifting, that of the ten two were privates, one a gunner, one a signalman, one a leading aircraftman, one a corporal, one a sergeant, one a lieutenant and two were captains.

In January 1945 we brought out *Comment from Italy*, two and a half times longer than *Verses* and including stories and essays as well as poems. A New Zealander, H. Brennan, appeared again, this time with two poems and three short stories, all of them very talented. Sidney Finkelstein a T/4 in the US Army, walked in one day with an essay on 'The Unknown Verdi', a fine short piece full of intelligent enthusiasm; that had to have a place. Major Baxter, with a flurry of self-deprecation, handed in a poem about his two daughters. 'The Silent Children' is a moving short poem on the misery of knowing that your children are growing and changing all the time without your seeing and sensing how. Many years later I met in London a senior Army Education Corps officer and asked after Colonel (as he later became) Baxter. 'Oh, he and his daughters were drowned some years ago, sailing a dinghy on the Thames.'

Comment contained a preface from Benedetto Croce. An Italian professor among our friends knew him well and arranged for us to visit him. This was towards the end of 1944. Mussolini had more or less left him alone – his reputation provided a fragile circle of security – but he had been living, by now seventy-eight, in a sort of exile on the Peninsula. The Americans had carefully and admirably sought him out in his villa in Sorrento and ensured his safety during the turbulent days of the surrender.

In charge of the trip from Naples was a small, ebullient journalist; he told me to be at a certain street corner very early on a Sunday morning. When I arrived, petrol – vividly coloured and so presumably stolen from the Allies – was being siphoned hugger-mugger into a battered little black car. That was an operation I was not meant to see, so they delicately asked me to stand a few yards away.

We arrived at the fine Palladian villa well before nine and were asked by Croce's amanuensis daughter to wait in the high, tiled hall. A pair of elegant politicos passed us, fussy as White Rabbits, clutching the day's newspapers which were already marked in places for Croce's attention; they disappeared through the double doors to the Master's study. The journalist immediately skipped over and put his ear to the large keyhole, from which he gave a series of dramatic reactions to what he was hearing – of which the gist was: 'Ah, the crooks. I see what they're plotting; trying to get the old man to support the line on . . . . , which they'll push in Rome next week.' I did not know how far he was melodramatising what he heard. Sad to think of that great old man who – as well as writing for over forty years aesthetics, historical studies, literary criticism, editing *La Critica* and publishing much else – had been thrown out of his Chair at the University of Naples when Mussolini came to power but had still continued to oppose Fascism; and now, in his old age, to be coaxed at by those little perfumed plotters.

We had only a few minutes with him, but he readily agreed to write the preface if, once he had read some of our work (the material for *Comment* was not then ready, but we gave him *Verses*), he thought the enterprise worthwhile. About three hundred and fifty words arrived not many days later. Even in English the prose is oratorical, lyrical, melodic, tender, generous, and unworldly.

The preface began: 'What do they think, these men, these youths, these adolescents who for more than five years, far from their homes and their loved ones, torn from their studies and from their work, cut off from the hopes which they cherished, have played death's game . . . Do they bear in the depths of their souls, more or less consciously, the mystery of a revelation at hand, of a new world to come?'

I met Croce once more, after he had returned to his apartment in Naples on the Via Roma. Some acolytes, including one or two professors who were close to him and had brought me along, shuffled around a large library with books mounting to the high ceiling. After a while the Master, as always accompanied by his daughter, appeared, his air one of simplicity and modesty, of hearing other music. For a short time he moved graciously among us, with someone identifying each new group. Then he was gone.

The collection of what we thought to be the best new poems by four poets who had first been published by the Club appeared in July 1945. *Four in Hand* was printed on the fine new American paper provided by the cigar-smoking major, and had a pictorial dust-jacket by Frank Bowman, a Club member. We were not ready with another collection until some months into 1946, and by then I had moved up the hill to become a staff captain in Education, was lecturing a couple of times a week at the Istituto Orientale downtown, and was preparing for demobilisation. *Voice from*

Italy, edited by Basil Kift, was a mixture of writers we had already published and new ones; a mixture too of stories, reportage and verse. It still reads well; and for me movingly because it contains one of Andrew Shonfield's earliest pieces, reportage on the burial of a soldier killed when his motor-cycle crashed. In a sentence or two, Shonfield caught the pathos of the occasion.

'I notice Jamieson, who was his friend, sobbing behind a tremendous wreath of flowers . . . And as he sobs the flowers shake and then vibrate individually upon their long necks. Shaking and shaking, the enormous wreath looks like an awkward shield which hides a schoolboy face giggling at some sudden grotesquerie.'

3

My own connection with the Club had been becoming less close for some time. Before joining Education I had been sent for a few weeks to brigade HQ as an Intelligence officer, where my senior was that thoughtful man I mentioned earlier, who had taken to himself, though he need not have done, the burden of presiding at an execution.

Leaving the troop for brigade HQ was like quitting a sec. mod. for a grammar school. Here the Other Ranks and NCOs were batmen, clerks, signalmen, storekeepers – neat and soft-handed, with hardly any admixture from the harsher working-class trades. The officers' mess was civil, if not intellectual; minor public-school in general tone. The brigadier was a regular, an amusing and amused man who refused to fuss anyone, because he assumed they would all be decent chaps who did a decent job.

During that short tour of duty I met yet another of those groups – temporary, but complete in their day and terms – which formed themselves within the Services wherever there was enough room for social movement. Just before the ill-advised American attempt to cross the open ground before the monastery, I was told to go up as near as possible to Cassino, to the forward Intelligence unit, and bring back the latest information on the state of the battle. Movement well up had to be in darkness. I found the unit on the southern or back slope of a hill which faced the monastery, spread out under linked tents. They handed me a copy of the briefing which they brought up to date every hour or so. I have no idea how efficient they were, how well they compared with their German opposite numbers, how they had been selected or whether other procedures within the British army would have produced a more effective group. It was their cohesion of manners which most impressed. One or two of the group of eight or nine might have been regulars, but regulars with more intelligence than the average, capable of being sent on a sequence of difficult training courses; intelligent upper middle-class army-family stock. The others were unmistakably Oxbridge, so articulately, so confidently, so relaxedly, so assuredly pre-war Oxbridge (and at least middle middle-class) that they could have been characters from *Brideshead Revisited*. The ways of moving. The gestures, and the voices were easy, but as formal as if choreographed. Most revealing of all were the forms of their speech, the phrasing rather than the accents. Unfinished sentences, most of them oblique and many of them verbless, a complicated code much more powerfully indicative of a closed group than even the physical marks such as the loose chokers in the necks of their battle-dress blouses. I was seeing and hearing all this whilst sitting in a corner reading the brief. One pair at a nearby trestle table were in the intervals talking about classical civilisation in southern Italy.

A week or so before I was due to go back to the unit I was offered the chance to go to a school for Intelligence officers somewhere in the Middle East, with likely promotion following on transfer. It was tempting, but by then I had been with that troop for about three and a half years, and neither Mary nor I envisaged a spell for me as a peacetime officer, no matter how elevated. So a jeep took me down the road and back up to the Vomero.

Now that, in early 1945, the end of the war in Europe was plainly not far off, my interest in adult education and its post-war importance was growing rapidly. British armies round the world had for some time been receiving the pamphlets of ABCA, the Army Bureau of Current Affairs. Its driving force was W. E. Williams, a fiery, wiry Welshman, later Secretary-General of the Arts Council, but probably best remembered in association with Allen Lane's Pelican Books. At some point in the war, probably as it became clear that the tide was turning and that soon millions of men would be coming back to a Britain they were thoroughly out of touch with, someone became convinced that more should be done to prepare those men. Most of those in the High Command – though I suspect Sir Ronald Adam, the Adjutant General, was on the enlightened wing – were thinking only of giving advice on the practicalities of resettlement, within a society assumed to be going on much as it had before.

The Beveridge Report had been published in 1942 and Butler's Act on our educational future in 1944; two flagships for the post- war period. By 1944 there was an unusual feeling in the air among servicemen, not often articulated cogently, but indicated by banal-sounding phrases: 'We don't mean to go back to what it was like before'; 'Things have got to change'; 'I'm not standing for that lot again'; 'We didn't go through all this just to settle back where we were'. There had been a sea-change among men who had been, most of them, ill-educated, not encouraged to have many expectations or to look forward to any change for the better, to progress, to movement.

Even during the war only a minority had been brought into contact with more open societies such as America, Canada, Australia. Most had seen societies much more economically backward than their own, so they could continue to feel superior to them, and had in no way been introduced to other countries' political ideas, open or closed. The tone of propaganda had changed during the war, but most remained patronising: the *de haut en bas* tones had yielded to the self-consciously pally, that was all. But the ice-blocks were cracking. That waiter-service for the officers, on the ship which took us to the Algiers landings in 1942, had begun to look outdated by late 1944. The War Office still issued material of the 'simple souls but hearts of oak' variety, most of which assumed that people knew and accepted their places within the hierarchies and were one and all nationalists and royalists. Most of the gunners I knew had another pattern of attitudes, however: they were chauvinistic – that was deeply ingrained by education and most later persuasion; very few were politically aware, but those few were almost all socialists; very few, though they followed the army's rules where they had to, were at bottom deferential to rank, and the remnants of deference decreased as the war went on; and most men were not royalists – they had 'very little time' for the Royal Family.

It follows that the concept of an Army Bureau for the spread of knowledge about current affairs was not likely to commend itself to most in the War Office; indeed, to many in the War Office and outside it would seem likely to promote subversion. So it was extraordinary that the powers allowed ABCA to be set up. It may be that Philip Morris, one of the great educational pro-consuls of the time, who was Director-General of Army Education towards the end of hostilities (itself an unusually inspired appointment), put his weight behind the idea. The favourite explanation for ABCA's start, which may well be a typical and topical myth, was that W. E. Williams had been called in to promote in a traditional manner the education of the troops in those later stages, that he proposed what became ABCA, met strong resistance but pursued his case as far as Churchill; who said it should go ahead.

So ABCA was born and the pamphlets dispatched regularly. They seemed to my inexperienced eye models of exposition for adults who had little background to the issues they treated but were assumed to be intelligent enough to grasp an argument clearly presented. They did not talk down, and underestimated neither the subject nor the capacity of the readers – getting across without selling out. They were factual, concise, and entirely without the chauvinistic blarney which disfigured so much in official handouts. They were rare English examples of that *haute vulgarisation* which the French respect and the British fear. To those soldiers willing to listen and think about them – and they may have been a minority, though probably a larger minority than the conventional powers would have been happy to realise – they could have come as a revelation. 'They', in so far as the ABCA pamphlets were assumed to have come from 'them', had not talked to ordinary soldiers so directly and tonelessly before. The tones they had known had moved on a short line between the bossy and the wheedling. The simple but awe-ful thought then struck me that these men had virtually never in their lives listened to a writer trying to talk objectively, honestly, about life and its problems; that never to have met the works of Jane Austen or George Eliot or Thomas Hardy or all the rest was a huge limitation, to be regretted not because it indicated that they had not had access to some socially-defined (and, to some who felt they had that access, socially confined) High Culture, but because they had been denied entry to one of the most important of all liberating experiences – the opportunity to recognise that it is possible to try disinterestedly to look at and give some sort of meaning to your life, not to move only between prejudice and gossip, disconnectedly and repetitively.

Each troop had to designate one officer to introduce the men to the subject of each pamphlet. I suspect that ABCA's clarity often got mangled in the process of mediation. Still, there they all sat month after month, being introduced not only to the main issues in social security policy or educational planning or industrial prospects or trade unionism or local government, but – more important – being introduced also to the idea that these things concerned them and that they could have, should have, a say in the discussion and resolution of them.

It used to be commonly said that the shaking-up experiences of several years of war, whether abroad or at home, had prepared the ground for the election of the Labour government of 1945. I still think that is probably true, though nowadays such a link is often played down. The Services vote was not large enough to put Labour in. That probably owed more to disaffection on the Home Front. But I believe ABCA's succession of pamphlets and the regular talk plus discussion sessions based on them all over the world did a great deal to make many soldiers vote for Attlee – not because ABCA's activities were barely disguised socialist propaganda (they were not), but because they helped reduce the power of the mandarin voices, accelerated the decline in deference, made soldiers realise they did have a right to think for themselves. They still, most of them, admired Churchill for his pugnaciousness and steadfastness. Their vote for Labour was not a vote against him as a war leader. It was a vote against the Establishment from which, for all his populist appeal, he came and in peacetime stood for, and a vote in favour of their new-found sense of themselves and their significance.

4

The war in Europe ended early in May 1945. We had been expecting the end for so long that, when it came, it had little emotional impact.

By mid-1945 the resettlement courses had been established in London: a week for chosen officers to learn all the main elements, from the practical to the fairly simple psychological, about the business of settling in again, so that they could pass it on when they got back. A travel warrant appeared after the usual delays and ordered me to report to Capodichino airport next day. There stood a roughly-converted Lancaster bomber. A handful of us climbed into seats like sawn-off deckchairs, clutching canvas bags and transit rations. Throughout the journey the Polish crew talked and sang over the engine noise and vibration. At Peterborough they twice tried to land but were warned off by a Verey light arching just ahead of us. The third time they swore, and Polish swearing is as rich as Polish stew, ignored the light and landed. The crew immediately raced across the tarmac. One of our deserted group, a legal officer reporting back to London, guessed they were running gold up from North Africa via Naples, and wanted to get shot of it before whatever skeletal customs procedures Peterborough had could catch up with them.

I reached King's Cross hours later and made for the West London Reporting Centre; Mary had been sent multiple letters to every address she might be in at around that time, asking her to come to London and leave a message at the Centre saying where she had, I hoped, found for us to stay. It was by then just about three years since we had seen each other. Her three or four days there before I arrived were a nerve-racking mixture of anticipation and uncertainty; she went to the Centre every few hours, then back to the Royal Court Hotel in Sloane Square, each time having to persuade the receptionist to let her stay, even though the pressure on rooms was unceasing and even though she had passed the term of her original booking. So I arrived, and found her. We held tight, silently, for a long time. The Royal Court found it possible for us to keep the room until my course ended, and then the army gave us all a week's leave. We went to Leeds and Stalybridge and stole three or four days alone in an almost empty Cornwall. Towards the end, Mary slid off her bicycle into a ditch and we realised she was probably pregnant; as she was. Then back to Italy for what turned out to be just over nine more months.

Once back, I found that, personal relationships apart, the experience of seeing Britain again after so long had been disturbing

more than joyous. I wrote a short essay about it but was out of
practice and it was portentous. I wrote about eavesdropping all
the time in London to find out what people were thinking, but
being put off by the same old voices and the virtual preoccupa-
tion of so many people with the prospect of better food, more
varied clothes and fresh amusements: I had assumed a great
many people would be thinking about the implications of the
atom bomb, but only a very few were. I had thought the implications of Belsen would be a hard pill even for twentieth-century
civilisation to swallow, but for most, apparently, they were no
more than a nine-days' wonder or horror. During the week in
London, I heard one favourable comment about the new government: 'Now we have a Socialist government, we must do all we
can to pull it through.' The speaker was a pre-war refugee from
Hungary.

Back with the regiment I fell into becoming, half unofficially,
our resettlement and education officer, trying to answer a range of
questions with little more than the guidance of that short course.
In its own terms, it had not been an inept course. On practical
matters it was clear and competent. But the most important
questions men asked could not be answered unambiguously:
'Should I try to get further qualifications? Would I get a grant?
Even if I did, my wife might object to living on a grant not a full
wage. And she wants to start a family soon.' More complicated
problems introduced faithless wives, or the worry of setting up
home again but with a child there who is not your own, or
parents-in-law who never liked you, have enjoyed having their
daughter to themselves again in your absence, and will not give up
easily.

I was unqualified to deal anything like adequately with such
knotted problems, but I listened and then wrote letter after letter,
especially to bodies in Britain who might be able to help. Most of
them tried. My ABCA experience led me to seek special help from
the WEA, the Workers' Educational Association; their general
secretary, Ernest Green, another now almost-forgotten pre-war
pillar of popular education, gave help well beyond anything I
could reasonably have asked for. After some months of this
welfare and advisory work, it seemed natural, at the beginning of
1946, to become brigade staff captain for education.

Someone at the Istituto Orientale for university-level language studies, situated in the old part of Naples, had learned that there was an officer nearby who had a degree in English Literature and, what's more, a postgraduate degree as well. I was approached by a dapper, sweet-smelling, round professor who was enchanted to learn that my degrees were from Leeds. 'Ah, that great scholar Professor Wilson,' he breathed. 'What a stable to have come from.' It was useless to tell him that F. P. Wilson had left for Oxford long before I was aware of Leeds University. The halo of Wilson circled me from then to the end of my time. The professor was a consummate name-dropper. As we entered the library of his big, bachelor's flat on my first visit he asked without warning: 'And how is my good friend George Bernard Shaw?' glancing as he did so at a large photograph on a nearby wall. In the background was Vesuvius; in the foreground were four or five professors and in the middle of them the lanky figure of Shaw. My host was next to GBS, smiling widely but looking as though he had squeezed in there just before the bulb popped – which was, I soon learned, exactly what he had done.

He was a barrow-boy of academia. His students all had the same guide to English and the same edition of the set texts. The paper in all of them looked remarkably like that black-market toilet paper spirited from the captured ship. Any student who wished to succeed would have those texts and in a viva would take care to respond to questions, all drawn from the book, with answers in exactly the form given in the book: 'What do you wish in this post office, miss?' 'I wish please two threepenny stamps and a postal order for two shillings and sixpence.' 'Wrong. Think again.' 'I wish for two threepenny stamps and a postal order for two and ninepence.' 'Correct. Proceed!' His guide to English etiquette, also a highly desirable text for any ambitious student, showed a delicate sense of English manners and a fine eye for the placing of adverbs and capitals: 'If your hostess graciously asks you to carve the joint it is Not Done to roll up your sleeves to perform the task'; 'You should not quarrel Audibly with your wife at the dinner table.' His students swore he had spent a total of only two weeks in England, some time in the Thirties. One might have guessed the Nineties, from the succession of dinner parties where careless cads had to be warned off rolling up their sleeves to carve, and married couples carried on sibilant wars.

Before giving my first lecture I was taken to meet the Rector or

President. A shabby, war-dusty room, with another small man behind a large cluttered desk. Conversation began quietly enough but soon erupted into angry shoutings, flashing eyes and bangings on the desk. I never learned what had caused all this, but had the impression that it was only another skirmish in a running war. The two of us went down to the lecture theatre. As he opened the door which led to the platform we were assailed by an uproar. The very large lecture theatre was crammed: they were on every inch of space as well as on every seat – on the steps, the floor and the window ledges. Many of them were clearly ex-servicemen, and many had obviously been waiting a long time, since they had the remnants of their lunchpacks on their knees. One might, in advance, have expected it to be a bewildering and embarrassing sight, but it was not: it was moving and heartening. They had been years without access through a native speaker to the English language and literature which they had chosen to study, and their moment had come at last. Their faces glowed with expectation and welcome.

The professor was not to be done out of making a fine speech. He introduced me as a scholar of profound distinction, one of the prize pupils of that great man and colleague, Professor F. P. Wilson. There hung in the air the clear imputation that he too had been one of FP's brightest and best. I would introduce them with surpassing brilliance to that masterpiece of our Shakespeare, *Macbeth*, and intersperse those golden hours with incisive introductions to the language itself. How privileged they were! And what is more – here he paused and raised his arm before bringing it smack down on the rostrum – 'He is doing all this – for free!' I had assumed I was, but this was the first actual confirmation. The students burst into sustained applause, hammering on desks and drumming their feet.

I saw him no more in the class and hardly ever again anywhere. No doubt he had an informer or two who told him I was keeping the students happy so he could go about his other business, fighting the Rector and cooking up yet more twin-language textbooks, printed on toilet paper provided by the crony who published for him. I worked from such a copy of *Macbeth*, treading a delicate path as I corrected what even I could see was often a wobbly Italian translation, whilst not making him a figure of fun to his students.

Rather more than twenty years later I walked those corridors again, a middle-aged man about to talk to students who looked hardly into their teens. The high-pitched, always verging on the choleric, voice of that professor, whose name I no longer remember, seemed to come through the still shabby walls. But he was already dead.

In the intervals of army duties and lecturing, I wrote my first essay in the explicit hope of publication: 'The Journey of Sydney Keyes' – not a distinguished piece of work but with some of the insights youthful enthusiasm can inspire. I had little idea where to send it but finally chose *The Poetry Review*. The editor replied saying that in his view I was an important new talent, that he was privileged to publish me and that payment would follow. I imagine he said that to all the boys and girls, for though the essay did appear in the issue of January–February 1947, no payment followed.

Then I began work on an essay about Auden. He had been my favourite living poet ever since Leeds in the mid-Thirties, and the interest had increased throughout the war, especially after the publication of *Another Time* in 1940. At first I was thinking only of another essay of about the length of that on Sydney Keyes. But this grew and went off in new and unexpected directions so that when I did finally leave for England I had what looked likely to be at least a monograph. It became, some years later, my first full-length book.

On 26 May 1946, only a few weeks before I was due to be demobilised, I had a cable announcing that our son had been born. I remember saying to Andrew Shonfield, though I don't know where I dug up the phrases, 'We have a man-child. A man-child has been born to us.' That seemed wording suitable to the momentousness of the event. In the weeks before the birth Mary had been searching for jobs advertised in the educational press and applying on my behalf for any which seemed at all likely. I still had half of the Frank Parkinson postgraduate scholarship from Leeds with which, if the war hadn't intervened, I could have had good hopes of going to Cambridge to work on a doctorate. It was still possible to try for a Cambridge place and to hope that a second year's grant could be found somewhere. But Cambridge was already filling up with its own returning servicemen, accommodation was scarce, and accommodation suitable for a couple with a very small baby even scarcer. We decided that I would let the balance of the scholarship lapse.

I was finally demobbed about a week ahead of time because the University of Hull had called me for interview; the brigadier approved that immediately. It took a good few days to go by train from Naples to Calais; most of the lines were in poor shape even a year after the end of hostilities in Europe. Huge army cookhouses were placed at intervals and at even further intervals transit camps for one-night stops. Throughout I sat happily next to a man called Bill Connor who had a well-deserved pre-war reputation as the *Daily Mirror*'s eloquently withering columnist, Cassandra, and was going straight back there. We met again years later and remembered how we had helped pass the hours by inventing advertising copy. Our finest was for Critch, the powder guaranteed to cure 'crutch itch', the itch in our crutches from which we all suffered throughout that journey. Somewhere in Germany the train stopped at the ruins of a city station. We walked out of what had been the entrance and faced a waste of brickyard, a town reduced to rubble for as far as one could see. It was Pantelleria on a much larger scale.

Eventually I reached Stalybridge and saw Simon, our first child. Mary's parents were, as always, helpful in every way possible; and we went to Leeds to show off the baby. I went to a nearby demobilisation depot and changed my coupons for a set of civilian clothing. It was a very cleverly arranged outfit, as clever as the organisation of the ration book or the launching of 'Utility furniture'. It hit the absolute or dead mean of taste and did not – here was a gain – distinguish between officers and others. There was a limited choice of suit colours, rather as there was of spectacle frames in the heyday of National Health optical services. I do not remember a choice of styles. One wandered down the aisles in the Ashton-under-Lyne drill hall, looking for the right size. Mine reminded me too much of my first long-trousered suit, bought with a 'cheque' for repayment over twenty weeks and costing thirty bob. I offered the demob suit a few months later to a cowboy painter and decorator, but he insisted on giving me half-a-crown for it, probably so that he could all the more confidently rebut anyone who accused him of stealing it. There was a brown snap-brimmed trilby, which made me look as though I was heading for an early Death as a Salesman. That was kicked around by the children years later. But it would be wrong to be snooty; this was inevitably mass provision, but it had as much as could be managed of a human face.

5

So that was the end of five-and-three-quarter years. Not a heroic period for me and for those I was with, most of the time; little horror, some pity, more boredom and a submerged resentment at the waste. Why did we not choose more heroic roles? With rare exceptions my colleagues were capable of courage when that was called for, as it was a few times. I knew no one who had deliberately chosen ack-ack as a relatively safe arm. I suppose most took what they were offered; and when their Regiment was converted to a mobile role they took that; if they had been converted into airborne troops they would have accepted that too. Unless their feelings are very directly engaged, more men habitually go with the grain of what life offers than strike out. A few were making, silently, more of a stand; were reacting against more dramatic roles and the styles of some of the people who assumed them. It was an involuted, an inhibited, set of attitudes, neither to be praised nor excused; and in some ways very British.

For most of us, these events took half of our twenties. For those newly-married there was the loss of the few years of the special kind of youthful freedom before the family begins to arrive. We put up with it in a marking-time sort of way, as if disconnected from real life; that was to start afterwards. It was harder for those at home; they were not, as we were, cocooned from the pettyfogging, wearing, day-by-day difficulties of making ends meet, always against the same drab background.

The most miserable among the servicemen were those who could never lift their eyes even to what was new and different around them. One had to watch that they didn't sink into a self-destructive gloom at the never-relieved thoughts of home and, at the worst, of worries about home. But most of these kinds of servicemen did not need special worries: they were totally and all the time lost, because their small worlds – Nuneaton, Hartlepool, Bethnal Green – had been all-embracing, and they could scarcely exist in any other place.

I can think of no more convincing explanation for this extraordinary phlegm by almost everybody else, at home or abroad, than that we had no choice and that in such circumstances people do go on going-on, that the days become weeks and the weeks months and the months years. How much longer would we have gone on? Probably for yet more years.

And we came back, when many thousands did not. Set against their loss, any loss of ours was inconsiderable. Now we were no longer fed, clothed and sheltered by the Army, were looking for jobs, and perhaps had a wife and baby to care for. But what mattered most, what counted overwhelmingly, was that we were at last free to begin shaping lives of our own.

PART TWO

WANDERING TEACHER

A schoolmaster should have an atmosphere of awe and walk wonderingly, as if he was amazed at being himself.

W. Bagehot

The true teacher defends his pupils against his own personal influence.

A. B. Alcott

CHAPTER 4

✿

REDCAR AND MARSKE
1 9 4 6 – 9

The appointing committee at the University College of Hull had an air of consequence combined with courteousness and a wish to put you at your ease. The philosophy professor, Tom Jessop, exemplified the style. With double-breasted, charcoal-mixture worsted suit – and double-breasted waistcoat with a hunter watch on a gold chain – he was portentous but kindly, as befitted a nationally eminent Methodist layman. The whole committee was gentle. They had *gravitas*, certainly, because this was serious business; but not an excessive weightiness; a small University College still not funded by the University Grants Committee had to strike a nice balance there, and they did.

Mary had sent in nine or ten applications for jobs on my behalf, giving a *curriculum vitae*, names of referees and all else needed. Nothing grand, in the academic hunting order, none to Oxbridge or the big redbricks. Smaller universities or university colleges, rather, which were looking for assistant lecturers at £350 a year. One extra-mural department was advertising also, Hull; and the British Council had a vacancy in Sweden within a university English department. That was the chancy joker in all those modest applications: I suppose I liked even then the idea of introducing Britain through her literature.

There may have been almost six years of war, but in the universities the socio-academic pattern held. None of the eight or nine small places took up references, the essential gateway to a possible interview. Clearly, a Leeds first was heavily discounted on that *bureau de change*. Day after day little notes arrived, usually two lines long and cyclostyled in purple ink. They all had the same kind of message: 'I have been asked to inform you that the appointment has been offered to Miss Jennifer Trump, B.A. (Oxon)' – or '(Cantab)'.

I remember now – the censor has nodded – that there was another joker. When several rejections had come in and we were beginning to feel nervous, I applied for a graduate-traineeship in management with the John Lewis Partnership.

John Lewis was not interested either, I think probably for two or even three reasons. To him 'graduates' would be from Oxbridge; and he might suspect a first. So, a first from the provinces!? And one who had run an *arts* club in Italy after hostilities ended? Far better a reasonable Oxbridge second, with a blue. Even now as I walk past that John Lewis flagship in Oxford Street, I look up and wonder – perhaps a career might have been crowned up there, in the general manager's office? More likely, an early agreement to separate because this particular graduate trainee seemed not to have a vocation for paternalistic higher retailing.

As to the universities: ten years later I asked a professor of English, again at a smallish provincial place, how he was going to sort out the very numerous candidates for a similar first appointment: 'Oh,' he said, 'I think I'll eliminate for a start all except those with Oxbridge firsts.' Perhaps he was then driven to eliminate all without an Oxbridge doctorate. He had himself a provincial first degree but an Oxbridge doctorate. Of course, Oxbridge admit and train well some brilliant people; given all their advantages, it would be remarkable if those two places did not; they also admit some who are no more than modestly talented and a few quite unfitted but with the right connections. The skewed British educational system ensures that a good number of very bright people never have the chance to think of Oxbridge; and the provincial universities are as sparing with their firsts as Oxbridge, and with their doctorates.

In mid-1946 University extra-mural work had just been given a big boost. Many in the Labour government were grateful for the opportunities it had long provided in the provinces – especially in the Welsh valleys, Lancashire, Yorkshire and parts of Scotland. The success of the Army Bureau of Current Affairs had indicated the response to and importance of adult education – on the left, in the middle and among the more civilised Tories and senior civil servants.

That mid-Forties non-vocational injection would be hardly thinkable in the late Eighties, is against everything universities are now supposed to stand for and that government favours. But, ironically again, in 1946 Churchill – who was by then in the wilderness, and who had been persuaded of the importance of ABCA – might have been imagined smiling quizzically but fairly favourably upon it.

As is the case with most of us on such occasions, I assumed from looking round Hull's waiting-room at the dozen or so in attendance that I – incidentally still in uniform, so soon had the call come – would be low on the list of possibles. There was the inevitable man of much confidence, with a rolled umbrella and a record of some years already in the trade, part-time at a very large redbrick university. Six of us were appointed, but not the umbrella man; perhaps he seemed too assured for that insecure provincial citadel. Some of the six are now dead; all the others are retired after mixed careers in and out of academia; one, Muriel Crane, remains a very good friend.

The committee called the six back one by one. Surprisingly, they had decided to appoint me on the third rung of the ladder – £400 a year, not £350. Probably the lecturing experience in Naples and the Three Arts Club had influenced them. Though pleased, since a pound a week more was a substantial lift, I did not then or for some years see the significance of their move.

Waiting in Stalybridge that evening was a telegram announcing an interview, in London the next day, for a British Council post in Sweden. I did not know what the practice was in such instances but decided that having that day accepted the job in Hull I could not try for any others. I have kept a soft spot for the British Council. It has from its start and with some justice been called a suede-shoed Oxbridge body, but when eight small universities and university colleges did not bother to take up the references of a well-qualified Leeds graduate the Council went as far as to offer an interview.

I

University extra-mural departments divide the whole of Britain between them, and guard their areas as jealously as French departmental prefects. When I joined Hull its province ran from

Middlesbrough in the north, down over the Humber and through Grimsby just into deep Lincolnshire; east to the bleak coast of Holderness and west to the far side of Selby, with York as a West Berlin shared with Leeds – which was, at the start, not as active extra-murally as Hull.

Hull's new head of department, G. E. T. Mayfield, despatched me to the far north of his territory, to the Middlesbrough, Redcar, Darlington area. The northern Dales are magnificently, windily open, and remain unspoiled. Middlesbrough itself, on the Tees estuary, was in the early nineteenth century one of the most rapidly-growing of all the industrial cities; it still had the air of having been cheaply thrown together for the benefit of industry: street after street of poor housing, a mean little centre, a dirty and smelly circulation of air, grey light above the chimney-pots; virtually no indication of a sense that people have a right to try to live with dignity and grace. They were busy at that time putting up nearby a huge complex of even more evil-smelling installations – many of them became, I believe, victims of the recession of the Seventies. As always, the predominant mood of people was cheerful and friendly. I had an elderly blind student who lived in a small house near the works, always enveloped by the stink of refinery emissions; from her benevolence of character you might have thought fortune had placed her, comfortably-off and sighted, in Provence.

I started work from Stalybridge, before we had found accommodation up North, which meant being introduced to the first of that huge range of establishments which cater for lower commercial and professional itinerants: the commercial travellers' and occasional peripatetic lecturers' small hotels or guest houses. Those which called themselves hotels, though they might be no larger than the guest house two doors down the street, were preferable, since guest houses had landladies rather than proprietors or managers, and landladies tended to appear, like over-zealous, self-employed guard-dogs, from the back passage whenever you came or went – just to 'make sure you're all right'; which meant to keep an eye on you.

Hotels had an atmosphere slightly more distanced and anonymous, even if they too had only a dozen rooms. In both kinds of establishment most rooms had by then wash-basins; added long after the houses had been built, so the pipes marched over and up the always flowery wallpaper. Other 'private facilities' were still rare, and so was central heating, though a few had shilling-in-the-slot gas-meters in some bedrooms. There was a communal bath down the corridor, opened only with the key kept in the office. The dining-room and the lounge were usually warm. Except in the best places, and those were known as exactly as truckers know the best pull-ins, only the more tired 'travellers', those who had spent the better part of their working-lives moving from one such place to another, took supper (or, usually, high tea) in the 'digs'. They had lost the energy to seek out restaurants and weren't fussy about what was served.

Breakfasts were usually good; as we always say, in an attempt to find some culinary virtues, that's the one meal the British respect and do right by in their public provision. Still, some places would try to get away with serving the cheapest of streaky bacon and the smallest of eggs, no tomatoes, mushrooms or sausages and certainly no fried bread. Against those the commercial travellers soon struck, so such places went downhill or improved their breakfasts. Sitting in the bay-window of the dining-room on a Middlesbrough avenue facing a good breakfast on a crisp autumn morning, with the wind coming off the Dales not from the factories, you could almost forget for a very short time the poverty, the illiberality, of expectation postulated by almost everything around you on behalf of those who passed their lives there.

At such a breakfast one morning there were at the table for six where I sat five young commercial travellers; like me, all or most of them newly from the Services. This was before the days of the executive briefcase; our plastic old-style briefcases or attaché-cases were on the side; so, like the props of a small chorus-line, were five trilbies. They were all alike – light chocolate-brown (the current phrase was 'nigger-brown'), snap-brimmed, turned up at the back, well-brushed; I think they were called 'Robin Hoods'. It was a uniform, as were the hacking-jackets with two vents at the back and the tapered trousers which rested just on the arch of the foot. That uniform, completed by the *Daily Telegraph* at the ready, remained until at least the late-Fifties, when I saw it on members of a course for aspiring executives at the Henley Administrative Staff College.

The conversation, as always happened in those first years of the Attlee government, turned to politics. The travellers one and all abused Attlee and all his deeds. They were reciting the mantra, saying

what they thought Their Kind of People on the First Step of the
Ladder would be expected to say – especially by their bosses. It was
routine, conventional, biased, unthinking. They were stroking
each other, not communicating but massaging one another's – and,
more important, their own – egos in preparation for the day's re-
entry into the harshly competitive, rigidly right-wing world they
had put their trust in and hoped to climb within. I decided the
occasion needed a dissident voice.

That was the first and is so far the only occasion on which I have
been collectively and loudly abused from a bay-window, hurriedly
thrown open; the chorus-line came to life for at least this
presentation. They leaned out as I walked down the avenue, calling
'Fucking Commie' and the like until I turned the bend.

That incident from so long ago prompts me to realise that I am a
once-born socialist and will remain one. I recognise virtues in
Conservatism and so why some good people embrace it; but I could
never vote that way. The test is the sense of community, of
fraternity; and that of Conservatism is at bottom a form of
patronage. Similarly, I could not vote for the very far left; their sense
of fraternity is often too bossy, 'for your own good'; their
'community' is often 'communitarianism' and so finally levelling
and centralising. We should feel members one of another, but also
retain all we have of sparky, spikey individuality.

This sense of both belonging to others and of responsibility for
our own consciences may to a large extent have come from my early
Primitive Methodist years. It remains, all those years after I realised
I had lost that religious belief which our neighbourhood instilled
more consistently than any other principle for living; the belief is
not likely to come back.

The best commercial hotels were in Scarborough. The most
successful had a good holiday trade but reserved a few rooms for
their regular 'commercials'. Out of season they were usually full of
commercials. Until I had a car, and later when the weather was too
bad to trust the high and winding coast road, I stayed at our
Department's favoured establishment; in a three-sided close with its
fourth side open to the long road which ran opposite the side of the
railway station. High tea was hearty in the Yorkshire manner but
did not vary; or perhaps it seemed not to vary because I stayed there
on the same day each week. Masses of excellent piping-hot chips

cooked in beef-dripping, not vegetable oil, a large slice of gammon (the farms in the hinterland made sure their regulars didn't go short), an egg, several slices of bread already buttered, a large pot of tea and a glass stand of buns, cakes and 'fancies'. Those teas, and Middlesbrough-style breakfasts day after day, explained why there was much talk of heart attacks among the older men. After such a tea, I went to my class and the commercials settled down in the lounge to do their books and exchange the gossip of the week.

Once back, I listened to their Willy Loman stories, but was never asked to reciprocate. That I lectured to adult classes for the University College of Hull seemed to strike them with the same strangeness as if I had announced I was touring manager for a regional symphony orchestra – altogether out-of-the-way and a bit 'above their heads'. But no resentment at what might have seemed a toffee-nosed occupation. Unlike the snap-brimmed trilby chorus in Middlesbrough, most of the Scarborough regulars were middle-aged; and a little sad and drained. They had had years of being away from home most weekdays, of making up their books night after night, of anxiously checking on how orders were coming along, aware all the time that the over-arching figure of the Area Sales Manager in Leeds, all the time 'on their backs', would be even now going over last week's figures.

I used to think, for both the common features and the contrasts, of Matthew Arnold as one of Her Majesty's Inspectors doing his reports and also trying to write creatively in similarly difficult circumstances; but the Scarborough travellers couldn't sometimes stay with well-to-do friends. They had at least some comfort as a group, a slightly desperate comfort. They were past the age at which they might have been called to take over in that Leeds sales office, and past the age at which they could have changed jobs; they were the ageing brothers of the even more anxious newspaper canvassers of the Thirties.

At about half-past nine (an interesting time, since it showed that most of them did not go out to the pubs, which even then stayed open until ten) tea and biscuits were brought in, the order-papers put away, and the conversation broadened. Not to areas outside the trade but away from that week's stories to remembered anecdotes with a wider, an archetypal, significance. One night I overheard – they were not talking directly to me or I would have suspected leg-pulling – the story of Ronnie X's downfall. In its collectively-remembered quality, it was like the old myth about commercial travellers telling each other dirty jokes in a train, jokes they knew so well they didn't need actually to repeat them but had only to announce 'Number 57' to roll with laughter as a body.

Ronnie had been a traveller for years, selling women's underwear (most of them were in small consumer or fashion goods). Trade had been bad for some time so he secretly became representative also for a firm selling French letters. Good money that, since he already had a car and a lodging allowance from his first firm. The punch-line, which was delivered with practised timing, was prompted by an innocent or apparently innocent question from a newcomer, if there was one; if not, the group would give a series of 'Oh ay's' as the climax neared, and then raise their eyes – a signal that the narrator could go straight into the finale: 'Then one week he got his orders crossed! That did it! Never got another steady job.' Did they really believe that story? Perhaps it or something like it had happened once upon a time. But how had so many of them come to know Ronnie X? The whole tale and its telling had the air of a tribal legend.

Within a few weeks, we found somewhere to live in my territory: half a house on the main road running out of Redcar towards Middlesbrough, a 'through' terrace house dating from about 1910, with a bay-windowed front room, another room immediately behind that and a kitchen at the far back; a classic style in lower middle-class housing.

The landlady-owner was a flowery-genteel elocutionist from Middlesbrough, a past-mistress of the off-putting rhetorical question, especially when you asked for some simple and useful facility which might be taken for granted in a rented and so-called furnished house. 'Curtains for the front room? You really feel you need them?' – in a manner which suggested that the best people nowadays had all discarded curtains, as a comic working-class custom. She had a fine line in entirely verbal patronage. She picked up my *Concise Cambridge History of English Literature*, glanced at the blurb, turned to her constant lady companion and enunciated, as though she had come across the complete *Encyclopaedia Britannica* in a room she had the privilege of owning: 'Imagine, my dear, the whole of our great literary heritage in the one volume.' I hope she gave it to her prize pupils thereafter; there was an ingenuous romanticism behind the gentility.

The house was in dreadful condition, not fit for a very small baby without massive antiseptic cleaning; the furniture and carpets looked as though they had been picked up as a job-lot at a house clearance. No doubt they had; such set-ups were common immediately after the war; there was money to be made from stranded young families, and the houses themselves steadily appreciated in value even though hardly any care and maintenance was done on them. We had half the house and, by an arrangement I've seen nowhere else, that meant we had the downstairs front room, the other tenants the downstairs back room; the bedrooms were similarly distributed, and the kitchen shared. The other couple had a small baby too; the husband was an accountant just moved down from Scotland to make his way. Such an arrangement could have been a source of recurrent friction, but I cannot remember a cross word in the whole year we were there. Without abusing her, we formed a front against the genteel-mean landlady; and we shared things. They had a large zinc bath which we borrowed so as to bathe in front of the fire in our sitting-room; I expect we had something they borrowed.

Redcar was then a dreary little town. In part a weekend lung for Middlesbrough working-class families, it preferred to think of itself as a rather proper dormitory for people who could afford to live there and work in Middlesbrough, or for the comfortably retired. It had a social life of its own and its own town council. The town clerk, a man of substance, lived a couple of hundred yards down the road from us, in a prick-neat house and garden. The whole set-up was too small and so too parochial even by English standards.

In 1946, to be a newcomer in a place like Redcar could bear hard on you. You didn't know a butcher or a grocer so had no place in the queue for titbits off-rations. An essay could be written on the power accrued, by butchers especially, during the war and for as long as rationing lasted – of meat until as late as the middle Fifties. Even if they were not corrupt, and I imagine most were not though some were 'keen', sentimental folklore set in so that a butcher would say – or his wife more likely, since she usually served – that Mrs So-and-

So had been loyal to their shop throughout the war and naturally they would see her all right now.

We were succoured by coincidence. Our regimental MO, he who had injected me with morphine as I was bumped on a broken door across Pantelleria's volcanic fields, was practising in Redcar, with an established family. One of their many kindnesses, in that notoriously bitter winter, was an introduction to their butcher; which meant that when the Old Loyalists had been served we might be offered, very much *sotto voce*, half a rabbit. I doubt if we have had a rabbit since rationing stopped; it says too much.

The educational and cultural pinnacle of the town was Coatham School, a day grammar school with some history and much sense of its own traditions. Probably not a bad grammar school in its own terms, once you had stripped off the sillier social habits. That was not easy; the headmaster ranked below only the town clerk and the vicar in the minute dance of the social order. In our time he was an amiable but scatter-brained man who congenitally took up new ideas so long as they were both simple and eschatological. His latest was Christian Science. But the school was officially of the Church of England persuasion, and each year at least a bishop and sometimes the Archbishop of York himself appeared to take confirmations. In our time the Archbishop, Cyril Garbett, came and, as was proper, was given the headmaster's study to robe himself. The headmaster appeared and offered the Archbishop a sheaf of literature which, he said, might be found interesting; Christian Science leaflets. The Archbishop's reply had the magisterial quality which most of us only wish we could find on remotely similar occasions, if any there are: 'Sir, for such offerings this is not the time nor the place; nor am I the man!'

Unknown to us, a distant relative lived in Redcar and soon came round. Her husband was a friendly, helpful, unassuming man, a long-serving clerk in a safe job. He showed no signs of the insecurity which those who set great store on respectability can show if they are working in a harsh commercial environment; he was, I think, in local government service. They had one child (everything they did was modest), a daughter on whom they doted. All three were small, as most in our own family are, probably because we all came from the poorer end of the working-class. In his family's terms, therefore, the husband had done well. They had a semi, a car (it was their mid-Thirties Hillman Minx I bought for £100 when they decided they could just afford a new model, in the middle of 1947). Their lives revolved steadily with the seasons round a fixed pattern: the garden, chapel, odd 'runs out' in the car, pleasant holidays in unadventurous places such as Southport, going to the 'pictures' occasionally, and having tea in Middlesbrough after shopping, also occasionally. 'Occasionally' was a much used word and well-packed, in that environment; it meant 'So you see we can break the routine from time to time, but nothing in excess.' Above all, they were devoted to looking after the home and maintaining its atmosphere of cosiness, neatness and welcome. If you saw the wife in the street without knowing her, you could have guessed simply from her tidy, composed appearance that she knew how to make a home; and that that home would be bustlingly cheerful, without quarrels, sulks or grudges, resolutely close and affectionate.

You can make such a guess with some middle-class, middle-aged women too, even if they are sitting confidently but quietly in the foyers of large hotels, not at all inhibited as working-class or lower middle-class housewives might be. In them too the composure comes as much as anything from the sense they carry that they belong to a world outside that setting, a centre they command and which is more real than any public foyer; no uneasiness but no bossiness; they sit right, and put public anonymity in its place.

I have sometimes found myself muttering: 'There's no home' or even 'Man goeth to his long home', as a charm against suburban domesticity. Indulgent; and the long vowels make the melancholy attractive. It is not easy to 'make a home', to practise the familial and neighbourly arts, those of one who 'sweeps a room as for Thy laws' which I first met closely in my in-laws, after the war, in that distantly-related couple and their daughter in Redcar. Those parents are long dead and those particular homes and the kind of peace they could hold gone, like millions of others. As though they had never existed. No: the style is passed on to those who want to carry it on, whom it suits. For those who have no faith outside, it is one marker – there are a few others such as, paradoxically, the urge to speak freely as an individual, whatever the cost – in what otherwise would be a meaningless flood.

When all has been said about its limits, we should also stand back and recognise how much better this suburban style was and is, as a way of life, than many alternatives. It was not aggressive; it believed in being companionable with those around it and had many well-practised ways of being so, all the well-lived-into, helpful neighbourly practices. Not many questions about the good, the true and the beautiful were asked, but some were lived-out; and nor did they tear one another apart. At their best such people achieved a pattern of domesticity and a sense of being connected to one another which were a quiet triumph.

Auden used a comfortable, undramatic limestone landscape as the symbol of domesticity and the suburban:

> . . . Dear, I know nothing of
> Either, but when I try to imagine a faultless love
> Or the life to come, what I hear is the murmur
> Of underground streams, what I see is a limestone landscape.

One of D. H. Lawrence's tiny master-strokes appears, quite unexpectedly, in *Women in Love*. We have been living for almost two hundred pages with the intellectual and emotional convolutions of the two emancipated modern girls, Ursula and Gudrun. Those two are at the Water Party when unexpectedly their parents, dressed in their best and looking what they are, innocent and unknowing, walk across the scene. It is as though a sketch by a naïve Sunday painter has been superimposed momentarily on a Picasso. The girls laugh at their appearance, at their mother: 'with much more of the shyness and trepidation of a young girl than her daughters ever felt, walking demurely beside her husband, who, as usual, looked rather crumpled in his best suit . . . She could not understand that there could be anything amiss with her appearance. She had a perfect calm sufficiency, an easy indifference to any criticism whatsoever . . .' But the girls are still callow enough to laugh at this vision of 'the shy, unworldly couple of their parents'. It is a remarkable cameo of the deep rightness that ordinariness can sometimes have.

2

After almost a year in that half-house, a student in my class at Marske, a tiny straggly village a couple of miles down the coast road between Redcar and Saltburn, told us of a bungalow for renting there. It lay up a snicket behind the main street, using the back garden of one of the shops there; not very well-built but attractive, a Mrs Tiggy-Winkle sort of place surrounded by a small garden. To us it was greatly preferable to the half-house, especially since we wanted to increase the family. The doctor's widow who owned it still lived in their big house-cum-surgery over the road. Embattled, rock-solid Tory, professional middle-class but very kind-hearted, she was an admirable landlady – once she had decided we would do, odd though we looked to her. She marched us over the road to inspect the property, waved at it whilst assaulting some monstrous recalcitrant growth, and uttered a mordant and vibrant sentence which conveyed all her forcefulness: 'Need to do something about that garden. IT'S THIGH-HIGH IN TWITCH GRASS.' So we moved in mid-summer, a comically small load. Some weeks later the local remover shifted two of our friends from Redcar to Saltburn. As he passed our snicket he told them: 'Moved some people up there the other week. They had nowt but bloody coal' – the half house had been economical with the coal rations, at least – 'and bloody books.'

We settled in very well, that summer of 1947; our daughter Nicola was born in August of 1948 and we stayed until the early autumn of 1949. During that first year in Redcar there had been little time for writing; learning how to live a family life after the hermetic ways of the army, learning how to teach, just keeping up with the weekly demands of four two-hour classes, plus always increasing numbers of weekend schools, pushed aside all but small items of writing.

By the time we moved to Marske the class preparation was containable. There was no space in the bungalow for a workroom, but there was an old wooden hut, detached, just at the back. Using enormous blanket pins, I hung from the roof old and smelly carpets found there so as to form a fairly draughtproof tent, bought a four-bar electric fire and settled to prepare classes and write. If all four bars were on and anything else, such as a vacuum cleaner, was added, the house circuit blew its main fuse. But that was only on the coldest days.

It all provided a reasonably workable pattern: preparing for classes, and if possible adding some writing in the morning; a walk on the windy beach with the pram most afternoons and more writing if any time was left, family tea, and so out to the class. The car had been laid up throughout the war and wasn't in bad shape. No heating and only a six-volt battery, so journeys of fifty or sixty miles each way on winter nights over those quite remote hills, especially down to Scarborough and Bridlington, meant you needed heavy clothing. On the worst nights, when the headlamps and windscreen wipers were on all the time, the battery would fail. But you could wind the windscreen open and switch off the wipers; that, though the snow or mist froze on your face, let you just see the verge – and later the cat's-eyes – and so got you home.

That early writing was of two kinds: pieces about adult education, of which more later, and general writing. During the summer of 1946 I had watched the local Bench in action at Stalybridge and looked at the habitués of the public library reading room. T. R. Fyvel, then literary editor of *Tribune* – George Orwell having given up that post in 1945 – showed interest, and the first of the pieces, on the local Bench, appeared in October. At some point there was an essay about railway station bookstalls. They were all, I saw much later, sketches towards elements of *The Uses of Literacy*, but that project did not properly form until the beginning of the Fifties. There was also a months'-long strip-cartoon history of British trade unionism, produced for the journal of the local Labour Party. I know of no extant copy; and a good thing too.

The Auden essay begun in Naples was expanding and occupied most spare time and presented most difficulties. Professionally I was alone, except for departmental staff meetings every few months or so; but they were made up of about a dozen lecturers from half-a-dozen disciplines, and concerned themselves with administrative regulations and general issues about teaching adults. There was no regular contact with a group of literary and like-minded people as in an internal department, no daily access through the library or the senior common room to a range of literary periodicals and not enough spare money to buy other than the *Manchester Guardian* (then edited by a former adult student, A. P. Wadsworth), the *Observer* and the *Listener* – which, with the *New Statesman*, was in its heyday. For almost all the time I was talking to myself about Auden and much else.

It must have been by late 1948 or early 1949 that the essay on Auden had grown to about 35,000 words, and taken Auden's work up to 1940. I sent it to Bonamy Dobrée, deliberately asking only for his opinion, not for a recommendation to one of his publishing friends. He said it was 'useful' (a code-word for 'not too bad') and suggested I send it to his old friend Herbert Read at Routledge. I should not send it to Chatto and Windus since the reader there would be Cecil Day Lewis and about his poetry the essay made some uncomplimentary remarks. I forgot both the offered recommendation and the warning, and a few weeks later sent the typescript to Chatto.

Cecil Day Lewis replied saying they would like to publish but the essay should be extended to about 60,000 words and cover Auden's work up to the present. Would I like to discuss his proposal over lunch? When we met, he was courteous and in every way encouraging. Back home, with the extra-mural lecturer's great boon, a fairly free summer, ahead of me, I more than doubled the length of the essay within the three months. Moved by Day Lewis's openness, I moderated the criticisms of his work. That is to say, I removed those references which were snide rather than straightforwardly critical. At first, I wondered if that was a correct decision but later decided firmly that it was; the most common error of young critics is to try to be clever-clever towards their subjects. It had taken his un-self-defensive kindness to make me see that references of that kind were unjustified anyway.

Chatto accepted the expanded version, but by the time they published it, in 1951, we had been living in Hull for almost two years. It still managed to be the first full-length study of Auden's work. As we left Marske for Hull, as we were actually seeing off a by now medium-sized removal van, the postman delivered a publication I had ordered with acute trepidation some weeks before – *W. H. Auden*, by Francis Scarfe. My book was even then being edited at Chatto. Had I been overtaken at the last minute? No: Francis Scarfe's was a long essay, a monograph; a good one, but not purporting to be more than a short introduction.

The most striking feature of my *Auden: an Introduction* was precisely that it was the first full-length study. When it appeared Auden was in his forty-fourth year and had been well-known, with a reputation increasing all the time, for about twenty years. I had written the book between the ages of twenty-eight and thirty-one, was unknown, living out in the provincial sticks, and this was my first book. I give this detail because it helps make a point about the

later professionalisation of academic letters. By the Sixties at the
latest it would have been unthinkable for a young unknown to
produce the first book on a famous poet in his mid-forties. Even if
several books had not already appeared from older and more
mature pens, contracts would have been signed and warning signals
sent out – most of them from the USA. The fifty-year-old
heavyweights would have long before moved in.

It still surprises me that I could sit quietly all that time in the
oriental-tent-hut at Marske preparing the book, should wait a long
time to see it published and should still be first. But then,
departments of English literature in Britain and in North America
were still by present standards very small, and many of the older
men who had been holding the fort throughout the war were not
looking for new fields. But why did no younger lecturer turn to the
subject soon after being appointed? Perhaps being an extra-mural
lecturer favoured me; no club, few distractions, no one near to jostle
with or against.

The book itself was not a particularly distinguished study. I can
now think of a dozen writers who have done better work on Auden.
I hope George Fraser was right when he said that the value of my
book was as an expression of a young man's love affair with the first
living poet he had, in Dobrée's phrase, 'made his own'. So there was
at any rate a freshness about it and its insights. The later life of some
of those insights taught me one of the rules of academic borrowing:
don't attribute all the perceptions you admire in other writers; just
put them in your own words as your own ideas or – if you are feeling
circumspect – refer to them as if these are things we have all known
by intuition ever since the poet began writing. Then even the
original critic may not recognise what you have done.

I wondered whether the book would be reviewed in *Scrutiny*
since its chief editor, F. R. Leavis, had some time before announced
that in spite of his early promise Auden had now proved to be a poor
poet. It was reviewed: the reviewer said mine was quite a good book
but he wondered why anyone should go to the trouble of writing a
good book about a bad poet. This drew objections from a reader.
F. R. Leavis moved in to defend his reviewer. I then wrote to Leavis
saying his intervention showed he had not read my book, so how
could he comment. He sent me a letter of apology beginning: 'Dear
Mr Hoggart, I am abashed . . .'

Random House published the book in America but Auden told his editor there he would rather not read it; he must go his own gait. He overcame the inhibition later, thanked me for it but said he thought I was all in all over-generous. But that was after about a decade, when I first met him, in West Berlin.

Those early Redcar–Marske years revealed three professional characteristics which now seem congenital with me, or at least embedded: solitary working (partly enforced, partly taken to naturally), the lack of a clearly-defined sense of direction, and yet a drive to go on, usually to the point of overworking. It is easy for a solitary worker to recognise professional academic groups which have grown up with each other, which continue for decades to go to the same parties and there quickly to hive off into their own cliques where, as they mount the ladders, they increasingly carve up their increasingly top-level specialist empires between them. Groups from the same year at LSE are especially recognisable in these ways, and usually both gifted and thrusting.

There are other groups, such as those of people who have come under the influence of an exceptional tutor (if he or she has good contacts all the better, and that does often happen) and who for years afterwards carry a special confidence around with them, even though some may have been merely lucky and their talents no better than average.

The most clearly-directed groups are from Oxbridge. They are the ones who announce to their friends in their first or second years that they mean to become President of the Union or the dramatic society, that they will not aim for a first – which might suggest a dull swot or putative scholar – but will apply for the BBC (this has now become old-fashioned) or one of the quality weeklies or Sundays, that in ten years they expect to be editor of this or that; and so on. They assume a metropolitan, public-eye, media-engaged life. Until I began to meet Oxbridge people regularly, I had never heard conversations like those.

Many people in both kinds of group honour their promises to themselves and work hard – but within the group's terms and their clearly-defined lines for the measurement of progress. By contrast, my own constant attention to work was directed from within, in part a form of self-justification. But not entirely; it was also a push for meaning outside the day-to-day. Nor was it in the end a solitary matter; it could only operate in the apparently engrossed way it did because it was surrounded by the realities, the affection and the responsibilities, of family. But again it was physically isolated, since there were few academic or intellectual young families in those remoter North Yorkshire areas.

A paradox here is that I have always tended to invoke a sort of group in writing, a group which can be addressed as 'we' – as though out there are numbers of *bien pensants* (of course) who are ready to listen carefully. After hearing me lecture in New York in the Sixties, Lionel Trilling said he admired the British ability to invoke a 'we', a civic and civil intellectual collective, but it was unavailable to him, an American. So were the tones which went with it in a public lecture. Perhaps we – some of us – take it for granted long after it has ceased to exist, that shared circle; if indeed it ever existed. It is certainly a very British 'we', characteristically a puritanical 'we'. Its normal opening runs something like: 'We ought to be careful not to . . .'

I admired those who seemed to need none of those three impulses: isolation, group sense or clear direction. Especially poets, who were tuned to other aspirations. At Leeds in the third year I was taken by my poet friend Dorian Cooke to see another poet who worked in the civil service; probably in the executive class, since Leeds wouldn't have housed many in the administrative grade. He was educated, civilised, soft-spoken, appeared at ease with himself, happy with his wife and baby, wanting to talk only about the writing of poetry. Was he an efficient civil servant? I would have guessed so, but not markedly; not a 'high-flyer', not a great striver on that side of things, not one his superiors would tip for promotion and a march up the ladder, not 'promising' in that way because that was not the way in which he wanted to promise. There was a sense of an inner dignity, in that enclosed but not imaginatively-isolated flat just below the University, which I had rarely met before and was surprised and moved by. For some years after I used to see his name, which I have now forgotten, in little poetry magazines; no more than that. He was a Mary; and Marthas are often attracted to them though knowing, of course, that they could never be like them; and only partly wanting to be.

The range of intellectual fare in Redcar and Marske was rather restricted, easily identifiable and cosy. The right newspapers, a few journals, fewer books, the Third Programme and an occasional film –

all made an economically-woven fabric of intellectual interests. I remember in particular Trilling's *The Middle of the Journey* in 1947 and *The Liberal Imagination* in 1950. A new major critical influence had arrived; the most European – even English – of rising American critics. Koestler's *Darkness at Noon* had appeared in 1940 but lost none of its force in the second half of the decade. His *The Yogi and the Commissar* came in 1945. Of native English writers (in more than one sense) Orwell most forced himself on our attention, *Animal Farm* in 1945, the *Critical Essays* in 1946 and *1984* in 1948. We had seen some of those seminal essays on language, 'The Art of Donald McGill', 'Boys' Weeklies' in occasional and often-short-lived journals – by now the names seem faint, have to be retrieved; but not their flavours: *The Critic, Politics and Letters, Polemic, Humanitas*. Graham Greene's *The Power and the Glory* and *The End of the Affair* began to appear on our class syllabuses. Middleton Murry exhausted the remnants of our patience with him by arguing for 'the one just war', against the Soviet Union. Most of all, Eliot's *Four Quartets* and the abridged edition of Toynbee's *A Study of History* held our long-sustained interest.

There was very little public artistic activity in the whole of North Yorkshire. The idea had hardly penetrated to the local councils. There, as in many other places, the Labour government's permission to local authorities, in 1948, to spend on the arts the proceeds from up to sixpence in the pound from rates revenue was rarely used. But it was not a bad time for films, some Italian, some French, and the Ealing comedies. Just before we left Marske we saw *Passport to Pimlico* and *Kind Hearts and Coronets*. A teenage school-girl from a family up the village street was always willing to baby-sit for extra pocket money. *Whisky Galore, The Lavender Hill Mob, Bicycle Thieves, Bitter Rice* and Cocteau's spectacular *Orphée* followed soon afterwards.

3

There was another and in the long run more important reason why Redcar and Marske, from 1946 to 1949, were not as isolated as they might have seemed. Quite soon, a great deal of thinking and writing was going on all over the country about the nature and purposes of university extra-mural studies. There was an excitement – about the best ways of teaching adults, about the subjects most suitable for the needs (not necessarily the same as the wishes) of adults, about whether experience with adults really did lead to some redefinition of those subjects – an excitement which was not to be found at that time in the internal departments. The only similar ferment was in the Sixties, when some (but not most) of the new universities, notably Sussex, tried to 'redraw the map of learning'. Even there, and then, the subjects themselves received most of the attention, the needs of the students relatively little.

A considerable number of men and women, some of whom became well-known afterwards, chose to enter university extra-mural work in 1946 and 1947, and a fair amount of their time was taken up explaining, to themselves as well as to others, just why; why what they were doing seemed to them more interesting, more worthwhile, than internal teaching and for that matter than intellectual journalism. We knew our work was, to the larger academic and literary world, unfashionable and quaint, and that saved us from many distractions. There was a touch of defensiveness in some of us, but it was less important than the fact that we felt, either at the start or after our first winter, that we had a 'call'. From a great many names I pick three only, because each influenced me. Both E. P. Thompson and Roy Shaw started work for Leeds University's extra-mural department, Raymond Williams for Oxford's.

Roy Shaw became a particularly close lifelong friend. Born in Sheffield, he had had a harder working-class childhood than I and was seriously ill several times until his marriage and well after. But he had extraordinary persistence, supported by both a strong sense of the need for moral purpose in life and an attractively vulgar sense of humour. He managed to get into Manchester University as a mature student, and in turn became one of the great adult tutors of his generation.

Raymond Williams started as an External Tutor for Oxford in 1946 and did his fifteen years for them. Like Philip Larkin, who took over the Hull University Library in the mid-Fifties and whom we knew there and later during his visits to Leicester, Raymond Williams was three or four years younger than I. They both died early, Raymond Williams as I was beginning to draft these chapters.

At such a point, at such moments, perhaps (as it was then for me) for the first time, one begins to feel left behind, 'living on borrowed time' as older relatives invariably said at such conjunctions.

In those late-Forties, some of us talked about the Great Tradition in university extra-mural work; and our gurus were Temple, Mansbridge and Tawney. Temple had just died, Mansbridge died half a dozen years later, Tawney remained active almost up to his death in 1962. To see his noble, lushly half-hairy, egg-like head – with a small furnace of a pipe protruding from under the brown-edged moustache – on the platform of the Workers' Educational Association's annual conference was to feel yourself in touch with a strand of British social and educational history which should speak to the best in you.

That history had begun in the middle- to late-nineteenth century, at Cambridge and Oxford. A few people there, fired by social concern and especially concern for the ill-educated 'toiling masses', fired also by a belief in the power and virtue of education, persuaded their universities that it was a duty and not a dilution of their purposes to establish 'university extension' classes, evening classes for voluntary adult students, above all in the provinces. The idea spread, though very gradually; and, after all, there were not many universities when it all began.

At a conference in 1903, the Workers' Educational Association was formed. Dons, trade union leaders, religious leaders had come together to consider the special educational needs of working-class adults. That impulse was due chiefly to Albert Mansbridge, then a Cooperative Union official and only twenty-five years old, and to Temple who was even younger. Almost forty years later, Temple became Archbishop of Canterbury and was still writing and preaching about social injustice; 'one of the greatest moral forces of his time', his obituaries said. The extension class movement, in spite of its good intentions, had, like water finding its easiest level, become by the turn of the century too much the preserve of middle-class people.

It is the old English story: to him that hath shall be given; for him who knows what he needs provision shall be made abundantly; and that provision, in that form and style, will keep out those who need it more, but don't know they need it. Mansbridge argued that if those working people who were willing to make the considerable effort demanded were given a few key opportunities like those of internal students – regular tutorials, personal attention, guided study, essay writing – they would do as well as internal students. He is said to have asked for the best available tutor so that his argument could be tested, and that Temple supported him; hence the appearance of Tawney. Mansbridge had thus defined what became known simply as the tutorial class.

Out of the University Extension movement, but even more out of the Workers' Educational Association, there emerged the Great Tradition. The pinnacle of that tradition was and remained for half-a-century the tutorial class, and its first and one of its greatest practitioners was Tawney; he established the first two classes, in Lancashire and the Potteries. Even though that was well before our generation came onto the scene, some of us still felt proud to be following in the line Tawney had established, so powerful was 'the Movement's' sense of mission and purpose; in the North, at least.

The tutorial class had the simplicity and tensile strength of most greatly inspiring ideas. It assumed a group of twelve to fifteen adults, willing to come together regularly under the same tutor, for a two-hour meeting. Willing also to commit themselves to attending, so far as ever possible, twenty-four of those weekly meetings throughout each of three successive winters (roughly from October to March). They had to promise to involve themselves in continuous study, steady background reading, and the writing of regular essays and other written work throughout those three years. A very tall order, a very puritanical order, straight out of the serious, self-improving tradition which was so strong in parts of the working-class, fed by church, chapel, trade unions and friendly societies. Characteristic also was the strongly-held belief that this work should lead to no tangible reward, no diplomas, no 'credits'; knowledge and self-improvement were sufficient rewards in themselves.

On any test the achievement of the tutorial class tradition in its heyday was impressive. Most people in the universities did not and do not know that; to them extra-mural work was marginal. If it had been competing directly for funds instead of being largely financed by direct grant from the Ministry of Education, that indifference would in most academic staff have turned to at the worst hostility, at the least competitive jealousy.

Many of the early tutorial class students went on to become **graduates, journalists, university teachers, Members of Parliament.**

This is not difficult to understand, given that so few of even the brightest among the working class, in those early decades, had much chance to develop their capacities even up to the point of reaching the local grammar school. At their most striking, the early tutorial class students were self-selected autodidacts to whom such a class gave their first opportunity to move up and out through study. But that, though important, was not the central purpose of these classes even from the beginning.

Tawney, who showed that the tutorial class idea was right, could work, was deeply impressed by both the talent and the application of his students. He was an exceptionally gifted teacher, so these talents probably blossomed under his hand more than they might have under another's. He and other early tutors also said that their tutorial classes helped redefine their subjects, that social history or industrial relations began to look different if you discussed them for three years, week after week, with adults who had had much living evidence of social history and daily experience of industrial relations. For me much later, similar implicit but powerful challenges to the definition of my subject – English literature – led me to move out to an area I called contemporary cultural studies.

It might be assumed that those who came to this work more than forty years after Tawney would not find such potentialities in so many of their students. By that time many of the most gifted in the working classes had been 'creamed off' into higher education. Nevertheless, studying literature week after week for two hours with tutorial classes, I too – and those who started at the same time – was impressed by the capacity, the intelligence and imagination, which the most unexpected students could show, whether they were motor mechanics or low-paid clerks, or retired shop assistants or what used to be called 'ordinary housewives'. That indicates two important and related points which the British still find hard to accept: first, that the 'creaming off' into higher education even up to the late Forties had been (as it still is to a considerable extent) partial, aslant, selecting its winners by certain accidental and/or fixed and easily measurable criteria only; second, that if one did not accept the usual rules for what constitutes 'brains', the latent ability of many people was far greater and more various than those rules were capable of measuring. But that second point raises a larger issue than even the early Grand Masters felt themselves forced to confront; they had enough on their hands with the more evident disparities of the first sort.

Here is where the experience of Raymond Williams and E. P. Thompson particularly comes in, and my own. For all three of us, the largish books which first brought us to attention were begun during those early years in extra-mural education. Partly this was because extra-mural university teaching, for all its stresses, does give you – if you are willing to work unusually hard – up to one third of your time free each working day (you take classes in the evenings and prepare for them in the other third of the day); it also provides, because your autumn and spring terms are long, a wonderfully expansive summer gap (though summer and weekend schools increasingly interfere). These are less important impulses to the writing of those books than this fact: that the experience of adult teaching itself shaped and informed the very nature of the works themselves as they developed. Raymond Williams's *Culture and Society* would have been a different book if it had been written over years spent teaching internal undergraduates in a traditional university setting. Similarly, Edward Thompson's *The Making of the English Working Class* is rooted in his direct experience of taking tutorials with working-class adults in the rugged but friendly industrial townships of the West Riding of Yorkshire.

All three books – to add my own *The Uses of Literacy* – were written during the first half of the Fifties. We did not talk about them with each other, though I seem to remember each of us knew the others were writing studies which were important to us. I do not know how the others moved along the structure of their books as they took shape. I know mine was a two steps forward, one and a half steps backward affair; and for a time one step forward two steps backward, before it reached what looked like the home straight. More important is that we each had a sense of the special social importance of our day-by-day work, a belief in the need for developed minds and imaginations – especially in wide-open, commercial, pyramidal societies – a sense of the many and major injustices in the lives of working people and so a deep suspicion of the power of class in Britain. Thus we all, in our different ways, started on studies which embodied our interest in cultural change, politics, and communication or lack of communication, between the parts of this greatly divided society.

CHAPTER 5

HULL: SETTINGS AND SETTLING IN
1949−59

Hull is about fifty miles up a creek, well east of the main railway lines and the main trunk roads, with dullish country most of the way across on the A18 or the A63. West is Holderness, fronting the northern shore of the Humber as it heads for Spurn and the North Sea, and that is even emptier; but haunting − sunk deep in the eighteenth century, church-ridden and tree-shrouded, with its vast village churches and magnificent elms (they have probably all gone now), damp, below the sea-line, smelling of vegetation, still in our day something of a squires' land and landscape; squires who were flushed out of their hides on important ceremonial occasions in Hull, men who with their East Riding cousins were the kind who became holders of that odd hangover of English titular positions, the stork-legged Lord Lieutenants. North to north-east is much prettier and plumper since it runs through or on the fringes of the East Yorkshire Wolds, through amply suburban Cottingham and antique, prim Beverley up to Yorkshire's favourite and seaside resorts: Bridlington, Filey, Scarborough, Robin Hood's Bay, Whitby. That's the south to north line; the social line in those places runs differently, and more convolutedly even than is usual in clusters of English seaside resorts. Thus, Scarborough is three resorts, by class; smaller resorts, before the age of the great caravan sites, belonged mainly to a wide range of families, the classless walkers and the sea-lovers.

In our time the southern outlook was most remote of all, since to get over to Lincolnshire and so to classes in Grimsby you had either to take a paddle-steamer for almost half an hour across the wide Humber or go twenty odd miles back west to the first bridge, near

Goole, and then back again south and east for even more miles; so
you stayed the night in Grimsby, where the commercial hotels were
like Middlesbrough's but the fish-and-chips were of unparalleled
excellence.

Now there is the Humber Bridge, only a few miles west of Hull; it
is spectacular and beautiful, but seems not to have greatly opened
up that broad bulge of Lincolnshire farming land. Nor has the
decision to name the sides of the river North Humberside and South
Humberside proved more than an ineffective verbal cosmetic. It has
not created the unity which the river has discouraged since humans
first found their way to each side to settle.

Even more than most cities, Hull in our time was a place of
revolving smells, according to the direction of the wind. Fish from
the docks and the fish-meal factories, oil from the oil-seed crushing
works, paint from the paint factories, wood from the timber yards,
chocolate from Needler's and mixed smells from Reckitt and
Colman's.

The city itself is almost entirely level, so cyclists used to exist at
almost a Dutch density. There is one slight slope within the
boundary, I think to cross a railway (other than that, level crossings
dominate and hold up the cyclists surprisingly often). That slope is
where the instructor takes you to learn how to start a car on an
incline. You are at sea level or even slightly below that, so the
cemeteries (the corpses must be wet until they disintegrate) are dank
and dripping to a degree even Leeds does not know. A natural haunt
for Philip Larkin; his recording of *The Less Deceived* has him
standing, long-mackintosh buttoned up, in the overgrown local
cemetery, holding his bike, trouser-clips in position, a stone angel at
his elbow. The Marvell Press did that operation. Jean Hartley, who
ran the Press with her husband from a tiny house, was one of my
students.

Wide 'drains' – drainage channels – used to intersect the roads
and run along the avenues (many have now been covered in); they
help discourage the streets and houses from slowly sinking into the
clarty earth. There are no cellars, and if you set out to buy a house
you soon learn to distinguish between 'subsidence' and 'settlement'
– the one might continue and bring the house down, the other looks
as if it has run its course; so, perhaps with some sturdy shoring-up,
you may expect to live there safely. Some of the local cowboy

builders, their collaborator-'developers', and a few dubious estate agents, were expert at making subsidence look like settlement or even at disguising it altogether, for a year or two.

The streets and the pavements tend to be wider than is usual in English cities; I do not know why. Perhaps the wide-open sky, the scudding clouds and the winds from the Urals conjure up a sense of all-round space you do not find in Manchester or Leeds or Sheffield, and so encourage space-making on the ground. Oddest of all, since it creates a faintly Andorran atmosphere, Hull has had for decades its own telephone system, its own call-boxes in their own colours, and slightly cheaper rates than the GPO, as it was. But if you want to reach outside Hull to the great and busy world you have to be connected, for a small charge, to that outer world-system.

I

For an academic Hull can be an engaging town and a particularly good place to settle if you want to bring up a family whilst pursuing a quietly productive professional life. When in 1949 Mayfield, who wished me to give adult classes within the university itself and generally to be nearby to talk to, said he wanted us to move down there we had mixed feelings; sorry to leave the coast and country-side, glad to be in a more lively place. But we stayed ten years.

On Saturday afternoons, walking round town, shopping, win-dow-gazing or just strolling through the more handsome bits, you usually met someone you knew on the well-marked trails: Paragon Square, Queen Victoria Square, Whitefriargate, the old wooden New Holland Pier, the local department stores – Hammond's, Bladon's and Thornton Varley's – the public library, the Ferens Art Gallery. The little snack bar there had its gentilities. They told the staff always to use tongs when they handed food to the customers. One day the waitress at the counter, on the point of passing an iced bun to us, noticed that it was dusty and slightly fly-blown. She lifted it to her mouth with the tongs and blew on it, with great delicacy. For high tea, there was Jackson's, a large and good grocers with an upstairs restaurant, or the Gainsborough, whose fish-and-chips were almost as good as Grimsby's.

Standards were high; the food was fresh, not frozen. The

traditions held, and said you should be proud of the food you offered, should not try to get away with the cheapest mass-produced stuff you could foist on people. The customers knew that and expected no less. One year we had a summer holiday in Cleveleys over on the Lancashire coast. The same standards remained there too: home-baked bread, home-boiled ham, home-grown tomatoes, all from the little shops just down the road on a tiny parade, and all full of taste. One of our more self-conscious visitors, up from the South, was so surprised he called it 'a moral triumph'.

So it was very pleasant to sit in a Hull restaurant, the children smiling with expectancy, to know you could afford it so long as you didn't go haphazard, and that you even had a car in the car park, second- or third-hand though it was. Round about five o'clock the unmistakable, burly, squeezed-into-their-weekend-clothes, Holderness and East Riding country working people started to make for their trains or buses; and the trolley-buses, loaded with families and parcels, their gantries sparking and crackling at the junctions and bends, headed for the municipal estates on the outskirts.

We settled in what all Hull calls simply 'The Avenues' – several wide tree-lined roads with another at right angles through their centre, and a large empty fountain at the central intersection, making a sort of roundabout. Even the smaller houses are quite large and the big ones very large indeed. Most had good-sized gardens, often with a coach-house leading out into the 'ten-foot', a common back-alley. Built for the successful middle class in the 1870s, they were now too big and too unsmart for most of those who could afford them. A few had become rooming houses or nursing homes or been converted to flats. But a considerable number had been picked up by professional families who preferred space indoors and out to smartness. Natural homes, therefore, for academics and only a mile from the University. We had an unsatisfactory year and a half in the echoing upstairs flat of a house owned by the University before, in early 1951, we found a house we liked and could afford. We were ready to have a third child and for that needed somewhere we could properly settle in; Paul was born in early 1952. We stayed in that house, happily, eight and a half years.

We soon realised that The Avenues were thronged with young academic families much like ourselves (and academics do tend to stick together): the husband not long appointed by the University and beginning to think about turning his Ph.D. into a publishable book, the wife preoccupied with him and probably his odd working habits (most husbands did help about the house, though), and with keeping the house in reasonable order whilst looking after a couple of children and perhaps with another on the way. Few wives thought of taking paid work themselves, at least in those early years; 'I'd like to see the youngest to infant school at five,' was the most common explanation. We tended to live in each other's pockets, within the little group we had become part of. There was a good and inexpensive nursery school just over the main artery, in Pearson Park where Philip Larkin first settled a year or two later. After that, for almost all the children, the municipal, local, infant and junior schools. Ours started to live in those familial Avenues at the ages of three and one; and left for Leicester when they were thirteen, eleven and seven – the longest we have lived as a family in any house; we really belonged, and they grew up with peers they still remember well.

The grocer, the butcher, the baker and the rest were no more than two or three hundred yards away on the nearest main trolley-bus route which ran from town towards the College. The grocer appeared one evening a week, took your order and had a boy deliver it on Friday evening. There were no supermarkets. You formed very knowledgeable relationships with each of the tradespeople – within the limits imposed by the fact that you were up at that still strange implantation, the University College, and so rather different from regular Hull people. You were assumed to be very proper; so genteel affrontedness set in if you fell below that expectation. A bachelor professor in one of the Humanities, an old Etonian, who shared our butcher, was in hospital for a few weeks. When he reappeared the butcher's wife said she trusted it hadn't been serious. 'Serious enough,' he said, in his self-consciously liberated hearty manner, 'they had half me guts out.' 'Not very nice, was it?' the butcher's wife said to us as she slapped the liver on the counter, and the huge beef carcasses swung on their hooks behind her. A theological colleague, tall and austere-looking, a considerable authority on the Russian Orthodox Church, similarly shocked his newsagent who had remarked on how cold it was. 'Yes, indeed,' said the reverend, as he opened the shop-door to go out, 'Proper brass-monkey weather.'

Like most of our friends, we felt we should have a telephone as soon as possible – the first in either of our families. And a vacuum-cleaner rather than a simple carpet-sweeper, and an electric washing-machine, though that had to be of a rudimentary kind. In 1949 and for some time after not all of these appliances were plentiful. A refrigerator came rather later and is still with us, though now in a support role. One radio only until the transistor revolution but a record player, with fibre needles, as soon as it could be afforded. For a good while many of us drew back our skirts at the idea of a television set; but children's pressures and our own emerging interest led to our getting one in the late Fifties, some time after ITV came on the air. To some extent, selective delicacy still holds: we have neither microwave nor freezer and, in true middle-class professional fashion, use our video (a farewell gift from colleagues at my last full-time job) chiefly for time-shift operations rather than for films from the video shops. Very choosy and fine-tuned – especially since we do have, of electrical goods: a dishwasher, two television sets, a sandwich-maker, a table-top grill, a trouser-press, several electric blankets (not used since central heating arrived), a rotary floor-polisher, a carving-knife, a blender and a whisk, six radios, a Hi-Fi system, a word processor and a photocopier; and a few other gadgets too obvious or small to list in total – such as an electric tooth-brush outfit, and one for making coffee illicitly in hotels.

All in all, life in The Avenues was amiably of the family, perhaps even uxorious. We were told after we had left that a little wife-and-husband swapping went on among some of the bolder members of staff; southerners, of course. But, like the man who played the piano in a brothel for twenty years and never knew what went on upstairs, we were entirely unaware of such things, if such things indeed happened. Our pleasures were less colourful: wives with a child or two in tow calling in for coffee during the morning, evening visits for a light supper after the children were bathed and in bed – tuna salad or 'tuna-bake' with coffee, say: cheap wine was still a few years off; a very occasional visit with friends to the theatre or even the York Mystery Plays – a sizeable organisation needed there, from finding late-night baby-sitters (ideally, grandparents) to packing blankets and thermos flasks of very hot coffee; the wind blew cruelly round the buttocks as the plays and the Northern nights wore on.

Memory invests much of this time with something of a sentimental glow. Excessive to remember Galuppi: 'Dear, dead women, / With such hair, too – /What's become of all the gold /Used to hang and brush their bosoms /I feel chilly and grow old.' But those healthy young mothers were very hard-worked and immensely cheerful; life was before them and they were comfortably off – not by any means prosperous but able to manage so long as the husband was helpful, not a drinker or foolish in some other way; university life is then one of the pleasanter fates. The wives were usually in print dresses or, some of them, in dirndls whose skirts swung like great bells; and sandals. Marks and Spencer's styles were only on the horizon, their food two decades away. 'The women of Clyro walk like storks,' said the bachelor Parson Kilvert. These women riding bicycles, usually with a child's seat over the back wheel, would have delighted him.

At weekends we often went, as single families or with others, to the local parks or the Dales, which were unspoilt deep farming country – different from the West Riding but in their own way as solidly and stubbornly Yorkshire; or to the completely spoilt, dreary nearby seaside resorts of Holderness – Hornsea or Withernsea – all pin-table arcades and the nastiest of take-away food (nastier even than it is now), the rock-bottom shabbiness offered to and accepted by the English working class when they are on holiday.

Summer holidays were taken as individual families; for us, to Mrs Fairey's at Filey for several years. Mr Fairey worked for the Parks Department and the unmarried daughter Mary at the local laundry. Mary had an ear for good stories about laundry practices – such as the habit of the girls, if they had laundered a particularly exotic gown, to delay its return so that one of them could wear it at the next town hop, launder it again and return it. The Filey arrangement, common in the north, was excellent. The visitors paid for rooms and cooking plus a small charge for 'the cruet'; but they supplied their own provisions – perfect with children, since only parents know their dietary vagaries.

At Easter, if there was a chance of a few days off, we went to 'somewhere healthy' such as the Lake District; and had full board with packed lunches. Christmas, for years until the roles needed to be reversed, was at the grandparents.

The most traditional, and symbolic, of all our family practices was Sunday dinner. I cannot remember our ever doubting that it should be the focal point of Sunday, except when the weather tempted us to a picnic. Our children follow the habit with their families.

Domestically, our regular intellectual pabulum was much as it had been at Redcar and Marske. That mildly liberal-socialist, not very taxing, intellectual life could be marked and measured by the succession of Sunday mornings, with the *Observer* shared across the breakfast table . . . noting approvingly the entry into force of Labour's social legislation; approving also the shedding of Empire, set off most markedly by the transfer of power in India, in 1947. When that disengagement came, it came with remarkably little fuss, whether from the right or the left.

Our intellectual uniforms were extremely predictable and identifiable. Early in 1957, in Princeton, I had coffee with R. P. Blackmur and we talked about some aspects of British domestic policy. He interrupted dryly and said: 'I will tell you what papers you take, and what magazines, what radio channels you favour and who are your favourite social and political commentators.' The old fox scored a hundred per cent.

We did our best to keep up with *Horizon* but it closed in January 1950; and with *Penguin New Writing*, which closed at the end of that year; just after the war it had had a circulation of one hundred thousand. The particular intellectual and artistic ferment of the immediate post-war years was subsiding fast. The Consumers' Association, founded in 1957, was characteristic of the end of the decade.

Picture Post under Tom Hopkinson was greatly favoured. We admired but did not like *Brideshead Revisited*. We enjoyed *Lucky Jim* in 1954 but couldn't get to see *Look Back in Anger* at the Royal Court in 1956. We saw *Roots* at the Royal Court in 1959 and sat next to, but did not speak to, a man with a copy of the Pelican *The Uses of Literacy* on his knee. Nor was the theatre strong in Hull at that time. The growth of the publicly-funded regional theatres came rather late to the East Riding; the Arts Council was less than a decade old; so in this as in much else the variety and spread of our arts interests was limited by geography as well as by family duties and shortage of money. But Mary and I, courtesy of her parents' willingness to baby-sit, did manage to look briefly at the Festival of Britain in 1951.

2

To any city away from the main routes and several hours from London a University institution becomes at once an important as well as strange feature. It takes a cosmopolitan and raffish place such as Brighton to swallow the newcomer with hardly a gulp. The practical gains are evident straightaway: buildings to be built and serviced, staff and students to be fed and watered; a big new employer. More interesting, and to an extent that is not true of most industrial plants (which from one angle universities are), they spread strangers in digs through all the town's arteries; a not-to-be-avoided social and psychological addition to the texture of its life.

Hull had a University College from 1927, chiefly and typically through the initiative and generosity of a local worthy, Thomas Ferens (the University College cunningly enshrined its sense of gratitude in the motto: *lampada ferens*; the University, the College having been ennobled in 1954, retains the tag). University colleges and new universities, more than the few older universities (Oxford's and Cambridge's mid- to late-nineteenth-century initiatives were splendid but unusual and not repeated), have usually felt an obligation to increase the sweetness and light available in their intellectually and artistically underprovided communities, and Hull was not behind in this.

It is a fact of life that if you live in a culturally well-endowed city and perhaps are some distance from the centre you may well, faced with such a wide choice, more and more postpone visits to the theatre, concerts, galleries. There will always be time later, especially if some more isolated visitor is likely to want to see the highlights once they finally make the trip to visit you. But very often that time does not come. In a modest-sized provincial centre you make the effort to go to the occasional concerts, plays or temporary exhibitions; they are the carefully-noted-in-advance highspots of the month or quarter; and you see most of your friends there.

One such crest of the winter season in Hull was a short series of chamber music concerts, sponsored by the university and held in its halls. They were musically very good and socially fascinating. The city and a bit of the county turned out in semi-formal dress; and of course the University itself. The Principal, later — his efforts and prayers being answered — Vice-Chancellor, attended whenever possible.

J. H. Nicholson was a bachelor who had read theology and thought of becoming a cleric but didn't; he had, among much else, held a chair in education at Bristol. A congenital smoker of the fag-sticking-to-the-lower-lip kind, he had a bullet head with gingery hair *en brosse*, and looked more like a leathery, shrewd French farmer than an English academic or higher education statesman. Not intellectually a high-flyer, nor one of the king-makers among heads of universities, he was all in all a fair-minded man — and lonely, living in an over-large, Principal's residence a couple of miles up the road to Cottingham. His position isolated his loneliness, so he had no close friends among staff and seemed to behave towards all of them, whatever their ranks, with a courteous but absent-minded distance, as though he was having to try to remember their names at each new meeting.

During vacations, he found relief by fishing in Ireland, and in term time in a long friendship with Beattie Pearlman, the middle-aged-to-elderly widow of a former lord mayor of Kingston-upon-Hull (the city's proper name) and solicitor, herself still of some but only a little consequence in the town. Still a name slightly 'to conjure with' in those parts, as some people were no doubt likely to say. She retained the big house on the front boundary road of The Avenues in which she had held municipal court, but made some money letting off one or two of the upper floors. To the right kind of people. So it came about that Mayfield and his wife Sammy — he was known as Billy — lived until the very end in the lady's attics; very pretty and agreeable attics they were, looking over the road at the tops of trees in the park towards Philip Larkin's similarly rook-haunted eyrie; comfortable, slightly over-warm, loaded with books, just the sort of snug nest that childless, middle-aged, literary couples like to make.

Regularly, after chairing long, tiresome and often acerbic meetings of Senate, John Henry Nicholson would drive his battered car (no Principal's Rover or, even less likely, driver), down the road to his friend's house where she soothed him with drink and a good meal. People made jokes about them, of course, but few (though for some the temptation must have been great) would have hinted that there was an erotic connection; there was, though, something touching about it. The mutually agreeable and advantageous semi-professional relationship lasted until he retired and went to live in York; she gave him a little home comfort which he entirely lacked in the official Barn; he re-created for her from time to time, by using her as his consort on some public occasions, a little more of the sense of importance she had once enjoyed as the wife of the mayor. So at the chamber-music concerts the central front row seats were kept for the Principal and his lady, and the seats on each side of them for cultivated civic dignitaries, senior professors and the like. Others sat where they would and could. Altogether pleasant little occasions.

After one such concert we came out into the November dark to pouring rain. I was dashing to open our car whilst Mary stood under an archway but was stopped by a man calling for assistance. He stood there soaking wet and worried. Cars were parked all round the university service road. He had backed so as to be able to get away and hooked his rear bumper on the front bumper of the car behind; locked like casual dogs. Then he had recognised, with moderate alarm, that the one behind was the Principal's. I asked him to get back in his car and rock it gently backwards and forwards so that I could bend between the two and try to unhook the bumpers. It took a couple of minutes, during which the rain poured well down the back of my neck. Then the bumpers disengaged, he sprang clear, tooted and was away. I straightened myself from the dirty bumper to find the Principal standing over me and demanding, in a classically imperious voice, what I supposed I was doing: 'interfering with' his car. Perhaps he thought the revolution had come, starting with plastic bombs being placed under the cars of heads of university colleges by dissident junior staff. He marched round and got into his seat without waiting for an answer.

It was not upsetting to me, just a comical, campus novel sort of situation. I told it as that to Mayfield next day. He, ever sensitive about the reputation of his extra-mural lecturers, immediately told his landlady, the former mayoress; she, also immediately, rang

John Henry Nicholson. He at once sent me a letter of apology in tones so courteous that they were positively grand, from the opening 'My dear Hoggart' through 'I am ashamed that I should have mistaken a simple kindness on your part' to 'I am, Yours most sincerely, John Henry Nicholson'. A silly incident but true to the best of behaviour in those sorts of places at that time.

Simple, too, like much else then. We swerved from basic and homely simplicities to a sense of the importance of the lights we were upholding; *lampada ferens*. Throughout the first half of the Fifties J. H. Nicholson organised, fought and manoeuvred to get his college full university status. All culminated in the official visit of inspection by the University Grants Committee – which was successful. Nicholson knew me sufficiently well by then to recognise me at one meeting in two; and so was able to tell me how cunningly he had planned the lunch for the visitors: not too grand or they'd think you wasteful; not so spartan that they didn't enjoy it, or might think you were showing off your careful husbandry at their expense. 'My great stroke,' he said, 'was finding a whole salmon. I like to think that had some effect on the outcome.'

The City Hall, a comely Victorian building at right angles to the Ferens Art Gallery, was the splendid setting for the annual degree-awarding ceremonies. Mayfield urged his staff to process with the others so as to indicate that they were a proper part of the university. We were marshalled in pairs and crept up the centre aisle to organ music so slow we were tempted to do a little jig between steps, but settled for ventriloquial conversation with our neighbours. At the base of the platform we separated to left and right and mounted the stairs to the high rake of the choir seats; a grand sight, much favoured by provincial universities with suitable civic halls.

On one occasion my partner did not appear, so a harassed marshal told me to walk in the centre. We reached the platform and I was ordered to the left by another harassed marshal. I murmured that the sheet of proceedings said my seat was on the right. He insisted I go left so I did, and found all seats occupied. It was clear that the main platform party was now on its way up the aisle, for the organ was reaching its finale. I got to the top of the stairs, just under the organ. Nothing. I decided to seek my seat over on the right by creeping between the organ and the back wall. There was insufficient room and my mortar-board fell off and rolled down the stairs.

By now the platform party were half-way up the hall; and the audience were enjoying themselves far more than they had expected. The all-oblivious Chancellor – a titled East Riding bigwig – rose to declare the Congregation open whilst the Chaplinesque figure still hovered hatless against the back wall. The resolute second marshal bounded up the stairs and hissed 'Sit', as to a recalcitrant dog. I squatted on my hunkers against the wall for the whole ceremony, looking like a discommoded Northern miner who'd wandered in and nicked a gown.

To some of us who belonged to the Department of Adult Education at Hull or to the Extra-Mural Department at Leeds our work offered not only the largely uninterrupted pleasures of introducing our subjects to people who had come of their own free will but also, in the first decade especially, the pleasures of political and ideological battles about the nature of our work itself, about what the WEA called the Movement.

Leeds had some tutors before and through the war, notably James Cameron, a teacher and philosopher of distinction who later held a succession of chairs. Leeds's organisation of its extra-mural work developed rapidly when it appointed as the first Head of Department one of its own tutors, S. G. Raybould. Sydney Raybould was stocky, pugnacious, a bluff Northerner to the core and a little stagey with it. The mark of a stagey Yorkshireman is his conviction that the height of wit is to be found in the dialectal *obiter dicta* of the greatest, and always native-born, Yorkshire county cricketers, those who call a spade a 'bloody shuvvel' to prove their directness. Raybould was a relentless planner and a productive writer – but only about the nature of adult education for universities. During the later Forties and the Fifties his was the most lively name in university adult education in Britain and one of the best known names in the field throughout the world, a name guaranteed to divide any group of tutors who were talking about their subject. He stood for the Great Tradition, the Movement, the tutorial class; he believed standards had fallen before the war; he had no patience with and a lot of scorn for subjects and teaching methods which did not stretch the students. He was a thorn to all who would not see things in his way, and engendered his own North–South divide. From the distance of another department I liked him, chiefly because I too was a puritan in these matters, and because he liked me and kept trying to persuade me to join him, and because I enjoyed his combativeness. I do not think we would have got on for long in the same department. He was rigid and could never see the case for literature; hard tack – politics, industrial relations, economics – those were the real things. Literature wasn't as soft an option as, say, local history, but it was on the soft slope.

It must have been about 1960 that Raybould and I were invited to a huge adult education conference in Canada; the conference, in Winnipeg for a few days, required us both to speak after dinner (huge pink steaks *au jus*, baked potatoes, ice-cream, water) in the enormous dining-room of the Royal Alexandra Hotel. We got on well in those days of close proximity, but Sydney did most of the talking. We were billeted in a motel on the outskirts of the city, so much on the outskirts that the downtown buildings shimmered in the distant haze down the straight concrete road. The view in the other direction was unsettling – the road ran straight west for so long that you could see the horizon curve. Even more surreal was our only available breakfast place, a petrol station just over the concrete strip, El Rancho Gaseterio. Petrol and food, as usual; but served by young girls in white leather cow-girl outfits and on skates, with rictal smiles as fixedly cheerful as those of plastic dolls. For me the most disconcerting element of all was Sydney's total indifference to everything around him. If seals in pinnies had appeared with our tray he would have said 'thanks' and carried on talking. If El Rancho had taken off, hovered fifty feet above the roadway and spun anti-clockwise whilst space-creatures served us, he would have reached for his plate of bacon and scrambled egg, knowing – willing – it to be there. He wanted to talk about the Ministry of Education's latest regulations on university adult education, only that.

From Winnipeg we took the transcontinental train to the Banff Conference Centre in the Rockies, for a week of good thinking. Sydney talked happily, even when we were up in the observation dome and passing through the more spectacular parts. I toyed with the idea of interjecting 'Look, Sydney, a giraffe,' but he would have blinked at me mildly and slightly reproachfully, as though to indicate that one doesn't interrupt serious conversations with silly jokes – and gone on talking.

From the Banff Centre they took us on a trip way up to Lake Louise. Sydney and I wandered to the edge of that mountain-fringed, brilliantly and translucently blue, expanse. He was still talking, but I invited him to consider the setting in all its un-Leeds grandeur. 'Yes, Richard,' he said after a moment's look, 'Now Section 3/4 of the new Regulations . . .'

Raybould, for all his manifest rigidities, was a great university Professor of Adult Education because he would let no one whose ear he could command forget the, to him, central duty of universities to those outside their walls who have not had the opportunities given to the usual students and the usual staff. He was supported throughout by his Vice-Chancellor, Charles Morris, brother of that Philip Morris who did so much for Army Education during the war. Many disliked the beacon they set up, but they were bigger than their critics.

My qualified but strong admiration for Raybould and sizeable identification with his principles reached their comic apogee when, round about the middle-Fifties, I went for an interview at the Cambridge University Department of Extra-Mural Studies. By then I had been almost a decade with the Hull department, but was not looking for a move. The Cambridge appointment, though, was especially tempting. When University Adult Education began, in the mid-nineteenth century, James Seth of Cambridge had been a founding father. Cambridge had commemorated him with the only named post in university adult education in Great Britain, the James Seth Lectureship; and this time they were looking for a literature tutor.

There was a large and I think strong field, but I was shortlisted for interview with six or seven others. We sat throughout a long afternoon in a small, partly book-lined room whilst each was called. Several of the others appeared to be former professors in what had been the universities of the colonies. Just before your turn came you were asked to go upstairs and sit outside the interviewing room. As they finished with one candidate, the next could therefore be in the room quickly. They may or may not have realised that the committee's every word could be heard by the candidate sitting outside. Before they called me in, I heard the head of the department say to the other members of the committee that he wished to make a couple of points. There were two good reasons for not appointing the next candidate. The first was that he was a Northern puritan, a sharer of Raybould's ideas – and they didn't want that kind of thing in Cambridge. They wanted someone with a lighter and more sophisticated touch. I remembered then the story of the pre-war extra-mural Oxbridge tutor whose courses were always about the Nineteen Twenties, which allowed him when he was in danger of drying up to rush to the piano and play excerpts from Noël Coward; he went on into Parliament.

The second reason was more practical than ideological: 'He is getting more, by two years of increments, than anyone of his age in my department, and that would cause trouble.' Thus did Hull's initial generosity or shrewdness come to trip me. It was clear that the head of the department did not want me, and only a stubborn committee member would push a candidate's case against the opinion of his boss-in-waiting. Nevertheless, a sturdy, Cam-bridgey-nasal woman's voice – which proved to be that of the critic and scholar Joan Bennett – said, both crisply and dryly, 'And he's done a lot more than any of your staff of his age have done.' A few years later I thanked her at the *Lady Chatterley's Lover* trial, where we both appeared for the defence.

They had to call me in, though it was a lost cause and one I was no longer interested in. I wondered whether to tell them with a flourish where to put their job, but my histrionic sense is weak so I kept tight-lipped, did not try to promote my claims and answered briefly. The chairman, a Cambridge economist celebrated for his prosecution of the need for cuts in public spending, opened with: 'You are a very expensive young man, Mr Hoggart.' I told him I didn't feel expensive. 'Wouldn't the advantages of living and working in Cambridge make up for some drop in salary?' 'Conceivably to me, but hardly to my wife and three children,' I said. No one asked for my views on university adult education.

Cambridge kept up its clumsiness to the end. They forgot they'd asked us all to wait; which we did till we were discovered by accident at about a quarter to seven. 'Sorry,' said a minor official. 'You should all have been told much earlier. Decided not to make an appointment.' The mail-train, the only one left at that time of day, was warm and decanted me at Hull Paragon round about five a.m., still smiling at the thought of being one of the dangerous Cromwellian zealots of the North.

*

Mayfield and Raybould did not get on and saw as little of each other as they could manage. The wooden toll-bridge at Selby, on the main road between the two cities, was like a frontier; you felt the atmosphere grow more severe and uncompromising, life become more real and earnest, as you clattered over it to WEA meetings in Leeds. The classes in York were a dagger pointed at Raybould's heart until a boundaries deal was struck. Further north, in Middlesbrough where for a few years both departments also held classes, one of Raybould's tutors, a solemn and conscientious man, complained to him not that I was trying to establish more classes than were agreed but that my one class was so successful as to pose a possible threat. The combination of pettiness and devoted application did not diminish in all those years.

Only the gentle WEA district secretary, Fred Sedgwick, whose bailiwick covered both universities' areas, could keep the temperature well down and provide a common meeting-place – his office – much as the Mayor of Brussels' town hall is said to provide the only place in that city in which the King and Queen can attend meetings, so powerful are the Flemish and Walloon rivalries. Fred Sedgwick had taken over from a puritan of puritans, George Thompson, with whom two convictions dominated: that the universities owed it to the workers to give of their best whatever the cost, and before their internal duties; and that no penny should be spent which could be saved for better purposes. So it was said that, having missed the last bus from Harrogate to Leeds after a meeting, he walked the score of miles, his shoes in his hand. His socks would take a beating; perhaps he took those off too.

That was in the Great Tradition, even though the story may have been apocryphal. As if in compensation, apparently subfusc occupations create their own dramatic anecdotes. After I had left Hull the story went round and was believed by otherwise sane people that, one winter night when the Hull ferry failed just before I should have boarded it for a Grimsby class, I hired a boat and rowed across that couple of miles of water, to arrive in time. A hundred yards on a park lake would have been all I could have managed.

Raybould's irritation and suspicion were enhanced by the knowledge that Hull University College had developed adult education in its area, and somewhat beyond, from its earliest days. Whatever the genuine interest behind it, that was also a shrewd political move. University colleges in the Twenties and Thirties relied chiefly on local benefactors and local aspirations. If such a college became a recognised presence as widely and as soon as possible, it both built up support and brought in more income. For years Hull's Principal, A. E. Morgan, and his close colleague T. H. Searls, first head of the Adult Education Department, spread their nets.

J. H. Nicholson built on their work. I never knew the formidable duo but came to see that Nicholson had a genuine passion for education in the wider community. He used to say – and many a vice-chancellor and professor used to say the same almost with tears in their eyes, long after they had ceased to take any adult education classes – that his happiest teaching had been in evening tutorial classes, that they refreshed him as nothing else could after a hard day on his internal work. You believed Nicholson, and could easily imagine that lonely bachelor in his early days teaching with skill and pleasure until nine p.m. and then taking the bus to his empty flat.

3

After the departure of Searls – he went with Morgan to the British Council – and throughout the war, Mayfield – the senior tutor in the department – had been the Acting Director of Adult Education. I do not know how strong was the field when they finally decided to reinstitute the appointment, though I understand there was some surprise when the man on the spot got it. He was certainly not then, nor did he become, a statesman of adult education; but was in other ways an inspired choice. He was new to his eminence when I and the others were interviewed that June day of 1946.

Mayfield distrusted all theorising about adult education, did not like reading about it, hated the politics of the profession nationally and internationally and, though he loved talking about good teaching, always did so *ad hoc* and *ad hominem*, from a set of well-honed rules of thumb. He thought Raybould more an academic businessman or politician, hard, dry-as-dust, than a scholar or teacher. Mayfield himself was happiest when talking about the practice of teaching in a detailed and particular way; and since his own subject was literature, those who shared the subject shared also his very particular and perfectionist attentions.

His preoccupying interest was in helping 'ordinary' (and he gave to that word an extraordinary suggestion of worth) people to appreciate the literature he loved; and for that the tutorial class was seen as the perfect instrument. He was unstinting in his willingness to talk about the work, so as to help tyros – until three in the morning if he was staying with you. If he came at last – or early – to the conclusion that you were not as serious about the work and its value as he was, then the air blew very cold. He had a patrician scorn for those who short-circuited the process of good teaching, was convinced this happened quite a lot in internal teaching (which was never visited by someone like him or by Her Majesty's Inspectors). He despised, and it was a moral judgment, those who confused good popularisation with triviality. Until they had proved their seriousness, he was suspicious of internal members of staff who offered to take his adult classes; perhaps they were only wanting to earn money for a summer holiday or to pay the rates, and had no interest in the Great Tradition.

Physically, he was not imposing and his public presence was slight. His style, and on the right occasions it could be impressive, came over best in talks to small groups and seminars rather than on public platforms or to committees (which never ceased to embarrass him – he hated both their formalities and the verbal codes for playing the committee game).

He was only a little over five feet tall and his legs were short in relation to his trunk – so that his small figure bore a jacket which seemed disproportionately long. He dressed well and expensively, was indeed dapper. He favoured large, wide-brimmed Borsolino hats, which gave him a slightly Continental air, like an Italian impresario in a not very expansive medium – chamber music, not grand opera.

I scarcely remember him ever raising his voice, though when you touched his funny bone he gave a harsh bark. His habitually soft and low-keyed voice commanded a complex keyboard of tones and a great variety of speeds. He had more capacity to express innuendo, dubiety, wry amusement, the feline and the sly in his voice than anyone else I have heard off the stage – which was imaginatively his second home. Observing Gielgud's complexly-nuanced performance, the mastery of the low voice, the dying fall, the sudden vixenish rise, the constantly half-arrested feminine gesture, in Pinter's *No Man's Land*, just before Mayfield's death, I wished he had been able to savour it. He loved the theatre more than any other literary form and, always supported by Muriel Crane, did a great deal to break a typically English distinction in adult education – you could have a class in the critical appreciation of plays; you could not have a grant for some dramatic practice in illustration of the critical arguments.

He intensely disliked administration; it simply moithered him. I saw him once, in his heavy smoking days, so put out by some administrative irritation that he lit a second cigarette when a sizeable one was still in his mouth, and for a short time smoked them both. He could be deeply interested in personalities, but always on his own terms. As to the problems of personality which beset every head of department, which can't be escaped and which often come just when one least welcomes them and from quarters one doesn't want to think about, such things could irritate him beyond measure. He tended to dramatise even his professional relationships, to divide his acquaintances and especially his tutors into saints and sinners, with some shifting between groups. Those he loved he loved dearly and, in general, consistently; those who were out of favour could do little right until some tiny gesture, probably unconscious on their part, set the wheels of their fortune turning again towards the zone of approval.

His greatest gift was as a teacher, both to his own students and to his staff. That second gift is rarer even than the first: the ability to help others see both what is involved in good teaching and how to acquire it in their own best ways. He visited classes tirelessly, which meant being out evening upon evening after a full day's work in the office. Usually he would ask the tutor to a nearby pub for a drink afterwards. Then the post-mortem began, very quietly at first and deviously; but it built up great force. 'I did wonder whether such and such a passage was the best way to lead into the novel at that point'; or 'I wonder whether you might have made a little more at that stage of the students' own experience'; or 'I think you'll find that, if you don't read so much from a typescript (however good it may be, and I am sure it is very good), and don't use abstract words but find exact concrete instances, the students will come along with you much further and faster.' It was all, after the first upsets to *amour propre*, marvellously helpful.

The 'brass monkey' lecturer in theology intrigued the proselytising teacher in Mayfield. Clearly there was a serious interest in teaching adults there and no interest in the fees, but the interest had not been translated into thoughts about method. One evening Mayfield found the lecturer, who was tall, gaunt and Savonarola-like, standing stiffly before a class of adults in a cheerless Goole classroom. As Mayfield sat down at the back the lecturer was saying, in a voice gentle but firm with intellectual reproof, 'Now I know that at this stage some of you are going to accuse me of the Pelagian heresy' (or some such). Since few if any among them knew what that meant, the class looked both startled and slightly guilty. Mayfield took the lecturer to the pub and suggested that the wind ought to be tempered to the lecturer's lambs, who liked him very much without understanding much of what he said. 'Be more casual,' Mayfield said, 'in both your manner and presentation.' He followed up that visit a few weeks later – and found the lecturer lolling over a desk, smoking a pipe and saying very casually: 'Now I guess one or two of you are getting all set to throw the Manichean heresy at me.'

The price of Mayfield's perfectionism was the loss of any writing by him. He did work from time to time on the beginnings of one essay or another, especially after he retired rather early. We knew in our hearts, and perhaps he did, that he was not likely to bring any of them to the point of publication. He was the natural brother of Camus's character who never got past the first sentence of his novel because he could not bring that sentence to its final and perfect form. He would almost 'keen' over other men's books on authors he loved, because he knew he had better things to say. One particular result of this block was that we lost what could have been a wonderful study of Chekhov's art; instead, he poured it all out at summer schools in illuminating *aperçus* scattered through lectures which could last over two hours once he was caught up. He became a literary midwife to his friends and colleagues, unable to give birth himself but able to ease others' birth-pangs. He made extensive and detailed comments on any manuscript offered him. In such work nothing was too much trouble; there, he was decisive.

An old cliché is right here: he lived for his department; it was a substitute family. He lived for it and within it not as a social or political entity but as, he hoped, a hive of good teachers going out night after night and weekend after weekend into the city and countryside. When he was moved to defend what he saw as the department's rights he could be tremendously, excessively, demanding even on those he most cared for. I suppose Sammy, who was a good deal older and as much motherly as wifely, recognised this early and learned to live with it. For him, as for a sizeable minority of us, his work had to be his life; he had virtually to live within the department, be bound up with it emotionally, relate all his acquaintance to it; it was second only to literature in the subjects he most talked about.

To outsiders – and perhaps sometimes to her – it could seem that Sammy was second to the department in his affections; but this was an error. He could almost ignore her at times; yet he could focus on the department's problems and on his books so single-mindedly precisely because he knew he had her total devotion; so much so that he rarely thought of it, simply assumed that background support was there. It was a selfish manner of marriage but not callous or false – and she knew, by his exhausting if ineffectual worrisomeness if any mishap befell her, that below the self-regarding surface she was the only other human being for whom in the end he had an unqualified love. And dependence. After her death it was even more than usually painful to realise the extent to which his reliance on her, on her unswerving attachment to him and so by extension to his department, had entwined itself into the deepest recesses of his personality. He was bereft, miserably lost; he read in a desultory way, wrote wandering letters, made a lunchtime half-pint last as long as possible at The Queen's pub on a nearby corner, lingered over his meals, took even longer than usual over his shaving and dressing, and did not survive her for long.

I had a striking experience of the stubbornness of which he was capable if he thought himself protecting the interests of his department. By 1958 I had become fairly well-known in the field, especially for *The Uses of Literacy*, of which he was vicariously very proud. One result was a large number of invitations to speak at weekend schools and day schools and on any available free evenings; all without payment, of course, since that is the Tradition.

I agreed, since this too is the Tradition, to as many as I could. I was at that time serving also on my first departmental committee (on the development of the Youth Service), travelling to London at least once a fortnight, and doing a great deal of inescapable ancillary work.

It all began to be very heavy indeed. Roy Shaw, who was by then, as I was, a senior tutor, had been allowed by Raybould to take one class a week fewer than the usual number. I asked Mayfield whether a similar arrangement could be made for me. We were good friends, but I should have been forewarned of trouble by his suggestion that we meet to talk the matter over not in either of our homes but in the agoraphobic lounge of the Station Hotel. It was an icy meeting; he was adamant. To give up a class! I might have been suddenly revealed as a mother heartless enough to propose off-loading a child to inexpert, anonymous hands. I continued to take a full pro-gramme plus everything else I could manage; and we remained friends.

But he was instantly full of protective anger when he thought anyone, but especially members of the internal English department, were upstaging members of his staff. So when, in 1956, the University nominated me for the annual Visiting Professorship at Rochester, NY, Mayfield was – I have never used this phrase before, but it fits here – cock-a-hoop, exultant at the discomfiture of his enemies as much as pleased for me.

When after almost thirteen years in his department, I told him Mary and I were becoming fed up with rarely seeing each other in the evenings and with the considerable number of weekend engagements which bore hard on all the family, and that I was disposed to apply for a – very rare – internal senior lectureship which had just been advertised in the University of Leicester, he was startled and upset. Within a couple of days he asked me for a drink in The Queen's; I wasn't sure what for but knew it was not for a Station Hotel confrontation. He had seen the Vice-Chancellor, Brynmor Jones – Nicholson had by then been gone a year or two – told him my intention, added that he was thinking of taking early retirement in the following year and asked if he could have permission to suggest that the VC would support me as his successor. Permission being given, he called me to the session at The Queen's.

That meeting highlighted the problem which, after a good number of years in the service, faces any extra-mural tutor who loves his subject but also looks forward to less daily travelling throughout the winters, less family disruption and perhaps some advancement. There is nowhere to go beyond senior lecturer, no chairs by subjects in those departments. The only chairs are held either by the administrative, executive, full-time heads of department or by people who profess a branch of educational studies relevant to the field.

The dilemma was sharp and clear. The chances of an extra-mural lecturer, with very limited experience of the life of an internal department, getting the Leicester job were slight; my strongest cards were the recently published *The Uses of Literacy* and the reputation of Arthur Humphreys, the Leicester head of department, for taking chances. I was very touched by Mayfield's move but told him I felt I should go ahead with the application, and he stopped trying to persuade. One side of him was pleased at the idea that just possibly one of his protégés might move directly into internal teaching at a fairly senior level; that'd show them yet again.

Always one has to come back to his love of literature. That never wavered; to his last days it was his constant source of conversation. He was a gut socialist, because he hated snobbery and felt instinctively on the side of those who had had to struggle, as he had from his Midlands lower middle-class background, for access to the riches of his civilisation (books, of course); but he didn't like to waste much time talking about or practising party politics. In his later years he carried a photograph of Solzhenitsyn in his wallet. That was where politics became alive and urgent for him – where the right to speak was involved.

He lived almost two decades after we left Hull. Apart from letters and visits, we used to exchange books at Christmas. More and more, his were scrawled over on the title-pages and inner covers with his roaming perceptions on the texts; small bright essays in themselves.

Mayfield could never have been one of the major public figures in university adult education, nor would he have wanted to be. Those of us who worked with him knew that, for all his finicality and intransigencies, he was a remarkable example of a dedicated lover of literature who was also and inextricably a dedicated teacher of literature. People such as these are very rare and if we meet them at the right moments in our lives can transform our own outlooks.

An intriguing remark by a politician in a recent review: if an author chooses to write autobiographically about ordinary things and people, he said, he 'must not expect their place in history to carry the narrative along'. Exactly. We do have good records of the simple annals of the poor and wholly obscure which we accept and approve at least as much as we do the annals of the famous, since they have a heart-catching and obvious exemplary quality; that is their 'place in history'. The records of the lives of the people in between – the Rayboulds, the Nicholsons, the Mayfields – slip down the space between the notable and the entirely unknown. They are now out of time and history. They were provincials, they worked in unfashionable institutions, and in unfashionable corners of those institutions; yet in their own ways they too were exemplary.

Having, in the first volume of this sequence, tried to record the life of the poor as I knew it in my childhood, I am now reaching the point where I began to meet some well-known figures. In general, I do not propose to mention them, to tell stories about them, unless a meeting, an incident, has more than anecdotal interest, seems to throw some light on the times, or is simply comical or odd enough to earn its place.

I will aim to walk that neglected centre-ground where the work of figures, such as those I have just described, may be seen to deserve celebrating more than is usual. They were neither greatly famous nor emblematic of 'ordinary lives'. They carried out devotedly for years, without regard to quick fashion or great publicity, work they believed to be important; and they made their contribution to the traditions of that work, added their stones to the cairn which had begun to be erected by the great early figures I have also described. All of them represented something of the best in an undervalued and often neglected but in many ways model area of education.

CHAPTER 6

TEACHING-AND-WRITING
THE 1950s

Professionally, the years at Hull, the Fifties, were years of teaching-and-writing. The hyphenated form is meant to indicate that the two activities were almost entirely enmeshed. This is one of the great advantages and pleasures of university external teaching. Your subject may and should be your central professional focus; but you have no captive audience. Your students come to classes by choice and often at considerable inconvenience; their backgrounds vary and their kinds of capacity; they are not examination-selected and semi-captive eighteen to twenty-one-year-olds. Without reducing the demands of the subject you have to ask yourself how you would implicitly justify to your students their expenditure of time and trouble, how best you can link their studies with their own experience, and what that must involve in shaping a course and finding the proper words to present it.

Some internal members of staff are 'born' teachers, and some – perhaps most – conscientiously set themselves to learning how to teach effectively. But on the whole the business of teaching, that difficult but inspiriting business, is not a subject which internal lecturers when gathered together spend much time in discussing. It is not at the front of their minds. They are more likely to talk about where their research work has arrived and perhaps about the possible interest in it of a good academic publisher.

One of the finest teachers at Leeds University in our day was Wilfred Rowland-Childe, a shy, unmarried, Roman Catholic, gentle, elderly poet. It had never occurred to him to try either tricks or simply helpful devices of presentation in lectures. He shuffled in, glanced briefly at his audience and then bent to his papers. His voice was low, not greatly modulated but not boring when you tuned into it. Some students would not bother to do that and did not reappear after the first lecture of the year's course. They missed an exceptional experience, an introduction to the nature of devoted scholarship which nothing in their previous education would have been likely to prepare them for. They would have heard him exploring, say, some new aspect of the minor metaphysical poets with the air of a man rapt that things should be after all thus rather than thus; and behind the words was a quiet humility before the fact that it had been given to him to see these new things.

But most of us should think about the nature of teaching our particular subject to our particular kinds of students from our first days at work. 'A loving heart is the beginning of all knowledge'; knowledge of our discipline and knowledge of our students; and of the right relations between the two. Again, the external lecturer is lucky here. He can if he wishes pursue his own research self-regardedly, perhaps in the hope of an internal job once his publications have established his scholarship. On that route he can pay little attention to the needs of students and get by with a casual, loose heartiness which will deceive many – especially since external students are usually humble, unduly humble, before someone who actually comes from the university. Or he can tease away at the tensions between the two poles of his duties.

Internal staff members' second main subject of conversation – after the progress of their own research – is the needs of students as individuals, from whether this one is bright enough to get a first and go on to Oxbridge for postgraduate work, to whether that one is being made miserable and ineffective by the demands of her boy-friend. On the one hand, intense talk about each one's corner of the discipline, largely unrelated to the intellectual needs of students out there in the lecture-rooms; on the other hand, a traditional pastoral interest which is one of the great merits of English university practice. But the middle ground, which could also be the best link between the two ends, is almost entirely ignored.

So for the external lecturer there is profit and loss from his isolated position. In the first few years of professional life the profit can outweigh the loss. You can almost feel yourself being pushed towards redefining your subject on your own, without others shaking their heads daily at the way you are going off the rails; you can try new ways of approaching each class, after successive early failures and some breakthroughs, with virtually no interference.

In some respects, extra-mural lecturers, who after all are university staff members, might seem to be treated with less than their due dignity. Since the Department of Education pays most of the costs of that kind of work directly, not through the arms-length quango mechanism of the University Grants Committee, the corps of His or Her Majesty's Inspectors have the right and duty to visit classes. The splendidly-eccentric HMI assigned to our area knew perfectly all the typically British inspectorial codes in gestures and speech. He would sit at the back in a sort-of-countryfied or cad's outfit which often included a purple weskit with brass buttons; in one pocket of which was a beautiful snuff-box he claimed had 'been Prinnie's'; he also claimed, and I have no reason to doubt it, that he was a cousin of Elizabeth Bowen; he certainly came from the Anglo-Irish gentry or near-gentry.

At the end, when the students had left, he offered you a pinch of snuff and, unless he was concerned about your competence, used a coded locution which I learned later to associate particularly with the Cambridge-trained, as they delicately compliment someone to whose lecture they have just listened: 'I *did* enjoy that. Thank you'. I never learned what he said to those whose skills seemed questionable. I know that after such occasions he, again according to the code, 'had a quiet word with the head of department'. In my experience that was the range and extent of interference with our work. Except that at Hull, for those of us who were tutors in literature, there were the occasional visits from Mayfield; to which no one could reasonably object. To have a head of department who had both kept up his subject and thought deeply about teaching it was an advantage few external lecturers enjoyed; most of their heads of department were administrators or, if they wrote, wrote as 'educationists' not as scholars in particular fields.

I have been stressing this intellectual freedom because of a curious incident in the late-Seventies. An extra-mural lecturer who was engaged on a thesis about immediate post-war practice sent a questionnaire to those of us he could find who had worked through that period. His questions seemed to assume we were under some political control from the Ministry as to the subjects we gave classes on and the way we approached them; or perhaps the assumption was that, even if such a control was not explicit, we recognised its shadow in the background and acted accordingly, whether to be more royalist than the king or to circumvent the inhibition. Some degree of political or ideological intent, whether from government or within the tutors themselves, seemed to be assumed.

'Objectivity' in teaching is always an ideal, but it was an ideal the best tutors put central to their work. Over the years, Roy Shaw had considerable personal struggles as to whether he should remain in or, once out, return to the Roman Catholic Church. It was typical of his attempt at objectivity in teaching that, at the end of a three-year class in philosophy, one of the students asked him now to make his own position clear, since it had not been evident.

My own single experience of an attempt at direct government intervention in adult education teaching came in the early Eighties, soon after the first Thatcher government took office. All the official cohorts, and especially the junior ministers to whose heads power quickly went, wanted to be model new brooms, especially in sniffing out incipient socialism. The previous Labour government had set up a new national quango, the Advisory Council for Adult and Continuing Education, and asked me to be its chairman. There was manifestly much to be done. The Conservative government soon made known its dislike of all quangoes. After all, they are paradigmatic of the consensus view of a democracy, in which a government sets up and listens to bodies which have as collectives no particular political allegiance but try to give such disinterested advice as they can after studying their subject. To a government which, even though it had come into office on a minority vote, insisted that it had been elected expressly to carry out a particular 'radical' (the word had been taken over from the other side) programme, it seemed unnecessary to ask a mixed group of people without the same sense of prior direction and purpose to advise it on any issue. You don't invite people to qualify and perhaps modify the fine, strong thrust of your own clear intentions.

ACACE's first term of three years came to an end soon after the new government took office. It would have been perverse, though not surprising, if the Council's life had been ended then, even though it had already shown how much still needed to be thought through in fulfilling its brief. We were given a further three years, but with the clear indication that that would be the end; as it proved to be.

The junior minister charged with responsibility for our area of work had that air of heady buoyancy combined with a simulacrum of Churchillian authority which first-time junior ministers acquire in their very early days; and lose after a few months answering questions in the Commons or meeting deputation after deputation from pressure groups. At the meeting he attended, one member presented the report of a sub-committee on the decline of classes in political education and how it might be reversed. After all, one of the main impulses behind the Great Tradition had been the conviction that in a democracy people, whatever their formal education, should be helped to be politically literate. The junior minister showed signs of perturbation and intervened to suggest that the promotion of political education was not in the Council's brief. We heard Tawney turn wryly in his grave. At the urinal just before lunch I found myself in the next stall to an HMI who had also been present. What did the junior minister think he was playing at? 'Oh,' said the HMI, 'he thinks he's doing what his Master wants. And the Secretary of State, as you know, sees Reds under every bed.' From clogs to clogs in just over a century.

I

But back in Yorkshire in the Fifties we had our idealism intact. Half of my own writing was for journals about adult education, most if not all of them now defunct: *Adult Education*, *The Tutors' Bulletin*, *The Highway* (the journal of the Workers' Educational Association). Sometimes alone, sometimes with others, I wrote essays with solemn, rhetorically-interrogative titles: 'What Are We Doing?', 'To What Good End?' and the like. Surprising that none of the titles began 'Whither . . . ?' We wrote about aims and first principles, and about the details of methods of teaching those kinds of subjects to those kinds of students. An exchange of this kind first put me in contact with Raymond Williams, who was then based on the south coast.

We distinguished steadily between the social justification for the work and any possible political direction. We were somewhat puritanical and very moral in our commitment. For a weekend school on the nature of moral judgments, shared with Roy Shaw, I wrote an earnest leaflet, 'The Sweetcake Country', which began:

Long long ago, in a certain country, the inhabitants ate nothing but sweetcakes. What is more, everyone ate the same kind of cake, little ones of strange composition. They contained, for instance, no milk but only water; no flour but only powdered chalk; no currants but only tiny pellets of dirt. But to make up for these (to us) important deficiencies in food value the cakes had several specious attractions; they were highly coloured, nicely varnished, and very sugary.

It was my first approach to a phenomenon I have since returned to often: that a consumer-persuasive, open society must be founded on and must encourage relativism in all parts of experience, since the customers must be assumed to be open to constant change in all things, in tastes, attitudes, assumptions.

Again we were, in comparison with internal teachers, in an exposed position. We could not join close, face-to-face groups of like-minded colleagues working in the same subject, happy to discuss that endlessly and, in so far as we looked outside, satisfied to make dismissive jokes about the popular press, popular fiction, pop songs and all the other trivialities of that world we did not feel we had to be part of. Our students lived in that world day-by-day; most of them did not greatly care for it, or for that matter seem to have been badly damaged by it. But the fact that they came to our classes showed they were making an effort after another perspective.

Their reasons for joining were mixed, some more mixed than others; from the prospect of simple enjoyment to a wish for a touch of cultural varnish, to the assumption that the study of literature would speak to their condition in new and profound ways. No one of them is wholly wrong. The hardest of all, because the best-founded of all, is the last. The approach has to be, as it has to be in so many things of importance to our personalities, a matter of indirection; literature studied for the good of our souls will not reveal itself; but if we try to read it with openness and understanding, the pleasure it gives will gradually show itself as relevant to our lives in unexpected ways. This is the hardest lesson for adult students to accept but should lie behind every class from the first; patiently and quietly but undeviatingly.

Another lesson, so long as the tutor is willing to take off the armour of specialist language and talk as clearly as possible, without reducing the subject (and this balancing act can be performed much more than many of us like to think), is that many of the students, even if they have had little formal education, are in some ways at least as bright as we are. The same lesson can be just as salutary to the occasional graduate who joins an adult class; he may be tempted to think that because he and the tutor are the only ones with degrees they belong to a select group-within-the-group; until a turn in the discussion or a quotation from a piece of written work reveals insights from a quiet, 'unqualified' student in the corner which all their qualifications have not given them.

Gradually, you build up almost as many different relationships as there are members of the class. In my very early days, at Middlesbrough, I once or twice more or less read an essay for the first hour and then invited discussion. Violet Turnbull, who had been well-trained by one of my predecessors, stood up and told me I had given them no way into a discussion. It had been, yes, an interesting essay, and no doubt I would publish it somewhere (she was right – it formed the basis of a chapter in my book on Auden); but it was not an introduction to the subject for members of an adult class. It gave them no purchase, did not open up questions which might lead them into understanding better the book being studied. It did not repeat itself, turn back upon itself, take stock, raise doubts, show a mind actually at work. It was, for the purposes of good adult teaching in literature, as useless as a learned screed about the geology of the high peaks to someone trying to master the first steps in mountain-climbing.

That was an error of underestimation by me. There are also errors of overestimation of what students can accept at a particular time in the life of the class. When the first tape-recorders appeared – bulky and heavy machines – it seemed useful to record the discussion in the second half of one of my classes at Goole. It might show how hard it is to give a discussion a coherent shape and development, how soon and how often it is interrupted, blown off course, broken into inconsequence or set off on new and more useful lines. The experiment proved that, and more – because, and it seems hard to believe now but at that time was true, none of us had, I imagine, ever heard our own recorded voices.

We sat listening, at first amused by the obvious distortions of that early equipment. Then I realised that two of the students, wives of local grammar school teachers, had faces frozen and red with shock and embarrassment. At the end they left silently and could not be persuaded to come to the class again. The reason was surprising, culturally intriguing and simple. They were Yorkshire women and to an outsider their voices would have sounded predominantly Yorkshire. But as wives of grammar school masters they belonged to the professional middle class, if to the less well-paid end of it. So their voices had acquired a slight gloss of educated gentility. Within their own heads this is what they heard; their minds filtered away the main Yorkshire strain and left them hearing the genteel elements; and those distinguished them importantly, crucially, from the body of people around them in Goole. They believed that and so, I imagine, did other residents of Goole with whom they came into contact; they were a bit different, posher. But the recorder, even when one had allowed for its rudimentary falsifications, told them what their voices really sounded like. Overwhelmingly, and in spite of the genteel overlay, they sounded broad Yorkshire, more like Yorkshire comics, Yorkshire pantomime dames, than grammar school wives as they imagined they should sound, as they wished to and had assumed they did speak; and that was unbearable.

Accidents like that were rare. More common was the slow but certain progress in a class which as meeting followed meeting turned it from a group of separate and often shy individuals into a small community, a civil society within itself, a society which had emerged from common aims, common disciplines and common courtesies; a society of a kind which few of us could have known before.

It was against this background that the redefinition of the subject, so far as it seemed to be forcing the need upon us, could best take place. In some WEA officials and a few tutors this took the form of asking for 'relevance' (another overused and wrongly-used word) in literature syllabuses. That meant G. B. Shaw, H. G. Wells, Jack London, Tressall, Sinclair Lewis and anybody else who could be fitted into the Co-op shopping bag of 'social realism'. For me it meant holding to the belief that the students were owed an opening to the best as I understood it in our literature, and could rise to meet the challenges of that best if given a proper opportunity.

It also meant believing that the methods of literary criticism and analysis were relevant to the better understanding of all levels of writing and much else in popular culture, and of the way people responded to them. This was not a lapse into the 'The Beatles are in their own way as good as Beethoven' nonsense, but equally not a refusal to see that the appeal of, and the response to, all forms of popular literature and art were worth study and might tell us surprising things about ourselves, about other people, and about our and their imaginations.

It is plain that I – and others like me – had in those early years a love-affair with the idea of teaching. *Eros paedagogus*. Out of old notebooks there still fall quotations from those who had thought earlier and further than I had – for instance, I. A. Richards. I do not know who now reads *Interpretation in Teaching*. What he said there was sometimes so simple as to sound like truism; but he had got there on his own, through experience, and by refusing to retain for himself a saving academic distance, or by leaning on his considerable Cambridge credentials; so he had earned the right to a gnomic simplicity: 'It is [the "travellers", i.e. the student's] judgment, always and only, that we have to train. All else is means and occasion only . . . It is, then, not our business to teach conclusions, but to help in the framing of questions.'

Or I liked to quote to myself, as I set out on foggy, clammy December nights for fifty-mile drives to classes, Shaw on the importance of learning how to read: 'And you must understand a printed page as you understand people talking to you. That is a stupendous feat of sheer learning, much the most difficult I have ever achieved.'

Again, the simple phrasing of one who has been there; phrasing which also points directly to another huge simplicity – that in the modern developed world, where all are said to be literate but are encouraged to remain literate only at a very low level, we begin to move out of the persuasion-chrysalis only when we recognise that almost all we read in daily life is special pleading, interested, out to woo us for ulterior ends, whether it is written by the advertisers or all the other commercial con-men, or by some kinds of politician, or by anyone who wants to persuade us to accept a packaged point of view without giving us the opportunity to find our own way there.

Then we see the difference between those kinds of things and the work of a disinterested writer who says: 'Life seems like this, as I see it in pictures, incidents and words – and how interesting and disturbing and comical and . . . it is'; and leaves you to take it as you will, to accept the meanings or not, according to the power of the writer's imagination and your own ability to respond to it. There is no hot breath; you are not being taken by the collar, urged to listen. You are being invited to attend a private session, a private enquiry into the appearances of life, into the making of sense. There is no more nearly-objective form of human communication, as Auden did not tire of saying:

> In grasping the character of a society, as in judging the character of an individual, no documents, statistics, 'objective' measurements can ever compete with the single intuitive glance. Intuition may err, for though its judgment is, as Pascal said, only a question of good eyesight, it must be good, for the principles are subtle and numerous, and the omission of one principle leads to error; but documentation, which is useless unless it is complete, *must* err in a field where completeness is impossible.

It took almost a year for questions such as these, about literature and its meanings for adult students, to begin to make sense to me. Before that, most was hand-to-mouth. Among much else, I remember trying to catch up with *Wuthering Heights* on the train which was actually taking me to a very early class. Walking on the water, somehow.

By the end of the first year, it had become clear that poetry gave the best challenges to both the students and the tutor, went most directly to the heart of the matter. There soon appeared in my commonplace book a passage from Flaubert on intuition and poetry which partners Auden's wider judgment quoted just above: 'Poetry is as exact a science as geometry. Induction is as good as deduction . . . No doubt my poor Bovary is suffering and weeping in twenty different French villages at this very moment.'

A work of prose would with time open itself to almost all students, but that was not true with poetry. Sometimes one felt that a few people, no matter how intelligent they might be in other ways, were tone-deaf to poetry. But if to poetry then surely also tone-deaf to important elements of prose? Perhaps; but the limitation didn't show so clearly there. I took to picking out basic, touchstone, elements as guides to responsiveness. Such as the effect and power of a particular word which insists on a special weight and stress. As does 'puzzles' in Hamlet's most celebrated soliloquy:

Who would fardels bear,
To grunt and sweat under a weary life,
But that the dread of something after death,
The undiscover'd country from whose bourn
No traveller returns, *puzzles* the will . . .

Or 'trouble' in these lines after the boat passage in Book 1 of *The Prelude*:

No familiar shapes
Remained, no pleasant images of trees,
Of sea or sky, no colours of green fields;
But huge and mighty forms, that do not live
Like living men, moved slowly through the mind
By day, and were a *trouble* to my dreams.

There were other and more elaborate exercises until I had to decide that some people – a very few – were indeed deaf to the workings of language in such and other poetic senses. Other people – again a few – found their hearing sharpened to an extent they had not suspected. As late as 1989 I was sent a book of poems by a woman who had been in my Scarborough class forty years ago. It was not her first volume, but we had lost touch. They were not poems a major publisher would accept, but they had a restrained yet muscular sensitivity to language and what that language was being asked to do. In an uneffusive letter the author said I might like to know that her sense of language and poetry had been wakened all those years ago, in class exercises and discussions.

It was all a strangely intense and often solitary set of enquiries. But we joined forces. Edward Thompson and I once spent a whole week at a WEA summer school exploring our agreements and differences on the meanings of Conrad's *Heart of Darkness*. In such collaborations we were in part giving ourselves reinforcement, still convincing ourselves of the importance of our odd profession, but at bottom in no doubt about that importance. The lonely sense of purpose could breed its own strange dreams. One elderly tutor who had criss-crossed the Yorkshire Dales night after night since the late Thirties, teaching economics, had worked for years on a vast economic-and-philosophic panacea for all mankind's ailments. I once held the great manuscript in my hands, but it never went into print. Most of the younger ones did not stay around to see that kind of old age; but we were in danger of professional afflatus, especially those who taught literature or philosophy. Even now, my own excessive distrust of internalised literary theory draws on the experiences, the stresses and strains and prides, of those early years. Clearly, 'relevance' lay elsewhere. Yet I expect there are external tutors in literature nowadays who run courses, with pleasure and success, on late-twentieth-century literary theory. In some good and some limiting ways, ours was a simpler age.

The ideas about the actual practice of teaching literature which came out of external university-level classes are, with little modification, applicable to internal teaching in universities and to teaching at other levels; most good ideas about teaching are widely applicable. Overwhelmingly, the principal aim, as I've said more than once, is to bring out the value of your subject to people for whom it may seem strange, above their heads, or who may have come to be introduced to it for a mixture of reasons, often mistaken; to bring out that value in the right ways, to connect properly, not to reduce or inflate or distort it, not to make it into a political weapon or a force for social dry-cleaning or a substitute for religion; and never to underestimate its difficulty if it is to be properly appreciated; but neither to make it seem a penance, an intellectual and imaginative all-bran.

Four elements have remained in the memory longer than others. First, how much a good class became a continuing interchange between you and the group, and you and each individual in the group. This was true not only of the discussion periods, which were a mixture of the planned and the free. It was true of the regular written work, usually essays whose themes differed with the needs of different students at different times. We heard of one tutor who saved himself a lot of work by simply writing 'Thank you very much indeed' at the bottom of every essay, and they all had the same subject. Others of us went through them with great care, at home, and would often write a small essay in commentary on them. Similarly, we thought of the best next private reading for each student. All this often resulted in direct correspondence; I still have books with students' addresses from the 1946–7 session. These were the essential struts of a two-hour class. To prepare for and run four such classes a week and take regular Saturday day schools and weekend schools made a full programme.

The second remarkable element, especially in the first few years, was the progressive slowing-down of the pace. In the very early days, when I might still be refreshing my memory of a book whilst the little, corridorless and dusty train jogged along to Whitby or Bridlington and the class where I would talk about it, I had assumed that two or even one two-hour sessions would be enough for almost all books. But gradually the books chosen for study became more and more important and the time they needed lengthened. By 1950, the third year of a tutorial class might be spending a twelve-week term on part of *King Lear*, with no sense that the pace was slow. By the end they knew more about how to read a book than they would have learned from a scamper through six of them in the one term; and the knowledge was transferable.

Two kinds of moving out from the obvious and the English texts developed. It seemed a pity that students for whom a new world was opening should not have the chance also to read Dostoevsky, Tolstoy, Chekhov, Stendhal, Flaubert, Proust, Mann, even if only in translation. It was a chance I had had and taken, since my foreign languages were restricted to French and a little Italian. I sought out the best translations (the department was generous at providing a copy for every student, though more and more bought their own, especially after paperbacks such as Penguins were joined by other imprints) and, where the language was one of the two with which I had at least some acquaintance, gave out stencilled copies of key pages in the original, so that the students could begin to see something of the richness which even the best translation could not capture.

Last, and perhaps most important of these four elements, those first five or so years of teaching led me step by step but inescapably to move out from the study of literature as it is academically defined to work on many other aspects of contemporary culture, chiefly but not only in words. I had, of course, read and admired Q.D. Leavis's *Fiction and the Reading Public* as well as similar material in *Scrutiny* and associated publications. Admired them, but not been altogether at ease with them. Something was missing in those analyses but it took me years to discover what. By then I was in the difficult process of writing what eventually became *The Uses of Literacy*. That book pays tribute to the work of Mrs Leavis, and it is a genuine tribute. But it was, for me more importantly, an attempt to adjust something in Mrs Leavis's approach – a distancing from the material in her, too wholesale a rejection of it and all it might imply. Helped by Orwell and C. S. Lewis, I became more and more drawn to the question of what people might make of that material, by the thought that obviously poor writing might appeal to good instincts, that the mind of a reader is not a *tabula rasa* but has been nurtured within a social setting which provides its own forms and filters for judgments and resistances, that one had to know very much more about how people used much of the stuff which to us might seem merely dismissible trash, before one could speak confidently about the effects it might have.

Ironically, Mrs Leavis came to say towards the end of her life that Raymond Williams and I had made reputations by climbing on her shoulders. We had certainly learned a lot from her and acknowledged it; but we stood on our own ground. The influences which more directly prompted me to move out – apart from the lessons I took from listening to students who themselves lived outside the academic closed circle – came from not only Orwell and C. S. Lewis but, more surprisingly, from Ezra Pound. Pound arguing that 'when language goes rotten' thought and feeling decay with it for each of us and for society, was yet another copy-book passage.

How long ago all this now seems to those of us who were engaged in it; how out of date to some in extra-mural work today. Because, it is said, nowadays you can find hardly anyone who will be able to match the demands of a genuine tutorial class (the adjective is a recognition that some of today's 'tutorial classes' are that in name rather than nature). Nor do we believe, the rebuttal goes on, that many of the earlier classes lived up to their prescription; much talk about their achievements is nostalgic distortion. To which one feels like making a rude old sweat's reply: 'Get your knees brown, soldier.' At any rate, these critics add, there are no Jude the Obscures left; they go to the remaining grammar-schools or move up their Comprehensives, to University.

But we do not find and educate all the bright talents among today's working-class people; too many social and educational factors get in the way. Instead, we tell them all the time that they do not need to, are not called to, develop their talents, that they should stay as sweet as they are – so that they will remain fodder for the usual unholy trio: the popular press, the more populist politicians and the admen.

More politically, it is said that the tutorial class tradition assumed that university adult education should make over working-class students into the image of the cultivated bourgeois – combining the Protestant Ethic with middle-class artistic gentility. It put too much stress on solitary work for self-improvement; it lacked an adequate sense of working-class solidarity and communality.

In spite of all the new technological aids to communication, the process of learning is still inherently slow, has its own natural rhythms; like childbirth. It can be helped along, both intellectually and psychologically, by work within a group; it is still in the end a matter of individual discipline towards some particular kinds of growth. Which is a quite different experience from that of simply being introduced to the arts and conventions of any particular social class. Part of the business of learning lies in the effort to understand, for instance, the literature of the past both 'in itself' and in relation to the social groups from which it came and which it hoped to address.

There is much evidence that many people today will seek further education and will meet high demands if they are approached in the right ways. The Open University itself is the best example. It began work after forceful opposition; there were plenty of people ready to dismiss its aims and prospects. Edward Boyle used to say that the Conservative Chancellor of the Exchequer of the day might well have killed it had he not died suddenly. If there proved to be any demand for it at all, some said, that demand would be for cheap, pseudo-degrees. But the response has been enormous and the wastage rate low, especially in view of the heavy demands made on its students. It is they who are in some senses the descendants of the early tutorial class students. Except by the incorrigible, Open University degrees are recognised as sound on any reasonable comparison; it works.

Yet almost two million British adults remain not literate enough or numerate enough to cope adequately with an urbanised culture which is above all confusing and deceptive. On the one hand it demands quite a high level of literacy and numeracy for survival, on the other hand it flatters people into thinking their low level of command is all that is needed to live the good life.

It is easy to assume that the great and widely-spread demand for further education by adults today is predominantly for vocational uses, retraining, refreshment or changes of direction; and such a demand does exist. But the full picture is more interesting. Just before its short life came to an end, the Advisory Council for Adult and Continuing Education ran the most thorough survey yet made of the demand for further education by adults. Of course it revealed that many want more education for practical purposes. But the most remarkable discovery was that a very substantial number of people seek further education for the traditional reasons. They express that need in lovely old-fashioned ways. They speak of wanting to be better educated so as to live a fuller life, so as to be more whole, so as to be able to understand their experience better, and the way their society is going. They want to understand and to criticise, but from a larger and less febrile perspective than they are generally offered; they are Arnoldians before they are anything else. Jude and his sister are not dead nor necessarily at university; they probably have Filofaxes; but they are still looking for larger meanings.

As I prepared to leave Hull after that first decade, to become an internal lecturer, Mayfield asked me to 'set down my thoughts' on the nature of extra-mural teaching. I do not know whether anybody read them but that request, from him, was like being approved at a passing-out parade of Mayfield's own heavy infantry; Llandrindod Wells almost twenty years on, with rather more official approval.

2

Through the first half of the Fifties I produced a piece of writing about adult education roughly every two months. Then it fell away. I had been paying dues to my chosen educational area, justifying to myself as well as to some outside having spent a decade in what seemed to most professional people a subfusc byway, the academic equivalent of the heavy ack-ack regiments. Once again, the idiotic British putting-people-into-boxes-by-presumed-status was in play and having its effect. We sometimes visited the Dobrées on our way down to Stalybridge for the year's great occasions. They were always affectionate and welcoming. They were delighted that I was beginning to be, if ever so slightly, known – not for writing about adult education and the universities but for directly literary essays; they also regarded those essays as steps towards what they assumed I wished for as soon as ever possible, translation to internal teaching. Andrew Shonfield reacted in much the same way. One of the students in a Bridlington tutorial class, a kindly and intelligent middle-class woman, told me in the second year – pointing towards a higher future I might be too modest to envisage – that in her opinion I was good enough to seek to be a grammar-school master; and that she would be willing to have a word with the head of the local institution.

After the book on Auden came out in 1951 there began a thin flow of invitations to review, write essays for compilations, talk to a few conferences and to broadcast. For the BBC; the first direct competition, commercial television, was still two years away. Yet the pace was slower in those days. The Auden book was well received in the press and on radio; but more than a year passed before I was asked to broadcast about him. That was in mid-1952, and a characteristic Third Programme occasion it was. The atmosphere was courteous; if not senior common roomish, that of an intellectual club; an atmosphere consonant with the tone of the discussions about aim and range which preoccupied the Third Programme's planners for years. My talk was not a talk at all; it was an essay in a prose meant to be read, not spoken. Even after half a dozen years of teaching it had not occurred to me, as a serious and interesting matter, that the spoken word moves differently from the word written to be read, that it need not move by whole sentences and paragraphs, can be ungrammatically colloquial, can gain by repetition and redundancy, should have above all a tone of voice of which the speaker is aware and knows how to use for what he is trying to say.

This way of thinking was not generally accepted among Third Programme producers; or it was given a special gloss. Some, it was said, were fully aware that the live voice is not the printed word and tried to guide anxious tyros – by advising them to imagine they were conversing with fellow members of that senior common room in the sky. That would have been a feat of the imagination for me. No doubt out of delicacy, I was not invited to make the leap; nor was I given any but the most simple, though handy, advice on presentation: make sure the pages don't rustle as you turn them over – turn each down at the top edge before you start; don't be afraid of pauses; try to get the stresses right. I read, I plodded through, an essay which, to become a good broadcast, would have had to be taken apart and put together again in a different way. It said some quite useful things about the relations between Auden's intellectual life and the changes in his poetry; but should have seen daylight in print only; it was inept and wasteful broadcasting, and would have caused all except existing Auden experts justifiably to switch off. The fact that some gifted individuals, such as Isaiah Berlin, can broadcast brilliantly – minds thinking aloud at great speed – without taking much thought about the character of the medium does not weaken the case for giving most of us advice on how the spoken voice best communicates; even the Third Programme found very few people like Isaiah Berlin.

It was two years before another invitation to broadcast came along and that too had its peculiar flavour of the times. Regional broadcasting was still flourishing, well-staffed and funded and with freedom to invent. West Region had a series, 'The Poem on the Table', invented by its Talks producers Robert Waller and Kenneth Hudson. The Third Programme had put out something similar in late 1952, but the audience sought for it was different. The Third Programme assumed its listeners already had a good knowledge of poetry. At Bristol, some interest but little prior knowledge was assumed; rather, it was felt that most listeners would be glad of guidance so long as they were not made to feel patronised. The series was obviously a form of adult education but did not sound like that. The producer took care to ensure that it was a friendly programme and not portentous or poetry-voiced. There was no reason of policy for it to have originated as a regional programme but a regional producer had the freedom to conceive it and the money to put it on. A poem was read, an enthusiast was questioned about it stanza by stanza so that understanding built up, and finally the poem was read again, this time – it was hoped – being much more intelligible to the listeners. The poem I chose was, inevitably, one of Auden's, a lyric: 'Deftly, admiral, cast your fly'.

Strange how often what seemed at the time isolated programmes now seem also to have carried indications beyond themselves about the nature of broadcasting, intellectual life and assumptions about people out there, in those pre-competitive days. The earnestness of the BBC up to that cataclysmic change in the middle-Fifties has been described *ad nauseam*, but usually shallowly. But at their best the Third Programme and the Regional system (and much else in the early BBC) were decent, serious and admirable attempts to use this wonderful new medium in the best interests of society as a whole and in much of its variety. It was bound to change, but its record needs not apology but praise.

I do not remember how one or two people at the BBC learned I was writing a fairly large book. Before the typescript of *The Uses of Literacy* had gone to Chatto I began to be asked to give talks whose subjects were plainly drawn from its material. There was a series of three in the spring of 1955 whose titles – slightly reminiscent of the style favoured by Methodist ministers on Hunslet's chapel notice-boards – call up the way the book had shaped by then: 'Tradition and Resilience', 'Unbent Springs', 'Present Trends'. A few months later there was one called 'Scholarship Boy', the title of a chapter which has brought me more correspondence – both intimate and relieved ('so others have felt as I have!') – from all sorts of people, including civil servants at under-secretary level and above, than anything else I have written.

The Use of English, a good professional and parish magazine for teachers which virtually ignored institutional levels and concentrated, with a strong Leavisite inclination, on common issues in the subject and its teaching, also published two long essays drawn from the by now very bulky typescript. Since I was always hesitant about sending unsolicited manuscripts, I expect those were asked for after I had given them at one of the succession of Use of English conferences at which we laid bare our latest thoughts.

I was grateful to Tosco Fyvel at *Tribune* for showing a similar interest and encouraging me to write those short, atmospheric essays on curious aspects of British culture which I mentioned earlier. Not many, but they all fed in. If you are living well out in the provinces, if you are investing most of your spare space and huge emotional energy in a book which grows all the time, which sounds odd if you describe it to friends, which threatens to get out of hand, and increasingly frightens you with the thought that no publisher will think it other than a five- or six-year self-delusion, then an unfussed, amused interest such as Fyvel's is a lifeline. Driving him round Strasbourg between sessions of a conference on George Orwell, just before his death in the Eighties, I told him this. He gave his Old Possum grin and said only: 'Ah well, you know, I thought from the first piece of yours I saw that there might possibly be something just a little bit different there.'

Early in the Fifties I did send off an unsolicited manuscript. In tutorials on modern literature I had found myself more and more teased, as well as attracted, by Graham Greene. Gradually a sense of common or related elements in structure, incidents and language – and of their relation to themes – grew. In the end there emerged a longish essay, 'The Force of Caricature', which F. W. Bateson published in *Essays in Criticism*.

But for most of the time, for almost all the first half of the Fifties, the book originally called *The Abuses of Literacy* absorbed my spare thoughts. It was a huge cuckoo in an already full emotional nest and at times I hated its voracity and its assumption that it had to be served first. Which was not possible; I had and did not want to neglect considerable family commitments; professionally, I was not prepared to let teaching suffer. I – we – survived, but the middle years on the trail were badly strained and I almost broke. The early years were easier because I did not know what I was letting myself in for, what inhospitable terrain lay ahead. The final years were better. Like a woman who in the fifth or sixth month of pregnancy settles harmoniously into the final straight, I knew then where I was going and that I could get there. I was past the awful point at which you find yourself saying miserably that there is no turning back, you are now in so far that to return were as tedious as go'er.

I had begun by wanting to write a sort of guide or textbook to aspects of popular culture: newspapers, magazines, romantic or violent paperbacks, popular songs, the sort of thing which is to be found in the second half of *The Uses of Literacy*, though in forms I did not suspect at the start. As I said earlier, I wanted, whilst respecting Mrs Leavis's work, to adjust it by setting it into the contexts of readers' lives. But that need broadened so much that it turned the book upside down; it was written back to front. I had begun by writing what became the second half, but the pressure of the need to provide a context led me to try to describe the texture of working-class life as I knew it; and that then became the first half. The demand of the themes in a work of non-fiction can take over from the writer – can get up and run away with the nail he thinks he has pinned them down with, as Lawrence said of the novel – just as much as the demands of a character suddenly come to life in a work of fiction. So there were two books, but hardly anyone noticed the join.

I showed the final typescript to two Hull colleagues. One was the Marxist sociologist of art, F. D. Klingender. In private relations he was a very gentle man but, like many such Marxists, uncompromisingly hard if he felt his ideology challenged. It was plain the book had upset him, but it took me time to discover why. He was of middle-class European intellectual stock and his image of the English working class did not square with mine; in my picture the radical working class figured hardly at all; nor did the trade unions or the industrial life of labourers; it was an inturned, largely domestic scene. Had I been presenting a comprehensive picture of working-class life these would indeed have been grievous omissions. Probably I should have made more effort to at least sketch in that wider part of the context. But my own experience had been overwhelmingly domestic, internal, home and woman-centred, and I did not want to appear to be claiming a larger, professional knowledge. Klingender came to see this, though not to relish the implications of my approach, my part of the whole; but we remained friendly acquaintances until his very early death.

The other reader was a historian friend. She too was disturbed by the book but for different reasons. She thought it was a dangerous attempt to cross or straddle academic boundaries. I would be attacked from both sides, scorned by both the social scientists and my literary colleagues. She told me not to try to publish it but to stick to my literary-critical last; and eventually, she felt confident, I would be offered a chair in English. That judgment upset me more than Klingender's; with him, I had had an intellectual dispute about part of the book's approach; with the historian I met the shock of the judgment that I had wasted six years of my free time. I had a sleepless night, but by morning knew there was still no going back.

In fact, most social scientists, here and abroad, were generous to the book, saying it suggested new and useful ways of looking at social change. Some French sociologists, in particular, said it implicitly rebuked their own over-preoccupation with abstractions by its hold on 'phenomenological detail'; some important American scholars were similarly open-minded. One English sociologist, in his cups at a professional meeting, said it wasn't all that bad but of course he too – being of working-class stock – could have written it had he ever got round to it. Many people I knew in internal departments of English kept fairly quiet about it, as though a shabby cat from the council house next door had brought an odd – even a smelly – object into the house.

Of adverse comments, the most interesting was that the first part of the book was 'sentimental' about working-class life. I have looked at it with that charge in mind and can find no sentimentality; it is an extremely qualified picture. But it does, where that seems right, speak with great warmth about some aspects of working-class life, some of the emotional aspects, and especially about the central place of women in holding homes together. I was forced to the sad conclusion that some intellectuals find it hard to take praise of good feeling, the celebration of where some people have got things emotionally right – and that when they meet this they almost instinctively reach for the label 'sentimental'. This is notably true of some 'radical left' intellectuals, whether from working- or middle-class backgrounds; they tend to resent a description of working-class life which shows most people as, politically, uninterested rather than aggressive; they berate the messenger the more his evidence piles up. Similarly some feminists have resented the kind of importance given to women in the picture I drew, mistakenly seeing it as a form of inverted male chauvinism.

The typescript went to Chatto and lay there for a good long time. I was told that Leonard Woolf, who was on the board, opposed its publication. But the book was accepted and I settled down to await the proofs. A good few weeks later, as we lay in bed with mugs of tea, the post arrived. A letter from Chatto, saying they had felt it wise to send the book to a libel lawyer. They realised I would be shocked by his opinion: he thought the book the most dangerous, in libel terms, he had ever read. Damages against both the publisher and the author could be enormous. There could be damages not only for specific libels; there could also be something to which he gave a legal name, as it might be 'consequentially-increased' or, more likely, 'aggravated', damages. By this the wounded party could be awarded further sums if the specific libel was contained in a forceful overall argument which gained increased force as it developed through the book. The 'abuses' in the book's title was itself grounds for that particular claim. He could only advise against publication. They could, said Chatto, take further legal advice but I would have to bear all – or it may have been half – the costs of that consultation. Another great deflation, as on the day of the historian's judgment; and another rally.

A few days later there was a sombre taxi-ride from Chatto in William IV Street, hard by Trafalgar Square, to one of the Inns of Court, where we met a sober barrister in early middle-age. He repeated the view that the book was very dangerous indeed and we settled down to considering page after page of alarums; a long process. It was possible to meet many of his objections there and then by adjustments, some slightly regrettable but others cute, safe and even better than the original. He demurred over a reference to the popular press's habit of having things both ways, of expressing moral outrage at some scandal whilst providing full details of it; I had called it 'Janus-faced'. The barrister said he didn't know who Janus was but the reference sounded libellous. After explanation it stayed. He refused to allow the use of some of the sillier, actual, come-on headlines from the same newspapers, but it was easy to invent my own on the spot. He said William Faulkner could find libellous a reference to *Sanctuary* as a pot-boiler, until I pointed out that the description is Faulkner's own, in his preface. Clearly, if you call in a literary drains inspector you must expect him to find things you'd never dreamt of under the floor-boards.

The sticking-point was the use of quotations from sex-and-violence novels. Most were from James Hadley Chase (known chiefly for *No Orchids for Miss Blandish*) who was at the time living in Spain and hardly likely to come back to England to claim he had been libelled. The barrister was immovable. He turned to Chatto's editor and said this stalemate brought back all his doubts about whether the book could be published, no matter what changes we had so far made. Plainly, he thought me thoroughly obstinate. Just as plainly, Chatto could not easily ignore his advice. I said I would think things over during the weekend, and the meeting ended. But not before a final happy shift. I suggested we lop off the first syllable of the offending title, so that *The Abuses of Literacy* became *The Uses of Literacy*, and there was satisfaction all round. It is anyway a better title, less hectoring.

On the four or five hour train journey back to Hull I decided to substitute for the libellous quotations my own sex-and-violence literature, and found that kind of pastiche surprisingly easy. The main problem is to avoid exaggeration, guying the originals; this may have amused me and the readers but would have spoiled the argument – part of which was that at their peak moments these novels, from the pens of the more successful authors, have a power which less successful practitioners cannot reach. They know, for example, how to conjure up violent sexual fantasies, and this requires an eye for detail and an ear for language; limited and put to limited purposes but not to be simply dismissed as a trick which any of us could perform 'if we had got round to it'. Ian Fleming is a more gifted writer than those I was looking at and so illustrates this general point especially well. He knows some of the main artistic rules. In *From Russia with Love* Fleming describes Bond making love with the Russian girl Tania in a hotel bedroom. There is little description of the act itself. But as the two OGPU agents crouched in the voyeur's cubicle film the scene their eyes bulge and the sweat runs down their necks and over their cheap collars; very erotic, and close in its oblique approach and effect to the early scene in *Madame Bovary* where Charles meets Emma, in the rain at the door of her father's farm-house, and is from that moment sexually trapped.

By Sunday night I had done all – remembering the while Aldous Huxley's short story 'The Farcical History of Richard Greenow', about a scholarly young man taken over at night by his female doppelganger, Pearl Bellairs, who writes enormously successful sentimental fiction. He dies in a lunatic asylum, still writing as Pearl up to two hours before slipping into his final coma. I was not tempted to lunacy, but it was a funny and a sobering exercise. I have met no one who recognised that the pieces were imitations. Perhaps James Hadley Chase, and even more likely Ian Fleming, would have. The barrister was satisfied and Chatto set publication in motion. But by the time the book appeared we were in the USA.

Throughout the decade, my relations with the internal English Department at Hull were slight. The Professor of English, Sherard Vines, was a minor poet, already elderly, and remote. Our only exchange was in 1951 when we passed each other on the shallow steps into the main building. 'Ah,' he said, 'aren't you the young man who has published a book on Auden? Congratulations. Good morning.' And off he toddled.

In 1952 or early 1953, the new professor and head of department, Ray Brett, sought me out and suggested I might like to give up to three lectures a fortnight to his internal students, on modern English poetry. No means of paying me, as I knew (it was simply an irony brought about by differing methods of financing that his members of staff could be paid for classes they took for our department), but he thought the experience would be useful, especially since I would want sooner or later to stop traipsing all over the East Riding and North Lincolnshire night after winter night and become an internal lecturer. It was a kind and thoughtful gesture and I accepted. Then he, in some ways still innocent of the sillier inhibitions of some of his staff, suggested I might if free attend the regular staff-meetings of the department. I went to two and was no more than coolly nodded at by one or two of the others; on the whole, they bent into a circle like a prairie waggon-train threatened by one Indian. With some embarrassment Ray Brett asked me not to attend thereafter; there had been objections to a part-time lecturer, from the extra-mural department, sitting in on their deliberations.

To think now of such things in that time at that place is like looking through a telescope the wrong way; at minute and self-important scurryings. Those who objected, probably only one or two, to an external lecturer possibly letting the side down were presumably excessively aware of being in a small and, to the great academic world, not very important department. The group of well-funded new universities of the Sixties had much more confidence; they knew they were going the way the world was going, the way the Robbins Report on the future of higher education had indicated. The University Colleges which, like Hull, became universities before the decade of expansion, tended to be concerned about keeping their academic noses clean, their dress well-adjusted, in all the ways recognised by the older and bigger members; they took their seats nervously at the great national university table or board.

Ray Brett nevertheless said he hoped that, when an expected vacancy in his department was confirmed, I would apply for the post. Since vacancies were usually advertised at assistant lecturer level, he would have to argue for an exception so that I could apply, being then about ten points up the scale. He was called into hospital for a minor operation and the advertisement, for an assistant lecturer, was drafted and published in his absence. He intervened from his hospital bed, but the appointing committee ruled that it would set a bad precedent to advertise one thing and do another; more nervousness; so my candidature was not accepted.

True to form, John Henry Nicholson called me in; for a splendid fatherly talk. 'It will seem a set-back, Hoggart, but believe me I have had similar set-backs. And you too will go far.' I believe he meant it and his handshake was warm. A shrewd old bird, and not really a smoothie.

CHAPTER 7

INTERLUDE–USA
1956–7

The huge, corrugated-iron-roofed customs shed of Pier Ninety-something on Manhattan was suffocatingly steamy when we landed from the *Queen Elizabeth* in early September 1956. A large American liner had tied up in the next berth half an hour before so the whole place was even more than usually crowded. We had been up very early to clear Immigration on board and had finally disembarked at about half past eight. By eleven the children were in distress; we could do little – you can't buy cool drinks in a customs hall.

It was evident that the overworked customs officials were, as we had been warned, taking back-handers. Even if we had been willing to do that, our dollars for the four or five hundred mile journey up to Rochester wouldn't have allowed us.

This kind of story is too familiar to need telling for its own sake. But what followed was intriguing for its first indications on the ground of an alien culture, linguistically at least. At about a quarter past eleven, I went up to one who seemed to be a senior customs officer, seated in the middle of the hall at a high desk, like an English auctioneer overlooking the bidders. I was about to utter my first words on American soil to an American citizen; as I spoke, I realised for the first time that to an American, and especially a New York, ear the English voice sounds light, pale pink, effete. What came out was even more English. I asked, in a very polite manner: 'Can you help me, please? I have three children'.

He stared at me callously and answered, before looking down at his papers again, 'Don't blame me, bud. See a doctor.' It was in its way witty as well as brutal; and the exchange an encapsulation of the different ways the two societies can handle speech in ordinary, everyday contacts. What I meant in unfolded speech was something like: 'My three children are suffering badly. Can you get someone to deal with our baggage, please?' I guess he would have understood that at once, even if he had reacted no more helpfully. That was more formal than, but something like, the style an American would have used. My formulation was altogether too oblique and elliptical, too English-coded. It didn't even say that the children were suffering; it took that for granted by saying we needed help because we had three children . . . and . . . but the rest was unsaid, didn't need saying, could in the English way be left to be assumed.

The result was to make him hostile, perhaps even more hostile than as a petty functionary enjoying his daily moments of power he normally was. If he had wanted to think for a few seconds he could no doubt have cracked the code; this guy with the thin Limey voice needs help because his kids are desperately hot and thirsty. But he was not inclined to, because he didn't like the voice, and liked even less the man's elliptical speech which left out the main thing he should have been saying. So he taught him a lesson, by pretending to take what he said as a simple, direct and complete statement of fact about the man's own predicament: 'I am in need of help because I have three children.' So – take it absolutely straight and suggest he could do with a vasectomy.

Since the rebuttal was so easy to place we didn't find it hurtful; and it was offset, when we did finally emerge, by the taxi-driver who took us to Grand Central Station and spent the journey amiably insisting over his shoulder, with an assured openness one rarely finds in England, that the atom bombs of ten years before had irretrievably damaged climate and atmosphere in New York; and if we doubted that then we'd better prove otherwise. At Grand Central, the children found the long, cool marble seats and stretched out until we left.

The interest of the customs shed incident was in the evidence it gave right at the start of our stay of the directness of much everyday American speech (in other situations, especially if they have anything of the formal about them, that speech can be periphrastic). By contrast, English speech can seem to them oblique to the point where it puzzles, and may even suggest you are trying to trip your hearer by a sort of knowingness, a linguistic nod-and-wink from the closed club of those more sophisticated Europeans.

It follows that irony will tend to puzzle also. At school in Rochester, Simon was put in a class composed of boys two years older than he was. His unusual articulateness at ten had presumably been taken to indicate the maturity of a twelve-year-old. He survived cheerfully, as a sort of mascot. One day the class was having a debate on the nature of the British Empire. Most of them did not approve of it. One large boy delivered himself of the judgment, 'My father could lick the whole British Empire with his little finger.' All eyes were turned on the English boy, to see how he would rebuff this insult. The teacher told us afterwards that the response was, 'His father must have a prodigious little finger.' The whole class had apparently been astonished at this disinclination to use the retort-direct, 'I bet he couldn't,' which would have led to the counter-retort, 'Sure he could' . . . and so on. The ironic and dismissive deflection, brought about by picking up the other boy's histrionic and banal image of the little finger and showing it for what it was, by using the reverse-excessive 'prodigious', a word not much in use by twelve-year-olds – all made a response which was in that time and place unanswerable. So everyone made agreeable expressions of admiration for such skill and the story entered the class's mythology.

I

The year as a professor at the University of Rochester had come about almost by chance. One of the largest Hull firms, Reckitt and Colman's, were much involved with the University and generous towards it. In the USA they owned French's Mustard, the soft, mild stuff spread along hot-dogs; and French's were based in Rochester. This was in the early Fifties when few English academics, except those studying germane subjects such as American history or literature, had been to the States. But to go there was a main ambition of very many. Europe was still recovering from the war and seemed old and shabby and tired. America appeared by comparison full of energy and intelligence in almost every discipline and area. It was important to get over there before you were much older. Fulbright's generous and imaginative scheme of 1946 had, apart from all else, made money for fares available to virtually any academic with an invitation. Presumably someone at one of the two universities suggested a Hull–Rochester annual exchange with Fulbright sponsorship, and Reckitt's/French's agreed to pay the salaries on their respective sides.

There would have been no shortage of professors willing to go for the 1956-7 session had that not been the year in which the University Grants Committee's quinquennial allocations for each of those institutions were to be announced. Once the block grant was known, the carve-up between Faculties and Departments could begin, and in that process professors argue as fiercely as market-stall holders argue for space but for much longer, with more polysyllabic words, and more arcane justifications in which sharp practice sometimes masquerades as moral vindication. No professor would risk being away during that operation, so Hull University, anxious not to lose a year of the scheme, was slightly stuck. It was at this point that Mayfield moved in and challenged them to accept that an extra-mural teacher, if they were to look below the professorial level, had as much right to be considered as any other. They finally agreed, and agreed also that my record suggested I would not be likely to let them down. Unaware of all these manoeuvres, we had already booked for a first family holiday abroad, in Brittany; then the jubilant phone call came from Mayfield. Within three or four months we were on the boat.

Looking back, one wonders how so large an upheaval was managed in the time available. It was managed; it always is, especially when you are young. The biggest upheaval is, again always, psychological: assessing what might be the effect on the family, and if it can be justified. Would the children suffer educationally, since the eleven-plus barrier still operated? That was solved when the local education authority agreed that Simon could take the examination by post, whilst pointing out that he would need some specific tuition at home; he got that from Mary and passed very well. More important was the likely effect of the loss of their friends; but against that one had to set the making of new friends, the general widening of horizons; and those seemed likely to be – and proved – much greater counterweights.

These are obvious enough losses and profits, but much more profits than losses, seen from a distance; at the time, the anxieties could be acute. Even as we stood on the pavement in front of our house in the late evening, ready to be taken by a friend to Paragon Station for the night train to London and the boat, one child took off and ran up the street, refusing to leave. Within three weeks of reaching Rochester the interest of so strange a place and the warm welcome and generosity of adults and children had put us all well on the way to settling in. As we left almost exactly twelve months later we felt very sad, sensed that we would from then on miss America, would for ever after feel familial towards it and the people we knew, and be slightly dislocated culturally, hovering over mid-Atlantic – would no longer have a view of the world and its ways which pivoted entirely on Britain's peculiar practices.

Naturally we had been homesick as we left and the children tended to cluster close at first; but after a day on the boat had found their ways to the cinema and such places. Fulbright gave me a cabin-class ticket and were agreeable to its being used towards cheaper accommodation for all of us, well down in the bowels much below the water-line. The waiter at our assigned table told us on the first day he guessed we were emigrants. Did he assume this about all families, or did we so obviously not have a holiday air? The Last of England.

At one point we thought we might have lost Nicola, perhaps blown overboard when they opened the decks – she was just eight and a slip of a thing – and we had a frightening twenty minutes or so before she turned up with the doll she'd gone down to the cabin to collect. Here was the old elemental fear – the hostages to fortune syndrome – surfacing again in its most dramatic form, all the more because we were away from our roots. It was my fault. She had told me she was going down to the cabin and I had nodded and turned back to my book without properly registering. The thought of that twenty minutes can still chill, and on such occasions I hear always in my head phrases like: 'oh, blown about the winds of the world . . .'

And now, far more than at the time, we can appreciate the stoicism and restraint of Mary's parents as they, then nearing seventy, saw their only child and her family go all that way for a whole year; no question of them or us breaking the year in two by a visit, as would be relatively easy to afford and assumed by most such families today. All the more a pity since Harry had seen no foreign land except a bit of Flanders before he was wounded, and **Doris none at all. They had to wait that full year, until we went**

straight from disembarking in Liverpool to Stalybridge, the children rushing in, looking taller, fuller, with different types of haircuts,
more liberated clothes and a slight upper-New-York-State twang;
but still overwhelmingly glad to see them again. That absence seems
now, in its length, its way of measuring time past, like a separation
typical of a hundred years ago rather than of only thirty years.

   An older man urging us to go when we were still undecided,
especially about the likely effect on the family, said his job had more
than once caused him to move house very long distances and often
with a dubious heart. But each time, whatever the other gains and
interests or even losses, he found the move had brought the family
closer together, gave its members a stronger sense of their own
importance one to another and so of the importance of the family as
a whole. This could seem limiting but I do not think that was what
he was describing, not a narrowing turned-inness. It was rather that
sense of mutual dependence and affection which severe illness or
incapacity in a family can also encourage; and in this I think he was
right. Even so, much the greatest cost was paid by the grandparents.

Rochester – and I can speak only of the Rochester we saw just over
thirty years ago – has the friendliness of a medium-sized city which
cannot and does not wish to think of itself as an exciting metropolis;
it believes it has more of a community spirit and is safer; it is
sensitive to being looked down on by people from the great
aggregations, and secretly knows it has better ideas about what
makes for a good life: space for private and public gardens (it calls
itself the Lilac City), the air coming off Lake Ontario, the Finger
Lakes nearby, sufficient good music, exceptionally good provision
of films (the Eastman–Kodak museum being there), not much of a
race problem or unemployment since its industries are mixed and
many of them very much of the late twentieth-century (Eastman–
Kodak, Bausch and Lomb, IBM); and those industries civic-
minded. Yet they did have a race riot in 1964. We were robbed
once, but that was slight and through our own carelessness. Our
landlord was a grasping Greek who seemed to think that in England
we all lived in or near castles and could be cheated accordingly, but
backed down when confronted by evidence of his shiftiness or
double-dealing. All in all and in general, Rochester is a decent,
undramatic city much like Leicester, only much richer.

The University of Rochester was a true child of the city in that it was of medium-size by American standards but quite large by British, privately funded and proud of it, academically in some ways modest, in other ways – like Rochester's large industries – of national and international calibre. Its staff and their manners mirrored their institution. Some knew they would move on and many did, regular movement for promotion or for tenure being a feature of the academic life for even near-high-flyers; but during their time at Rochester they did not feel, as some at Hull did, that they were in a backwater and only waiting for a call. Others stayed and over the years did work ranging from the splendid by any standards to the merely roller-coasting or the going-off-at-a-tangent. Almost all of them believed, making their own quiet translation of that American principle, that we had to be friendly one to another, and the more so because academic life in the States is regarded as more of an odd backwater even than it is in England. They acted out that belief in all sorts of practical and sensitive ways; they were good people to be with.

But not soft in the middle. By late-October 1956 we were well settled, the children were accustomed to school, we had some friendly neighbours and professional colleagues. Then one morning a friend rushed into my 'office' at the university and asked in agitation: 'What are you thinking of, Richard?' For a moment I thought he was referring to me personally; had I done violent harm to some of the mores of American university life – refused to see a student in need, seemed cavalier towards our calling? It was worse. Britain had with France embarked on the Suez adventure. I did not know, since we took no daily newspaper, and had no stomach for breakfast TV, or for the early morning turned-in-upon-itself local radio news. This first visitor was followed by a string of others, all equally shocked as well as outraged.

The end of that affair was the realisation, for some British at least, that our days as a big power were over, that our military adventures could henceforth be restrained by pressure from the super-powers. The colleagues in Rochester were not speaking from that perspective nor were they being self-righteous. They were all scholars in English literature or history, lovers of Britain and well-versed in her traditions. Their main emotion, and they were extremely upset, arose from precisely their admiration for Britain. They thought better of us than to relish seeing us act in that old-style gun-boat diplomacy manner. We were more civilised, surely, a particularly civilised society, and here we were acting in the imperialist way we once did but had over the last decade seemed to forswear.

Knowing nothing, I had little to offer, not even at that point the slight palliative that my colleagues at Hull, along with many others, were taking to the streets against government policy. I wish much more I could have told them about the BBC's stand against Eden's attempt to make them turn the news into government propaganda. Those who dismiss the British tradition in public-service broadcasting and (these are often the same people) those who give no value to the arm's-length principle in important areas of intellectual and cultural life – such people do not know, or choose to forget, the BBC's stand against Anthony Eden over Suez. That story, which I heard much later both from members of the BBC Board and of Eden's staff, belongs in another book. It remains the professional high-point of the Corporation's post-war history. Mountbatten, he who had looked so upper-crust as he addressed the commandos in that Scottish loch, comes out of the incident very well too, in his resistance to Eden; in a crisis he had the directness and force his class claims.

In retirement, one of Eden's appointments was as Chancellor of the University of Birmingham and he carried out his duties as conscientiously as his health would allow. He presided at one of the first degree day dinners of my time there. When people began to circulate after the meal, the Registrar came over and asked if I would like to be introduced to Eden. I said no, remembering Suez. 'Pity,' said the Registrar, 'he was saying at dinner how much he admired your work.' I felt stiff-necked.

2

A good number of Rochester's students at the time were from prosperous homes, prosperous enough to find the fairly high fees, and often came from towns up to forty or fifty miles away, many with beautiful evocative names such as Auburn, Henrietta, Seneca, Geneseo, Palmyra. Both men and women tended to be taller than their English counterparts ('with all that nourishment they're growing longer and longer femurs; you should see them out west,' a friend said). Their complexions were clear but less weathered, less suggestive of walks in the wind and rain, than the middle-class English. They tended, the girls especially, to be slightly plump as though all the corn-fed steaks they'd eaten had been effortlessly converted into body-lining; they had excellent teeth which paraded and gleamed when they smiled, much more evidently than teeth do in Britain. They wore casual and colourful but not shabby clothes; 'shabby' was not in their vocabulary, and deliberately dirty and ragged jeans and all their accompaniments were a dozen years off; no one could at that time have predicted 1968.

The girls especially were at first disconcerting. Not sexually. They were not prim or coy, but in some respects were almost boyish and asexual in appearance and manners, though research had even at that time shown that many of them were sexually active; others were well-behaved, small-town girls. They disconcerted because they set off so many contrasts with girls, women, one had grown used to seeing in Europe. At the most dramatic they evoked poignant contrasting pictures of all those 'little mothers' of the European slums, small girls with fourteen-year-old breasts like lemons and all the cares of the pram-pushing, toddler-holding world on their thin shoulders. In some respects, except in the bloom of the complexion itself, the American girls had the untouched, innocent and occasionally vapid faces of the classic English Rose. Given their rude health and strength they might have been thought to be relatives of Joan Hunter-Dunn; if they were, they were very distant cousins. Joan Hunter-Dunn's accents and body language were far more complexly class-defined than, happily, anything the girls of Rochester had inherited.

Some of the girls chewed gum much of the time but not in the slack, tawdry way which seems obligatory in Britain. You felt their dentists had recommended it for teeth and gums. Walking along the paths in pairs they would sometimes execute impromptu dance-steps, but they couldn't have seemed hoydenish or suggested what may well have been, two or three generations back, a peasant origin, even if they had tried. British girls walk from the knees, as though they are going to break into an anxious trot rather than a run; French girls walk from the hip as loosely as only young women **can, and that is a very sophisticated and erotic way of moving; these**

American girls walked with their whole legs but not sinuously: rather as though they were ready to run a mile.

Were most of them conformist? Some of the men were, especially those who lived in the fraternity houses. They had been to good private schools; they knew where they were going afterwards (usually to a comfortable job in father's firm); they had all the right views for the time of year; they were incurious to a deadening degree; they were wholly and unquestioningly caught up in the American dream and its rightness; and that gave them their blinding confidence. Few flashes of self-doubt had yet crossed faces such as those.

Others had a fresh and lively intellectual curiosity which is rare anywhere, and I was more aware of it in Rochester than I had been in British universities; their school system was less formal and tram-lined in its attitude to knowledge; or, more accurately, to the intellectual life. I learned years afterwards that a student in one of the sciences had heard me lecture on Auden. He later heard Auden lecture and read his own poems, had switched to literature and is now an internationally admired author of books on Auden, the editor of his poems and executor of his estate: Edward Mendelson.

What transformations, physical and psychological, this new continent and new society had brought about in so few generations. Did any earlier society give so much a sense of forward-looking, so little sense of the past? Or one many of whose younger members, though they usually had been given some simple but firm moral precepts, lacked so much the sense of self-doubt, of the intractability of both sin and virtue, so that in these areas they exhibited almost total ingenuousness? One remembers Randall Jarrell: 'You Americans do not rear children, you *incite* them; you give them food and shelter and applause.' Many of them had been indulged by their parents; that was clear from their un-star-crossed manner. How would they behave when, as was inevitable, life did cross them? Perhaps it never did, wasn't inevitable. How would they age? Are they now to be found in those well-turned-out, blue-rinsed groups who take the more expensive tours to Europe and her historic treasures?

Yet they were all in all remarkably friendly and open towards adults, and even to strange foreigners. They greeted you unfussedly and with consistent politeness. In class, they would stand up and say

courteously, making the 'o' in my surname very long and giving me
a doctorate I did not possess (but then no university professor could
be other than a doctor): 'Excuse me, Dr Höggart, but I would like to
say . . .' Or they opened conversations with a very soft-voiced 'sir' –
an opening English schoolchildren might use, but not undergraduates. Yet theirs wasn't the English schoolchild's 'sir', which is
prescribed as a form of deference to school-teachery status. Nor
was it the form of address I was offered at the Royal College of
Defence Studies in the late-Seventies. I had been speaking, with as
much justice to the complexity of the subject as I could muster, to
one of their destined-for-higher-things groups about mass communications in Britain. At the end the commandant called for
questions. A moustachioed major, red-faced and looking too
much like a stereotype to be real, stood up and said: 'Sah! Why are
there so many pinkos in the BBC? Sah!' The Rochester 'sir' was
altogether more civilised, redolent of older, Yankee, small-town
courtesies.

Most interesting of all was the American students' use of
language and what this indicated about their modes of thought.
Their most characteristic language when they were at work in a
class was instrumental rather than reflective, active, out to push
things along rather than ruminative, lingering or turning round
over ideas. They picked up what they habitually called 'concepts' as
if they were picking up the spanners of the mind. Sometimes when I
was lecturing in a broody sort of way, stroking a poem or an idea
here and there, I felt I could sense some were saying to themselves
'Why doesn't he give us a concept?' They would in discussion begin
'That concept, sir, seems to me useful in . . .' If their language was
then manipulative, this was not the manipulativeness of public
relations or political speech. It emerged from a feeling that the
world of ideas, just as the world out there, the great wide world
which had once been an almost empty land, had to be manipulated
– 'managed' would be better – by people who had forged the tools
to do just that. One should be able similarly to forge tools to
manage, to encompass, the intellectual world. At a lower but
related level, a student said early on – and his remark illustrated also
the openness they assumed: 'Sir, I admire your technique as a
lecturer.' I hadn't to myself called it a technique (though of course it
was, in so far as it had been thought about as what seemed an

effective way to introduce these things at this time to these students). But I would have been nesh of referring to it, to myself, as a technique; and no English students would have used that kind of language. They might have said to one another but not to me, in the played-down, insistently amateurish English way, 'Oh, Hoggart's quite a good teacher'; or not.

The best American students were more stimulating than the English not only because of this different approach to the business of thought but far more because they took hold of ideas freshly and straight. They carried into their university studies much less initial padding of assumptions than British students, much less intellectual hand baggage about literature and the way to approach it. They had not been trained in exactly what was expected of them if they were to be true 'university material', had not been taught to write 'clever' essays for A-level examiners.

Those American students who did waken to an interest in ideas tended to seem at first earnest, directly questioning rather than sceptical, uneasy before a throw-away joke on a scholarly matter, before learning worn lightly. They had come into the ante-room of the intellectual life and they wanted the inner courts to live up to what they expected of them, in weightiness and grandeur. This mood wore off in a year and then some were able to combine the demotic, dry, American wise-cracking habit with a due regard for the scholarly life, and the result was tonic.

Two incidents crystallised the extremes of student abilities and style. I marked an essay on Yeats which was not only pathetic in its near-illiteracy but plainly full of plagiarisms. The man had been stupid enough to go to the library and copy in a still unformed hand whole paragraphs from different critics. The essay was like a dish made up of elements of *haute cuisine* embedded in a large inferior hamburger. I gave the paper a fail mark. Next day there was a knock at the 'office' door and a very large young man appeared. Why had he failed? He'd put a lot of work into that essay and thought it had some good ideas. Yes, other people's. It became plain that not only was the word 'plagiarism' unknown to him but the 'concept' itself. If someone else had made a good point about an author what harm was there in recognising that and using it? If someone produced a better carburettor . . . The sense of knowledge as a continuing and developing personal process had not been introduced to him, and even after explanations eluded him. Knowledge lay around and you picked up the parts which best suited you.

He had seated himself on the corner of my desk, swinging his great legs and becoming more and more baffled and rattled, even after the most careful guidance. Suddenly he announced that his father was a big shot in the town's business community and wasn't going to like at all the idea that his son had failed with an essay. Was he going to offer me cut-rates in whatever the family business produced or in whatever service it provided? Or hint that Dad might send in the heavy mob?

Underneath he was an ill-educated, not very bright and very worried young man; so I gave him yet more advice and said he could resubmit. A week later back came a revised essay on Yeats, much like the first in the puddle of parts he had written himself but with the many quotations from other critics acknowledged, not individually as they occurred but at the end. Someone, perhaps Dad, had helped him with the introduction to the acknowledgments list: 'This essay would not have a shadow of its present stature were it not for the devoted labours of the Yeats critics whose names I here append: Dr Richard Hoggart . . . etc.' Since I have never written on Yeats this was an exceptionally large phoney bouquet.

Underneath the blind blundering there lies an important consideration. That young man was baffled not just because he was not very clever but because his culture had not introduced him to – had positively discouraged him from – the idea of intellectual discriminations, differences in intellectual grasp and ability. He could distinguish a cheap car from a better, and no doubt a good swimmer or runner from a mediocre. He had never been invited to understand that some minds may be better than others. He had been introduced not to the world of ideas but to that of opinions; and manifestly one man's opinions are as good as another's; that's part of the democratic faith. Add the assumption that other men's ideas/opinions could be taken over like other men's gadgets; that he or his father were paying plenty for his courses at the U of R; that he had according to his lights worked, had put some words on paper – and you had the whole foundation of his puzzlement. In such a mental context failure was unjust and unacceptable; it reflected the heresy that some men in some subtle, objectionable and hardly conceivable ways were, in spite of all the above egalitarian articles of faith, just better than others.

His exact opposite was a girl from one of those pretty townships down on the Finger Lakes. That she was good-looking, healthy and well-built needs no more than routine noting. But she also had a mobile face, expressions which changed as a lecture went along. She was one of those students whom you especially note in the first week or two because you think you recognise one who is trying to follow you closely, who is engaged, getting something out of it, feeling it on her pulses. Bright English students do not so readily show their imaginative excitement in a variety of eager expressions, though you soon recognise them too. This kind of girl recalls the remark of Henry James, roughly to the effect that American girls, faced with new experiences, tend to have exclamation-marks between their eyebrows. Or at greater length: 'She seemed, with little cries and protests and quick recognitions, movements like the darts of some fine high-feathered free-pecking bird, to stand before life as before some full shop window.'

The Department had asked me on arrival to plan a course on Modern English Literature. So: Hardy, Hopkins, Yeats, Eliot, Auden; and Joyce, Forster, Lawrence, Graham Greene, as a basis; a few others and a little drama. Perhaps because it was novel and given by an English native it proved popular. That was the course the girl joined. After a few weeks she came up at the end of the class and asked if she could say something. She then made what sounded partly like a slightly nervous confessional statement, partly like a discovery about herself which she was making even as she spoke. It was a statement about plenitude and about the threatened loss of innocence which only a sensitive student from that all-embracing culture could have made; the fact that she had the directness and honesty to make it was part of that culture too, one of its admirable characteristics.

She said something like this: 'I am enjoying your course very much. But it is disturbing me. Let me tell you about my background. I come from [she named a medium-sized town twenty or thirty miles south]. My father is a lawyer; my mother stays home but does a great many good works in the community. So does my father. They are good people and greatly respected. They are loving parents to me and my brothers. We have a pleasant life. In summer we have barbecues with the family, the neighbours, members of our church. In winter we skate on the Lake. I have to say, and I've only realised it after auditing your course, that I've been happy, it's been a happy sort of life. But now I'm shaken. I enjoy hearing you talk about, for example, T. S. Eliot and Graham Greene. I enjoy reading them after the lectures. But there's so much unhappiness, so much cruelty, so much accepting that life is grim and black and sinful. But it hasn't felt like that to us, not at all. And I don't know how to make head or tail of it.' Henry James again, forty years after he died; corrupted Europe and innocent America; but still the splendid exclamation-mark.

A couple of months later, in New York, I told Charles Frankel of Columbia about this incident. 'A good story,' he said, 'rings true. That's why I always say part of our duty is to corrupt the American young – like maggots boring into soft cheese.' He could say that; an Englishman could not, decently. Most impressive in that girl was her splendid effort at honesty before herself and her experience.

3

In the first months after we got back, in the summer and autumn of 1957, I tried to sort out some of the things, both large and small, we had learned during the year; not only something about America but even more, by reflection, about England from that vantage point. Notes made in the early weeks there would have had the clarity and confidence of the brief, startled, unqualified view. Notes made years later might have seemed denser, since filled out with afterthoughts; but those may or may not have been true to the experience; wisdom long after the event is always the easiest kind. These notes come in between.

Walking across the campus, an American friend and I were talking about our own societies and the combination of attachment and disaffection they evoke. I do not remember what I had said to prompt him to respond: 'Ah, but you see, I love America.' On paper such a statement may sound sentimental, out of the same bag as all those insistent, self-congratulatory anthems Americans launch into on public occasions. It wasn't. This man has one of the best minds I have known and one of the best built-in garbage-detectors. The assertion was honest and unrhetorical. To tease it further back a little: he meant America had been made into a nation in response to an ideal. He did not imply that dream had been fulfilled; he is a sharp critic of American society. He meant the idea of creating a nation in response to an ideal was heartening more than any other social act he could think of. His ancestors had come over in the late nineteenth century, German-speaking, getting away from religious persecution.

I imagine he also meant that he loved in America the sense still of possibility, the sense that however much the dream and the ideal might have been tarnished, there was still a chance of change for the better – what Emerson called the characteristic 'optative mood' in America, the urge to bring things nearer the heart's desire; above all, to people like him, in a moral way. This rather than the old European unexpectancy. In that year, Adlai Stevenson ran for President and the liberal academics came out in force on his behalf. It seems now no more than a naïve unfulfilled hopefulness and I do not know whether my friend would deliver himself of that brief assertion of love today. It caught both a moment and something inherent in America, in the sense of America. Few self-conscious, intelligent English people would utter such a statement at any time. They may have a deep affection for England, Britain, but its expression is more likely to be wry rather than direct, Orwellian in its dry double-take: 'England is a family; with the wrong members in control.'

Simon's teacher of English belonged to the same general intellectual, rather than ethnic, stock as my friend. His background was New England transcendentalist and he was entirely given over to the purposive life in that sense. His wife was said to be a distant relative of T. S. Eliot. He was quiet, earnest, the least wide of guys, nonconformist with a circumscribed nonconformity which had become a new kind of conformity. He was very kind to our son and greatly intrigued by his strange, quirky style. He and his wife moved at intervals from progressive school to progressive school across the land, following their kind of dream.

The American sense of possibility must be reinforced by the sense still of both space and plenitude. The space is being ruined, the plenitude is often based on shoddy, disposable, built-in obsolescence. The wide-openness is as often emptiness as beauty, or has the agoraphobic beauty of a Hopper petrol station on an endless road. That is an American not an outsider's recognition, as can also be the sense of wasteful and meaningless accumulation in the vast supermarkets. Europeans feel it more, find it harder to be at ease with this peculiar combination of space and unending invasive human activity. They know their own cities where the air feels as though it has been used and re-used time and again; they once had intimations of pure space in their own remoter regions. They have not, or not had until the last decade, so powerful a sense of stale, spoiled space as the tatty great roads, the huge self-defeating billboards, the tacky outskirts of cities, the mountains of wrecked cars, the nasty tourist townships of the Rockies and the unending aural pollution of pop from a million radios, produce in America.

Yet it is fascinating even at its most disturbing. Even such a television give-away programme as 'Strike it Rich' didn't seem in America so monstrously, vulgarly acquisitive and intrusive of personal distress as it did in Europe. There, it is a tawdry spin-off of a deeper and better impulse; in Europe it is simply greedy. And, though space has been so much spoiled, we have rarely felt as free, as eupeptic, as we did wandering down Virginia or through the Adirondacks in a large old car; we were after all being liberated from some of the hang-ups of Europe.

We came to enjoy the vivid rhetoric of those spaces: the enormous cars and even more enormous and colourful police cars, ambulances, school-buses, fire engines, the rhetoric of public noise and the largeness of publicly-expressed emotions. 'The service of a vast, vulgar, meretricious beauty', maybe; but also the product of large landscapes and the often Kodachrome-like light. Clothes were the most puzzling. One saw why men rarely wore the English three-piece suit, muted, heavy, subfusc like the climate; or the heavy country-jackets, sometimes patched and, most surprising of all to an American, sometimes patched in an upper-class way, as an upper-class statement.

But how to make sense of the differences in American styles of clothing which even we saw in so short a space and time: the sheer stylelessness of the almost ubiquitous bulging trousers, loose nylon blouses and TV, lipstick of thirty-five-year-old women trundling round supermarkets; the wealth-breathing, understated elegance of some rich women in the great urban centres; the fussy hats bobbing up and down on the way to church in the minor-professional areas; the broadcast commentary to a mannequin parade I watched in downtown Rochester: 'a fascinating outfit . . . an intriguing ensemble . . . a significant combination . . . conveys the gentle-woman effect for this winter'. It was the blown-up English English of the commentary which underlined the strangeness of the setting and the accents.

Throughout our time we were also in the state of suspension which being away from home and regular job, work and school, even for as long as a year, induces. Nothing suggests a continuing responsibility. The fabric of the house is not one of your problems; thoughts of career promotion are in the background; you have made proper temporary accommodations for the children which will hold together until the interlude is over; the ceremonials of commencement day can be enjoyed but not believed in; local and national politics are interesting but not your affair. In your normal academic life back home the divisions between work and leisure for you personally – family commitments are rightly another matter – have increasingly become blurred. In this period, this interval, they are sharper again, rather as they were in your schooldays. The only other period in which I have felt this kind of weekend detachment was in five years and a bit at UNESCO. The work there was arduous and long and I can recall only two weekends when I did not go back to the apartment with a full briefcase. But we felt much freer than in England.

Auden wrote about 'the vast synonymous cities' and 'the raw towns that we believe and die in' of America. There is something at first, and perhaps second, glance sad at the thought of anyone living out a life in the slapped-down-seeming small townships of the remoter Middle West. It would feel like sleeping and cooking on the stage of a poor provincial theatre, with no depth, no perspective, only the garish backcloth the advertisers provide as an indication of the life you are supposed to be taking part in, to be enjoying, and recognising as better than life in any other society.

Yet the truism that America is the worst presented of any nation holds firm; and not only of America's presentation of herself abroad, especially through television. She does herself constant violence in the presentation of herself at home, especially when – as is often – she goes mawkish. The other side of the mawkishness, the phoney **domesticities of America's presentation of herself to herself, and the** other side of the tawdriness, the makeshiftness, of space in America, is the capacity of people to make their own kinds of good life, particularly of suburbanism, in those spaces, and this can be as strong and attractive as the British form. It does not draw so easily on available, already-tilled and rooted soil all around; it has to strike roots quickly and often again and again, and it does. No less than when you are travelling by train at night across tiny, domestic Holland you feel, in America, when the dark space of the last hour is punctuated by the lights of a community, the sense of home, of family life going on behind those uncurtained windows; bright human assertions of belonging against the alien largeness of the land. So much outside can still seem like a clearing, not plotted and pieced in penny packets for centuries, but rough, unfinished, tussocky, the lack of enclosing garden hedges a sort of nakedness; it is easy to feel like castaways but on a quixotically generous, enormous island.

One of our neighbours in the little wooden houses of Rochester had moved up from New York to a new job. Early on, his wife gave a classic wail: 'It's all so strange. I don't even recognise the disc-jockeys.' Within weeks she had settled, was exchanging hair-do's with a neighbour, had coped with a fire in the kitchen and was making a wonderfully glutinous pea-and-ham soup from her Italian mother's recipe; that especially was an icon. The pattern shows particularly in those new settlements of little boxes on otherwise bare hillsides some miles out of town. Even thirty years ago, the houses would be full of things, things everywhere – multiple televisions, transistors, hi-fi gear, cameras, videos; and the gardens cluttered with aluminium picnic equipment bought by mail order from Cincinnati. Yet that is not in most people acquisitiveness; they don't really believe in possessions; they give away very easily; about goods they are transcendentalists. If you are a visitor from Europe they will load you with goods, their own goods, a 'shower' (the old pioneer word for gifts to help you settle in is exactly right) of goods. The nonchalance of the easily-filled belly perhaps, not the pinchbeck assumptions of Europe, but a larger, more loose-limbed assurance for most, not just for the traditionally well-to-do. The lengthening femur of the American West compared with the little bow-legs of rickety, lined men trotting-up snickets in Lancashire to borrow a hand-cart so as to shift a fourth-hand mangle.

In the American style is a touch of the innocent and Adamic.

There might have been transferred, on the move from Europe, the more grasping, hoarding and ostentatious of European manners; but the writ of at least some kinds of puritanism didn't run there. People lived – the weather helped – much more out-front than we did; they did not twitch curtains, not only because there were rarely curtains to twitch but because so much was exposed anyway. They fetched cans of beer openly, cooked steaks in the backyard, called out to one another across the vestigial boundaries between the houses, walked easily into each other's kitchens.

As I was writing these pages, a distant relative reminded me in a letter of an incident in my childhood, entirely forgotten by me, which makes the sharpest of comic contrasts with the American scene as I have just described it. My grandmother had sent me for two ounces of loose potted meat, as meagre a portion as you could buy. And make sure the neighbours don't see it, she said. When I got back to the tiny house there were two women visitors, distant relatives from a few streets away so not all that close. I kept my school cap on and was told by grandmother not to be impolite, to take it off 'before visitors'. Which I did – and the potted meat in its screw of paper fell to the clip-rug. 'We 'ad to laugh, yer know,' they inevitably said.

I used to laugh, and sometimes still do, at the ways in which the American conviction that no other nation has ever got things quite so right expresses itself, in the ordinary matters of everyday life as in the larger political forms. It may not have had one of the great physical empires of history; it has created the first all-embracing international empire of an ideology; or, better at this point, the first all-embracing international extension of itself and its caul of habits and assumptions to all its citizens. As we saw in Africa and Italy, Mother America assumed she must extend her breast, endlessly gushing with what they liked best, with what best said 'America' to her children, wherever they might be. Perhaps the British should have sent their troops Tizer and mobile fish-and-chip shops. But the 'he never expected much' habits held there.

It is by now clear that in our day America still seemed, and I am choosing the word carefully, unreal. Even her major disasters recalled the movies more than life, real people and real blood. The country seemed hard to take seriously, to have nothing to teach.

This was a myopia but widespread; and the Americans had in return their own form of it towards us. In a way all foreign countries seem unreal until we have spent some time sharing their day-by-day lives; but the unreality of America to the British was different. It was based on a vague feeling that America was still an accidental offshoot of Britain, a rather wilful, soft and boastful offshoot. It was reinforced by the delayed acceptance of the fact that we were no longer a great imperial power. We had let much go in the decade after the war and were to let even more go in the early Sixties.

We had not fully realised that in terms of power we were now in the second division. When that realisation set in many of the British became crabby, like demoted NCOs, full of rankers' bile and old sweats' mickey-taking (still the salt of the earth, of course, and fine chaps to have in a tight corner, no doubt, as the English Establishment kept on saying).

So even for people such as us, who might have been expected to know a little bit better by 1956, it came as something of a shock to learn that the Americans didn't think of us from one day or month to another, did not feature our major news prominently, or quote our major papers, or pay much attention to us at all. One colleague found all this so disconcerting that he refused to take the *New York Times* and had the *Guardian Weekly* flown out; contact with reality again. American scholars in English literature knew our main names and their work in the discipline. They also picked and chose discriminatingly across the whole of Europe and the rest of the world, in so far as they moved outside their national scholarly boundaries; which they did more than their British counterparts.

We all have our self-deceptions. In Britain our greatest continues to be that we are all classless nowadays. Oddly, the Americans are much like ourselves in this, but more at ease in that Zion. They think it axiomatic that they truly are classless, whereas they have at least as strong a sense of such divisions as the Europeans. Not quite the same – less incised into the personality, not with the same signals, and with a propensity to change those signals much more often; so detecting-antennae can be less historically fine-tuned but must be quick-moving. As I sat next to Diana Trilling at a grand dinner in New York in the Sixties she did a breakdown of the class or status implications of each course, the waiters (men or women, black or white, gloved or ungloved), the guests and the way they were seated and the lines of conversation prompted by the host and hostess. Jane Austen, once she had tuned in, would have relished it.

For visiting English academics there was often a tendency in the beginning to find much in American academic styles comical. The preferred formality in public lecturing, for example; I was twice rebuked gently for not seeming as seriously academic in manner as my lay audience would expect and were felt to have a right to expect. Or the received idea that you should 'keep office hours', be in your room at the university during the working day. Our landlord, finding me at home one day – I was preparing lectures – asked: 'U of R closed, then?' The wife of the President of French's, coming in with clothes no longer needed by her own children, was also surprised to find me at home and asked: 'Aren't they giving you enough to do, then?' – at the educational factory up the road. The two men in the car-repair shop at Hull knew nothing about universities; they just knew that university people, people in posh jobs, kept their own odd hours. With the minority of less-conscientious American academic staff this pattern meant that, having kept 'office hours', they did little work at home even at weekends or in the evenings; they spent those times in the great democratic leisure pursuits, as the clerk or the plumber down the road did.

Those who came from particularly prosperous families often felt defensive about being academics. They carried an invisible banner, inscribed: 'We chose interest and honour before money'; and knew they were right. One told me his father-in-law could not bear to introduce him as a professor; he found a solution in saying 'My son-in-law is an educationist' – that sounds less odd-ball, more executively of the active world. Another high-level professional, told by his daughter that she proposed to marry the junior academic she had been going out with, remarked: 'Bit queer for a husband, isn't it; is he likely to go into Administration?'

For the visiting English academic, if he still had elements of the old-style English sense of superiority, the biggest lesson was that anything we could do they were now likely to be able to do better, and not only because of the weight of numbers, the wealth and the richness of educational opportunity – also because of the respect for knowledge. Their educational wastefulness ensured that their best, once winnowed out, were of the highest calibre – in scholarly slog, in brilliant exploration, in any aspect of academic work.

In the middle of the year at Rochester I spent a couple of days in Princeton and met a greater concentration of good minds in the humanities than I had ever met in a provincial university in Britain (my experience of Oxbridge and of London was limited). In the late evening a group of us drove to the home of a distinguished retired scholar. We sat in his garden in the warm night talking about the contrasts between European and American intellectual life, they in a manner more informed and alert than I had, again, experienced in Britain. We had a lot of wine. In the small hours, when the chill began to set in, someone suggested we visit the cows since it would be milking-time and I might be interested to see that. A few miles outside Princeton stood what was claimed to be the most advanced milking facility in the world. Hundreds of cows went round and round on carousels, being electronically milked and chewing electronically-measured plugs of the right food for the time of day, month, year. We went on talking – by now slap-happily – about tradition, the quality of life and the future now so manifestly before us. One of the group threw extra food to the cows and said: 'Break out, baby. It's your birthday.'

When working at the house through the middle of the bitter winter I wrote a British Council booklet on Auden, and intermittently wondered how *The Uses of Literacy* would be received. It appeared in February 1957 but, partly because of the buffer provided by distance, made no great impact on us. Whether inspired by that I do not know, but the University of Rochester soon after offered me a post. I was pleased but knew immediately that we would not stay. All the members of the family had enjoyed themselves very much indeed but knew too they would go back. The youngest said, with childish conviction, 'I'm English and should be in England,' and that in a way was psychologically true for all of us; and also professionally, for me.

So we came back, after the children's double summer camps and my double summer schools; we would miss our friends but have retained the closest of them; we would miss the long camping trips because they introduced us to space and other liberations; we would miss the brunches and the barbecues and the weekend-evening parties, even though some of them were like dry-runs for

Who's Afraid of Virginia Woolf; that too was America – articulate openness before their emotions even among the academics, perhaps especially among the academics.

I am not a 'pure' scholar who can work anywhere he is placed. I am not the kind of writer who does not need, or need any longer – because he already has nourishment enough to last for years – to be rooted in a familiar soil. I became greatly attached to much in American life. I still feel a powerful flow of adrenalin as the plane loses height towards that shore, of a sort which no other landfall gives – not Greece or Italy or South-east Asia or even Australia. But I am still suspended. If I became unsuspended, if America became at last 'real' and diurnal to me, then its tones, styles, manners and all the unspoken meanings would cease to be exciting and would become limiting, a soil I could not be nourished by. This is no limitation of America but rather a limitation in me; I am too immersed in, too much of, one culture; not a particularly fine plant but one which withers in almost any soil but its own.

PART THREE

✤

TAKING STOCK

He that hath wife and children, hath given hostages to fortune . . .

Bacon, *Essays*: 'Of Marriage and Single Life'

The lyf so short, the craft so long to lerne . . .

Chaucer, *The Parlement of Fowles* (after Hippocrates)

Old men ought to be explorers . . .

T. S. Eliot, *Four Quartets*: 'East Coker'

CHAPTER 8

'THERE'S NO VOCABULARY': ON FAMILY LIFE

If the sufferings of children go to swell the sum of sufferings which are necessary to pay for truth, then I protest that the truth is not worth such a price . . . I would rather remain with my unavenged suffering and unsatisfied indignation, *even if I were wrong*. Besides, too high a price is asked for harmony; it's beyond our means to enter on it. And so I hasten to give back my entrance ticket, and if I am an honest man I am bound to give it back as soon as possible. And that I am doing. It's not God that I don't accept, Alyosha, only I most respectfully return him the ticket.

Dostoevsky

Finally, when Bazarov's last breath had been drawn, and there had arisen in the house the sound of 'the general lamentation' something akin to frenzy came upon Vasili Ivanitch.

'I declare that I protest!' he cried with his face blazing and quivering with fury, and his fist beating the air as if in menace of someone: 'I declare that I protest, that I protest, that I protest!'

Upon that old Varina Vlasievna, suffused in tears, laid her arms around his neck, and the two sank forward upon the floor. Said Anfisushka later, when relating the story in the servants' quarters: 'There they knelt together – side by side, their heads drooping like those of two sheep at midday' . . .

Turgenev

Looking through old jottings, I find I first began making notes about family life almost thirty years ago, when the children were fourteen, twelve and eight – the move out of childhood into adolescence was just beginning, so it is easy to understand why the notes started then; they have continued intermittently until the present, when the oldest grandchild is fifteen.

This interest in family life – what it is, what it means – seems at first glance easy to explain in both of us. Mary was the only child of an unusually quiet-living pair and missed having siblings. No one to make jokes with round the table at meals, about school or church or the queer old woman up the road, or your parents; that kind of thing and much like it. I too was in effect an only child, surrounded by adults ranging from twenty-odd to seventy-odd years old. A family life, certainly, but mainly in its dourer elements.

Many of us have in a lifetime several houses, living places; they are separate and follow one another. We have only one home, and that if we are lucky we carry round with us in increasing states of consolidation. Its character builds up, if it is going to take hold and grow at all, like a coral reef; with its own peculiar appearance, feel, nature.

We were the first post-war generation of home-makers, not yet comfortably off, mildly beset by rationing and other shortages but cheerful and in good health; learning to live with each other, to do our jobs, and to look after children with, in the first half-dozen years, usually a new baby or one on the way. No other period in married life presents so many novel challenges; but then at no other time are you so resilient to meet them. The style of our married life, begun that summer of 1946, had been largely formed by a year or two after we had gone into our first complete house (in the spring of 1951) and, a year later, had the third and last child, Paul.

With us, the impulse we both had to 'make a home' meant that we created, naturally not always being aware of what we were doing, a wrap-around family. Even now after all these years we, and perhaps especially I, like to have them here – wives, husband, children, all. So that we can close the stockade if something horrible happens, or 'go out' – expire – together. An elemental, an atavistic, feeling which gives a new force to that old phrase about liking to have the family 'under the one roof'. I know we could never do it, and perhaps at the pinch would not want to do it, but I felt a twinge of envy when a colleague, on retirement, bought a very large rambling place which could accommodate almost all his extended family, each in their separate quarters, and also provide common areas. If there promises to be a severe crush, Mary might suggest that one of our groups delays coming for a day at some holiday period. I cannot do that. She is right; she loves their being here no less than I do, but knows one night's sleep foregone in the parental home is not of great account. My approach is partly the congenital working-class softness, excessive softness, towards kids, and partly a hangover from those occasions in childhood when, being orphaned, I was made to feel not wanted. How could one come within miles of risking inducing that feeling in someone else, least of all in one's own children?

It is a foolish hangover; our children and their children know well how solidly and permanently they are loved. But so it is. One of the discoveries of an enquiry such as this is of the power of such feelings, feelings you should have long grown out of. I know why many in the English mid-middle class and upwards send their boys away from home from the age of seven; but that habit, and what it tells about the nature of this large swathe of society, is the marker of the chief gulf in this society – educationally, socially, politically, and above all emotionally.

A result of this enclosed home-making instinct in us both has been over-protectiveness towards the children, and this may have made it harder for them to break away. They did like home, certainly; we comfort ourselves with the thought that they found home – its alarms and excursions, and above all its secure affection – more interesting than any other place, until they became thoroughly adolescent and aware of sexual stirrings. In different ways each of them could be, in adolescence, aggressive and casual; but not consistently, and no worse than that.

There are moments when a powerful quality in one's character, an unexpectedly powerful quality, is sharply evident. Such a moment came when I got back from a first visit, in the middle Sixties, to the Soviet Union. It was only for a couple of weeks and only to Moscow and Leningrad, to give university lectures under British Council sponsorship; and I had good company in another academic, David Daiches, and his wife. The weather was bitterly cold and the sky mostly a leaden grey. Moscow in particular was grim vistas down and across enormously long and wide streets. Faceless, drab, cementy buildings for as far as you could see. No colour from **advertisements; only the uniform red of uniformly-urging-on** slogans painted on huge walls. The hotel rooms were high and unfriendly and anonymous – in a different way from the anonymity of the Sheratons and Hiltons. The whole scene was agoraphobic, beyond the human scale, by the physical setting and by what it suggested about the unimportance of individual opinions and attitudes. In so far as it seemed to recognise the individual, in its public areas and manifestations, it had reduced that individual to a small anonymous unit to whom things were to be done – for his or her own larger good – by the remote authorities outside; and so it was claustrophobic also, pressing down on you. I was more than ready for home by the end of the first week.

When I got back to England and rode up the Tube's escalators (this was before they were sanitised by the GLC) I was delighted to see all the ads, especially the corset and swimming-costume ads, their colour and their appeal to the *homme moyen sensuel*, not as a productive unit nor as a worthy citizen. Thank God for the freedom to have dirty thoughts; at least it indicates that you are allowed to make up your own mind, think in your own way, indulge your own emotions.

As the three of us had stepped into the British plane we found ourselves laughing at the unexpectedly strong sense of relief we all felt. We had not been afraid; we had been depressed and to some extent strained by a paradox. Behind virtually any lecture we gave at home or in most other places lay unspoken assumptions: about the freedom of the writer to try to tell things as they seem to be; about the status of the individual, whether writer or not; and about the rightness of giving only limited powers and importance to the state. They were the ambient air within which our arguments could breathe. To give such lectures in a quite different climate was like trying to plant seedlings in what purported to be a bell-glass but was in fact entirely closed and a vacuum. That was at the heart of the feeling of claustrophobia.

We were late into Heathrow and I should have gone into a hotel. But I found a train from Marylebone to somewhere near Birmingham; with that and a fairly long taxi-ride I managed to reach Edgbaston in the small hours. The boys must have been away or perhaps stayed asleep. I remember Mary and Nicola running down. We sat on the stairs for a long time, me in the middle with my arms round them both – being bonded into the home identity again.

I

One of the most haunting small scenes in Western literature occurs
in *The Brothers Karamazov*, after the Captain has been assaulted
and humbled by Dmitri, in public and before his schoolboy son:

> At that moment the boys were coming out of school, and with them
> Ilusha. As soon as he saw me in such a state he rushed up to me. 'Father,'
> he cried, 'father!' He caught hold of me, hugged me, tried to pull me
> away, crying to my assailant, 'Let go, let go, it's my father, forgive him!'
> – yes, he actually cried 'forgive him'. He clutched at that hand, that very
> hand, in his little hands and kissed it . . . I remember his little face at that
> moment, I haven't forgotten it and I never shall!

Dmitri has no justification or provocation for the attack and
would not, it is indicated, have made it on a social equal. But the
power of the scene comes from much more than class differences. It
holds all the weight of a boy's adoring love for his father, whatever
the status or profession of his father; and of the near certainty that if
the father is in a lowly position or job the boy will eventually see him
lowered, reduced, humbled in and by the outside world – snarled at
by a foreman, ticked off by a member of the public, threatened by
the shop manager.

Watch a boy of four or five, going on his father's milk delivery
round, or walking to the end of the road as his father sets off in
uniform for a shift as a bus conductor – and you think how stage by
stage that boy will have to see his father in a much wider context
and so as, in the worldly sense, of little importance. The process
may be slow and, when the father is a decent husband and the home
happy, may never produce serious distress. A good home can see
you through adolescence to the point at which you can judge the
world's orderings against your recognition of your father's worth –
and your mother's, if she also works outside the home and is being
judged there – in more important, private, ways. The fact that a son
or daughter have gone on 'to higher things' educationally does not
necessarily make this understanding come more easily; brightness
doesn't always mean maturity. The parents of quite a few at Leeds
in our time did not appear for the graduation ceremony. Some
would have been put off from going by their sons or daughters,

either explicitly or by a feeling in the air; others would not allow themselves to be drawn, for fear they might 'show up' the new graduate.

Further along that line of thought lie the pathos, the misery, the appalling sense of loss which can be the reverse side of a family's strong sense of belonging. Hence, yet more scenes and lines which can wrench you as few can. I have a memory of overhearing a young mother phoning her mother about a death in the family. 'Oh, Mum,' she cried in a high, heart-broken wail, 'we've lost our John. He's gone.' The possessive and the two simple verbs are much more powerful than 'John has died.' They conjure up all the fear of the close family being broken up, dispersed, wrenched apart; and the fears that a child will slip away from you – in a crowd, on the beach, in a huge store or on a boat, and not be found again; 'he's gone.' And that somehow you may be at fault – '*We've* lost our John.'

Linked to that in a reverse fashion is a cry I once heard in Hunslet, also from a young woman, at the door of a house in which the father had just committed some act of violence, perhaps towards the mother: 'Ooh! *you've done it now*, Dad.' It caught up two horrible suggestions: that violence had happened before, probably regularly; and that this time the father had gone far too far, had stepped over a threshold from which there could be no return; this time it had broken a person and the family in a way which could not be mended; it was a dreadful epilogue.

Such memories, even though they may be culled from literature or even if they are from real life but do not concern your own family, nevertheless stay with you; they are illustrative. Do such unhappy incidents stay nearer the surface than happy ones? Perhaps. They tend to be more dramatic. And we are most of us more nervous of trying to describe happiness than the sad or shocking; a post-Victorian inhibition.

Yet I remember too the day Mary and I came back to Paris from a long and gruelling trip to the Far East on UNESCO work and landed, jet-lagged and weary from a long overnight flight, at a bitterly cold Orly airport. It was a few days before Christmas. As we cleared customs, there were the two boys waiting for us. They had found the time of our flight, met in London, flown to Paris, slept in our apartment and set off for Orly on one of the earliest buses the next morning. We glowed at the thought of all that. They wanted to be home for Christmas and home was at that time the Boulevard Haussmann. They could have waited a couple of days until we were back and had the flat and the food all ready. But they had decided – even though it might, given the vagaries of long-distance flights, have meant a very long wait indeed – that it would be a treat for us all to be together immediately on landing. They were grown up and well able to look after themselves. Yet still the gesture seemed marvellously familial.

It is plain how much of home-making is a matter of establishing roots, sometimes wider and deeper roots than either partner has known before. Roots downwards and tendrils outwards; they reduce isolation and build up identity. One side of me, when I am fully immured in home and working at my desk on what I enjoy, can feel like a little bantam cock. It is still not a deep assurance, and needs constant reinforcement. Very tired, in a hotel bedroom far from home, I can wake up at three in the morning and feel my personality crumble away, and loneliness, disconnectedness, reassert themselves. It is not self-pity. But the ghost of the boy to whom, with casual insentience, they threw the wrong size of boots at the Rotary Club camp for poor boys, the boy who – like his brother and sister – was referred to in his hearing as a problem, 'one of the orphans', that ghost hovers near the bed. No more than that, and sleep soon comes; and you go down to breakfast in the morning looking like any other visiting lecturer they've thought merits fare and accommodation. Nor are such experiences unique; it is the apparatus, the details, which differ. Most of us, whatever our origins, have our ghosts, those which say 'What have you made out of this start, these events, this material? And have you disowned us?'

It is the sense of wholeness and of continuity to death and even beyond, though I do not know what that means, which most surprises in this culture of the unitary family. Say to a parent of grown-up children that it must be some sort of relief at least to have them 'off your hands' and you will be likely to have the answer that they are never off your hands, that they will seek money and consolation until the end, your end. You immediately know that to be true, to be self-evident; you just hadn't yet thought of it. Similarly, phrases such as 'She'd had a good life. It was time to go', though to some extent helpful, are also ritualistic, and no one quite believes them. It is never time to go, for even the oldest member.

Where one goes early, a wife or husband, the survivor (unless below forty and sometimes then) seems more often than not to put up the shutters, the light of expectation goes out of the eyes; and even the skin and hair lose their brightness; it is as though they have written off themselves, and the rest of their lives.

Worst of all is a child lost by accident, plucked away. As is usual in responses to the most awful of events, an apparently banal and entirely unhistrionic remark can be more powerful and true than all the more obvious expressions of grief: 'To think he had to be taken away so soon' has nothing like the heart-rending force of 'I kept thinking of all the meals I'd cooked, to see him become that solid little boy from that scrawny scrap I first held in the maternity ward.' Sometimes one wishes we could be dramatic, melodramatic even, without being conventionally tatty in the manner of the In Memoriam columns of the local papers. They order these things better in Russia, so one has to go to that literature for a direct, apocalyptic reaction to the loss of one's child. As in the passage from *Fathers and Sons* quoted at the head of this chapter, when the conventional, countryfied, elderly parents of the revolutionary Bazarov have seen him die of septicaemia, and sink to the floor, 'their heads drooping like those of two sheep at midday'. Turgenev glides from the magnificently operatic 'I protest' of the father to the intensely homely image of the sheep in one move, and with no sense of discontinuity or incongruity. It is echoed almost twenty years later in Ivan Karamazov's spectacular rejection of God, the other passage quoted at the start of this chapter. Ivan too calls 'I protest'; very Russian, not very English.

From children to parents to grandchildren. We always say that the silvery-haired grandparents can more easily indulge the grand-children than they did their own children. But that is the shallower water. Grandparents think almost as often, day by day, of their own children (and now of their grandchildren) as they did from the beginning, though knowing and not at all resenting that their own children, much as they love their parents, by now think of them only intermittently except in periods of crisis. But the sense of continuity is being knitted all the time and especially at those periods of crisis. Our children have known only two grandparents and one of those died before they were as a group able to apprehend and share the meaning of the event. Their grandmother died when they were twenty-three, twenty-one and seventeen. They saw her fade out slowly, in bed at our home, as the cancer took final hold; they learned how to comfort her by sitting on the bed and talking quietly about anything which came into their heads. They helped surround her with love and they themselves realised, understood better, that love themselves; and they saw her into her grave on the Pennine foothills. It was, it is, one of the most powerful moments of coming together and of the recognition of endings and continuities that a family can have.

The pleasures of family life express themselves in pictures, rituals, jokes, words, smells. In the at first wondering look and then the sudden rush as you return to a twelve-month-old baby after leaving it with grandparents for a few days; the huge toothless grin of a six-month-old baby at the breast as you come in the door from a night away at a class; the expectant bouncing up and down of a ten-month-old, in the pram on the front garden as you come home for lunch. Most of all, perhaps because daughters seem more vulnerable, I remember the poignancy of our daughter at about eight years old – usually now seen sitting on the raised fire-surround in the back breakfast-room at Hull, the rather coarse-looking little pleated gymslip running over the unformed hips, the small, reddish-blue knobbles of knees – it is a period of bare knees, often cold, red and chapped – the long and creased boy-like fawn stockings and the heavyweight, brown, boy-like stubbly shoes. A graceful lack of grace, especially when she sat there with her little lap holding the cat, picking awkwardly and rather self-consciously at a tea-cosy she was trying to knit.

The rituals with our children were made up, as must be common, of the universal and the particular: a Saturday morning trip to the sweet shop or the newsagent's for comics, the annual round of autumn Feasts, the carol concerts, the Christmas pantos and a great range of Christmas habits – which can be added to over the years but not reduced, successive learnings to ride a bike round The Avenues, gathering to hear a favourite radio or television programme, getting round the settee for games of skill, going to the Baths on Saturday mornings before breakfast, singing over the washing-up after Sunday dinner once we'd handed that job to them – for years, Clarence 'Frogman' Henry was one of the staples – and trips to the nearby countryside on Sunday afternoons 'for a breath of air'. Tea anyday was a ritual since each could try to make the day at school comical. So was Saturday lunch which became a slightly indulgent prelude to Sunday dinner, and perhaps even to a trip into town and tea there.

It was on one such occasion in Leicester in the early Sixties, when I was cooking sausages for Saturday lunch during Mary's absence in town, that the last post of the week brought a remarkable letter: would I be willing to be considered along with existing applicants as a possible Vice-Chancellor for one of the new universities. 'What — *you*?' said Simon. Then, after a pause, 'Still, I suppose it's like the Leicester buses.' What about the Leicester buses? 'Well, shortage. They're having to use Pakistanis as conductors now.' Silly jokes, especially if they break the monotony of car journeys, go on and on, no matter how basically feeble they may be. In southern Germany we passed a garage owned by 'Rudi Knees' and that saw us through many a dull patch for years afterwards.

Of all the smells, I like best those of baking and cooking as you come in towards the end of the day. That they promise a good meal is not the main attraction. As the children gather round and chatter and their mother looks up with a smile, still absorbed, a bit flushed, it all suggests so much of the security, the extra trouble gone to out of love and the sheer sensuousness of secure family life. Not glossy but warm and welcoming and fresh. Untidy because that is inevitable when you make a meal, but not congenitally messy or dank with dripping taps and smelly dishcloths.

In the late Fifties, when Paul, the youngest child, reached manageable age, Mary took on some teaching in the local training college and I helped more in the home (a good line in tinned red salmon fishcakes) and with preparations for that teaching. She gave it up quite soon, of her own volition and without regrets, because she enjoyed more and felt more that she was doing the right thing when she remained, as she was, the pivot of a very full family life; as interesting and dramatic, she said, as anything she could find outside.

Of the children's speech I remember, first, some comments which took us by surprise and with a special tenderness and poignancy. Like the day our three-year-old looked up and asked: 'Shall I be happy all the days?'; or when the youngest, also then about three and riding in the back of the car alone with us, stretched his podgy arms round us without warning and said, 'You lovely people'.

Or the moments when comedy turned back upon us. As when we decided that Simon was just about old enough to know the main 'facts of life' – which means only the outline of a particular part of life. In the bath he asked something about the history of Victorian England, and eventually we reached the large size of many Victorian families and how they came about. I mentioned parental decisions or lack of decisions. 'What have the parents got to do with the size of the family?' he asked. He had provided the necessary, natural, unforced opening. I had got about four sentences into the significant explanation when he interrupted and, in a tone that at least partly suggested he wanted to remove me from embarrassment, said: 'That's all right, Dad. Thanks. Now can we get back to the Victorian history?'

Every family has its own pattern of emotional tones, manners, styles which make up a whole. Ours was loving but also liked to be flip and ironic; especially, in the others, in reaction from my own tendency to see a moral point in many things or, when 'doing things about the house', to assume that Sellotape is the answer to every problem. Was it Colette who remarked that a girl will always remember the way her father expressed his tenderness towards her – stroked her hair, squeezed her shoulder gently, used certain tones of voice – and will be unconsciously seeking those kinds of expression when she begins to look for her own partner? I don't know if it is so, but it sounds right. Certainly many children recreate in their own homes, sometimes knowingly, often not, habits, customs, dispositions, a general style and tone they have known at home and have simply 'taken for granted'. Once again, an old and 'taken for granted' phrase comes up full of new meaning.

The pleasures of family life are inextricably bound up with the pains, of which the main kind are the fears. Our worst, so far, have been two very serious illnesses, each of which might have proved fatal. Those were bad enough, hard enough to bear; but not, I imagine, as painful as being rejected by a child, cast off, refused the sight of your own child and your grandchildren; such things one knows or hears about. By contrast, the loss when they marry, though it is in some senses real, is a light and temporary matter.

They come back, with the grandchildren spilling eagerly out of the car and their parents smiling wryly at the division of attention.

When they are young you find yourself looking down at them from time to time, triggered by no matter what incident or word, and seeing something of the unhappiness they are at some point bound to meet; and you wish you could hold them and fold them, always. Yet at bottom you know not only that you cannot protect them except in a limited way; you know also that, as an American friend and father of four said, you can have little influence on their final character, no matter how much you try – about as much as a brace on their teeth. Too much is decided before you meet them; too much is decided by forces outside your remit and control; but you must still do what you can.

Yet sometimes, as we have waved off one of them going cheerfully to a school camp or some such, this fear has come in great waves. Suppose something terrible happens; suppose they just do not appear again. It passes within a few hours but whilst it has a hold it is entirely beyond rational control. Before having a family I had never imagined that such a feeling could exist, and in such power.

You see they are growing up as they more and more push forward to the newest experience which fits their new sense of themselves. You want them to grow up; yet you cannot avoid a sadness as they do grow up, as they leave childhood, and the family ways which go with it. You want them to push their own boats out, but the period during which they were in your harbour now seems unhappily short. This is the root of the temptation to indulge, the sense of the shortness of all the phases of life. You risk imposing a frightening weight of love on each of them, especially up to just before adolescence; and that weight of love can sometimes get in the way of their own emotional development. You have to try not to get between them and the growing up only they can find and live through for themselves.

You have to try 'to care and not to care', to let them grow in their own ways, to stand behind, not in front or even at the side, and increasingly as the years pass. Not that I realised all this at the time. So often you come to know these things long after they might have been of use to you.

The corollary is that they are perfectly placed to hurt you, deliberately or – more often – inadvertently. Like no one else, they can hit you where you live. Samuel Butler says that parents always have the whip-hand over their children and in some ways he is right, especially about the earlier years and not only for his own heavily-parental times. But, perhaps because he had no children, he is even more deeply wrong. In the end, at bottom, the children have the whip-hand.

How does one assess the effect one might have had on one's children? Are ours less anxiety-ridden than we – I especially – were, and to some degree still are? Are they more confident without being brash or cocky? Are they more relaxed and open with other people, whatever their accents and styles? After all, they all went to university. Are they less ridden by a sense of Them as against Us? One of them, when about thirteen, asked me three times in a week for more pocket money; he was on a stamp-collecting craze, and an entrepreneur at school kept tempting him with better and better offers. At the third request I demurred. He asked why, since he had seen pound notes in my wallet. I explained earnestly what he knew already: that money in a wallet isn't necessarily free, unallotted money. 'Oh, come on, Dad,' he said, 'forget the back-streets of Leeds and give me that extra couple of bob.' He got it. There was a bit of a liberation there.

In conversations about children and grandchildren, among people of our kind and background, the word 'bright' is a touchstone. 'Well, at least they've all turned out bright,' people will say slightly tentatively of their own offspring. And of grandchild-ren: 'He's a holy terror but very bright indeed.' In my childhood, in our kind of society, 'bright' was the unusual distinguishing factor, the propellant which might push you out and into another orbit. Nowadays, in people who have got into that other orbit, who are living in what seems a higher world than that of their origins, to have 'bright' children and grandchildren is one usually unspoken assurance towards the belief that they and in turn theirs will stay there.

What about indications that our children have turned out decent, kindly, honest? One wishes that and would be sad if a child, no matter how successful professionally, turned out to be a cheat. I know some whose children have done very well financially as stock market operators. Their parents talk about them apologetically: after all, the opportunity for a good education isn't meant to lead to that kind of thing, is the unspoken thought. It remains unspoken because we are inhibited from making moral comments, fear appearing pretentious, have lost the language because we are unsure of the validity of such judgments in the world outside, even though they may still speak to us inside ourselves. Our own children have all turned out 'bright' and we are very pleased about that. Underneath we are much more affected by indications, which we note but do not announce – nor would they make them explicit in this general and abstract fashion – that they reject intellectual and imaginative shoddiness and value charity towards others.

The one instance in which our generation and our kind of people feel free to speak in this way is when one of our children proves to be 'not bright': 'He/she isn't very bright, but has the sweetest character of them all'; 'He isn't likely to make a great showing in the world but everyone loves him because he's so sweet-natured. Some girl will spot that and realise what a good husband he'll make.' The psychological situation can, almost paradoxically, be made easier where one child is born disabled; say, with Down's Syndrome. This condition is not to be evaded by linguistic shifts and overrides the importance, the socially-marketable importance, of 'brightness'. It is virtually always said that children with Down's Syndrome have natures of very great sweetness, and perhaps that is so. More important is that in such instances the family is likely to close protectively around the handicapped one and all of them, no matter how 'bright' they may be, learn much more about the primary nature of love and the secondary nature of 'brightness'.

2

Most professional men of my generation hate shopping for food, furniture or clothes; I enjoy it. The related interest in things which claim to be 'bargains' now seems increasingly comical to me, as it has done for years to the rest of the family. This is the bran-tub spirit (there may be gold there), the Woolworth's syndrome, and as congenitally working-class as the addiction itself to those stores. Until I began to write this story – and found Woolworth's appearing again and again in different contexts – I did not fully realise their importance in the theatre of working-class life during the first half of this century. They worked according to a very few brilliant insights: that if you fix an upper limit of price, sixpence, your attraction will be far greater than that of places where your customers do not know 'what they are in for' in prices; and that long aisles of open displays, preferably piled high, are another powerful attraction, especially for those nervous of asking first to see goods and then to know what they cost.

All this goes to form the old-style working-class love of a bargain. There was always a man down the street who was mad on 'bargain-hunting', walking in home with bargains he had 'just picked up' at some one-day sale in a hired hall he had passed on the way from work, or been irresistibly offered by a mate. A hat-stand made out of antlers might look queer in a back-to-back but I have seen one; after all, it had been (the adjective does not vary) 'a real bargain'; and we all knew that Fred had 'a nose for a bargain'.

Against all current reason, the love of bargains has stayed with me and with others I know from similar backgrounds: the love of advertisements which don't try to be psychologically cunning but say straight out, 'Look, this is a bargain; come and get it'; ads for food, cars, clothing, furniture; small ads in shop windows and classified ads in local newspapers. The big department store sales are attractive because they do have genuine bargains and you can now afford any you reasonably want. But so are bring-and-buys, jumble sales, displays of gear for making your own beer and wine, church and chapel bazaars, auctions (especially shabby auctions in small country towns), discount and second-hand shops and particularly those where they accept goods, agree on a price and put it in the window, taking a percentage if it's sold; and now car-boot sales.

Today's bargains are centred above all on the postal service and must appeal, do appeal, more widely than to émigrés from the working-class world; but they hook us particularly thoroughly. I make the routine objections to junk mail, but can scarcely bear to throw it away unopened. I am not seduced by the idea of a free BMW and a hundred pounds a week for life; nor by the chance of a trip for two on the Venice Simplon Orient Express; I am by the idea of 20p off a range of goods if the coupons are handed in within three weeks. That's only a flicker from the past; if the coupons are lost I don't care; it's the thought that counts. The Argos and Scotcade catalogues, the booklets which fall out of the *TV Times*, the

American Express, Visa and Access special offers, the Discoveries Selection for readers of the *Radio Times* and all their siblings rarely go straight into the wastepaper basket.

I have not yet sent for a small electric shaver for the hairs within the nose and do not expect to; nor for an ioniser (*Which* says it's not at all sure about them). I would hate to find I had won a Personal Organiser. I have bought a car-boot-tidy (not very useful), Able-Labels (handy), little quartz travel alarm-clocks, an anti-wrinkle steamer (not worth the trouble), a long-reach window cleaner (leaves streaks), a battery-driven razor with a revolving head (gentle but not very effective), and an executive case (this was a present and is unexpectedly useful), a biro which writes under water and was perfected for space-flights (works, but the need is limited), inflatable neck-supports (a 'boon'), a detector of wiring or pipes behind walls so that you don't drive nails into them (it may be useful but the batteries run down between uses) and a tyre-inflator which runs off the cigar-lighter. One or two other items I have forgotten, but on balance and taken as a whole I suspect such things were not worth the total of money spent on them. But one should allow something for the pleasure of sending off, and of opening the packet; it might be a real bargain.

What causes all the little spurts of pleasure as bargains are sniffed out? Partly the satisfaction of knowing that now you can afford any you or yours are attracted by (you can come home bringing the booty over your shoulder); and partly something inherent in the character. Acquisitions of this kind are a sensuous activity; yet you do not feel possessive towards them once they have been obtained; you can just as easily give them away, and often do. It is this lack of acquisitiveness which makes the sensuous pleasure of the bargain sit alongside the puritan suspicion of the superabundance in supermarkets and the wastefulness they imply. It sits also with the readiness to give to a good cause much more than you've just saved on 'bargains'. In such free gestures, Mary and I come together like big-dipper chariots swooping up the same loop; her mother had a weekly allowance and had to calculate portions very carefully, even for visitors; so that's out with us; praise be.

We come then to the nature of the interest in money itself, a strange interest because it is not avaricious, not concerned to amass. It may like figures and counting, but is less interested in the sums of money than in what that money can buy (not necessarily for you) and so in what those purchases can signify. John Braine had the fascination in one of its more obvious forms, Arnold Bennett in a less obvious one. Virginia Woolf was mistaken to think Bennett's love of all the thisness of things and their prices indicated a lack of spirituality, of response to an inner being. Bennett's love of objects and their value expressed itself in some extravagant personal ways (the expensive shirts and all that). But these things were poetic to him, luminous, vibrating with suggestions of luxury, of a glamour and a freedom the Five Towns never knew and which were not merely ostentatious or vulgar. That hat, those gloves, that dress – whether they cost a lot or a little and whoever was wearing them – were a gateway to what a spirit was reaching after. They were, if seen for what they were, more interesting than disembodied, abstracted, sketchings of what a pure soul might be imagined to be seeking. In a different but related way Scott Fitzgerald was fascinated by these kinds of vibration, especially in his spoiled and careless, rich young women. The rich are resented not only because they have more money, but because they move and smell differently, less inhibitedly. Once, taken to a fashionable café-bar in Moscow, I saw girls tossing Dior scarves round their necks as they laughed; their hair was differently coiffured from most heads of hair one saw in the streets and I expect they smelt differently. Unmistakable; the daughters of high party functionaries, my guide said. Scott Fitzgerald and Arnold Bennett would have recognised them at once.

So money can be wasted, or at least given prodigally – for the right things, things which touch, or are made after a moment's thought to touch, that urge to generosity and largeness which could not express itself in the early years. I still tend to estimate conservatively what should be the value of a proposed present – at first; then, prompted or not, comes a second thought and the amount rises. There is still, after all, behind every dealing with money and things, the fear and the hatred of waste. That old phrase which I have quoted before – 'you'll pay for this' – is joined by 'it's a sin and a shame to be so wasteful', 'fancy good food being thrown away', 'he doesn't seem to know the value of money', 'I had to work hard for every penny I've got and am not going to squander it', 'a penny saved is a penny earned', 'take care of the pence, and the

pounds will take care of themselves', 'put something aside for a
rainy day', 'waste not, want not', 'I mean to get me money's worth'
and dozens of others expressing the fear of excess; the built-in rules
of thumb of the permanent siege economy. There are far fewer
apophthegms which run the other way, though they exist. Of those
common in our part of Leeds I can at the moment recall only 'penny
wise, pound foolish' and 'you can't take it with you.'

'He left her penniless' might seem nowadays little more than a
rather colourful figure of speech; it used to be literal. One tries not
to rebuke children who are wasteful at meals; at least they are not
wondering whether there will be anything other than bread and
margarine next time, and that's a gain; but the slight tremor is there
– waste is a sin. If you have been brought up in a home – typical of a
very large proportion of working-class homes before the war – in
which any sudden and unexpected demand for money could throw
the whole household economy out of kilter, in which try as you
might you cannot protect yourself against all possible demands,
then those unforeseen demands strike like a forceful wet dishcloth
on the back of the neck. So I try to anticipate every conceivable bill
for months ahead, even though I know we are lucky enough to be
able to pay them all without difficulty. But still when the rates, the
electricity, the telephone, the gas, the car insurance bills drop on the
mat I have half-a-second of mild alarm; can we really 'meet' them?

Intimately related, in this network of carried-over, residual,
unexpectedly slow-in-dying attitudes, is the hatred of being 'done',
'diddled', hatred on your own behalf and on behalf of all those who
can't fight back, since they are nervous in the English manner of
making a fuss or uncertain how to make one, especially against the
fast-talkers. The anger can be directed, on behalf of others, at
hucksters on fairgrounds or on one-day stands in hired church halls,
flagrantly cheating their customers with offers of watches, radios,
cassette and video recorders, carpets saved from fire or flood, and
bundles of tooth-rotting confectionery. On your own behalf and,
you tell yourself, in the hope that your complaint will help make
things better for others, you fire off letters to such as the National
Health GP who asks you, before attempting to make a date for you
with a local consultant, whether you wish to 'go private' for the
purpose; and to the consultant who leaves NHS patients way down
the queue for month on month but fits in quickly those who will

pay; or the dentist who rushes through his work carelessly since he is paid by items done, or the opticians who used to steer you away from the cheaper National Health frames towards the ones on which a bigger profit could be made; or, at the more workaday level, the garages who do skimped servicing but charge the highest possible rate, the cowboy plumbers, builders, electricians; and the supermarkets who play games with their mark-ups when some goods become more popular than they had anticipated. The anger has to do with much more than money; it has to do with the refusal to be seen as a milch-cow, is against the indication that you and other people are being seen as objects, and idiot objects at that, whom it is only smart to con. Of all this, the worst is the routine, endless exploitation of under-educated people.

I never fail to be surprised and pleased that, though not at all wealthy, we have a bit of a buffer against sudden shocks, and some available to help others. A test that the money's there, that there's cash to 'jingle in the pocket' but that it doesn't greatly matter, is the ability to walk through a big store and realise that within reason you could buy whatever might tempt you, in furniture or kitchen equipment or clothing; and that you are not tempted. To walk through Maples – well, Heal's, say – without a hiccup, with an unopened cheque book; to know you could change the sitting-room suite but are happy with the one you've had for decades – that is the classic test.

Much more important: it is good to know that the children and their children are well-fed and decently clothed; that their styles in dress and their accents are neither working-class nor middle-class; that they have good bones and teeth and complexions, are not pale, scrawny, rickety, pinched, or have any other characteristics in the litany of the underfed, and that the boys in both generations are or promise to be a good few inches taller than you are.

On the debit side, I think often of the ways in which I did less than I might have done for the children, fell down, let them down. Driven as always to do the next thing, pushed on by a rather stiff sense of purpose, not arrogance or plain ambition, in thinking it fell to me to tell other people where they did not understand this or that part of British society, I may well have not done enough for my own family in some respects. Not in material things but in such matters as finding time to play, to relax with them, quite simply to waste time with them. I did spend some time and do not want to exaggerate; and I broke off work when asked; but often had to be asked, reminded.

The image for all this is that at some point, quite early, I said I would try to write a book for them; whether they asked or I offered I cannot remember but think the latter. I never did. The entirely playful suffered; there never seemed time for that. Clearing up, the next assignment, had to be attended to first. I was fearful, too, that I could not write such a book, that the flow would be thin, the playfulness not there.

So time passed and the book was always in the future. When you look back at yourself from this perspective you realise you have passed most of the days as though there would be endless tomorrows, as though you would never die. Life is flowing past all the time but you persist in ignoring the flow, as though by that denial you can escape it and its costs. How much has been missed by this inability to live in the present? You feel guilty at putting off the good, the uncovenanted, the gratuitous things but go on doing so, and one day you wake and you are old and your children no longer need a book; they are not children; they are off and have their own children. They come back and that is good, but not the same; and the book has never appeared and now never will.

There was worse, something I recall with a flush of shame. Time, events, have revealed a capacity for mute and stubborn hardness which I never suspected. It is brought out only rarely and, now I have identified it, I try to divert it; but occasionally I seem incapable of breaking out from it. It is a capacity to turn stony, to resist attempts to soften me, to nurse a grudge not by words but through a locked-in silence. Once is too much of such behaviour; it denies the evidence of love.

One such scene still wrenches my heart. It occurred in Birmingham and I suppose, to give myself a small measure of excuse if not absolution, I was unusually tired and over-pressed, and something might have gone wrong in a quite exceptionally busy set of days, or I may have been resenting the demands of family on time I wanted for writing. I do not remember why I suddenly felt angry with Mary and the family, and bereft; perhaps they had joked at some neurotic compulsion I had been exhibiting. I was quite excessively cast down and went to the room in which I worked and stayed there alone, working in silence. The house then had for a time the gloom that hangs over a family when one of its members has opted out in anger and refuses comfort, denies them.

After a while one of the children came in and said, with the most open love in the world, 'Don't be like that, Dad. We do love you and we didn't mean any harm.' It was a wonderful and brave thing to do and I knew that even at the very time I was not responding to it but was remaining silent and hooded and unresponsive. I felt deeply ashamed afterwards, when I had unthawed; but I could not at the time break out; we can be two such people at once. I felt even more ashamed of the awful example I was setting a child who had had the openness to swallow his own pride and risk a rebuff and had also had the imagination to see how important it was for me to break out of such frozen, rigid, unloving responses. That is one of the worst things I have ever done towards my family and I cannot forgive myself for it – even after I have thrown in the scales for the defence all the obvious items about being orphaned, about thin-skinnedness, if I am laughed at from outside, about the plummeting feeling even after all these years if the assurance of love seems to be even for a moment denied. All these palliatives are not enough.

3

Two incidents, one public and one private, one at the beginning and one towards the end of the Fifties, threw a sharp light on central aspects of family life.

The Cold War, which had begun round about 1947 or a little earlier, to some extent had faded, as a constant emotional presence, by the middle Sixties. In the light of this it is surprising to remember that CND was not formed until January 1958. From the late Forties to the middle Fifties the landmarks were clear and the succession at the time apparently unending: the Berlin Blockade in 1948-9, the formation of NATO in 1949, the rising in East Berlin in 1953 and that in Hungary in 1956. That latter had the most powerful impact of all the sequence of risings behind the Iron Curtain, just as Hungary today still has a special hold on the Western European imagination, culturally and intellectually.

Families such as ours were greatly aware of all these things, and many in different ways and to different degrees were politically involved in trying to understand them and to feel surer about the right British attitudes and responses. In coffee-and-cake evenings the Cold War was, sooner or later, the main topic of conversation (followed by talk about the university and how it was shaping, and about the children and how they were shaping). Some were very active, especially in the local Labour Party. We joined the Labour Party in most of the places we lived, but found the local branches generally uninspiring and slogan-ridden. We should, it could well be said, have stayed to help them improve. But it seemed a lot of trouble for very little effect, and took up time better spent in writing.

As for marches and demonstrations, right up to the formation of CND and beyond, those did not greatly attract, whatever the virtue of their causes. Had we not been in America at the time we would have marched with Hull University's staff in protest at the Suez operation; that seemed particularly outrageous. Had marches been organised differently – very much more quietly – we might have gone on several. But the almost always simplistic banners, the routine chanting, the assertion of a 'solidarity' which often seemed more like that of a cheering-themselves-up crowd than of a thoughtful group concerned with large but very difficult issues, all this was unattractive. Some of the CND marches towards the end of the decade and after were different; but by then I had realised that I was not a marcher; the ineradicable impulse to go my own gait (not one I wholly admire or wish to defend or excuse, but can at least partly explain), the disinclination to join any club, team or group, had solidly confirmed itself.

Behind all for most families such as ours, and having priority over political issues, was the bringing up of the children. It is obvious that if we don't attend to political issues we may sooner or later not have children to bring up; but that is usually no more than self-evident or a debating point or both, and does not reach the level at which primary dispositions are formed and expressed in action. Our kind of people were greatly but not wholly and uxoriously engrossed in bringing up families; nor obsessively engrossed in pursuing careers for professional ends and promotion; other things were done, often via a range of voluntary bodies, contributions of cash and writing.

This explains the force which Nevil Shute's novel about nuclear war and its aftermath, *On the Beach*, published in 1957, came to have for us. It is what used to be called a middlebrow novel. But it seems to have captured something of the mood in many people, especially families, whether normally middlebrow readers or not, of that first generation to be haunted by the thought that their children might have no future at all. A neighbour, similarly placed to us, once told us she had regular nightmares in which the bomb had been dropped and she could find neither her husband nor the children. We all have such nightmares, but it was very much of the time that such a woman, the wife of an academic and mother of four, should have those dreams; and should have read Shute. Middlebrow or not, he had touched a nerve, caught the sense of a moment.

For me, and in this I seem not typical, the fact of the Holocaust was and is more haunting, though not more terrible, even than the threat of nuclear war. I can now recognise that individual human cruelty knows no limit. But that an advanced European nation could turn all its sophisticated powers to official, formalised, mass killing in obedience to an insane philosophy, that it did not have, in its intellectuals, its newspapers, its broadcasters, its universities, a sufficiently strong texture of critical resistances to such a lunacy – this is harder to accept intellectually and emotionally even than the cruelty; precisely because it is those kinds of resistances which we have liked to think would be able, in the developed world of the twentieth century, to prevent the public expression of the worst kinds of evil.

The Korean War began in July 1950. As well as sending out regular units, the British government called up members of the 'Z' Reserve for a fortnight's refresher training. I received my calling-up papers in the summer of 1951 and reported to a camp in Wales in late August. Again the long train journeys as in 1940, but this time with a first-class travel warrant, since I was a reserve officer. That was the least of the differences. Of the intervening eleven years, almost six had been spent in the army and most of that abroad. We had been married nine years but had been free to set up a home for five only – in Redcar, Marske and now Hull, with all the time a growing family. We had moved into the first house of our own that April. By now our particular family pattern and style had virtually set. My first book, on Auden, was just out and the itch which finally led to *The Uses of Literacy* was established like an intellectual tapeworm.

Whatever the stubborn survival of old attitudes from Hunslet, it was in important ways a different person who left Paragon Station that Saturday morning. I can still see clearly the stances and expressions of the family at the barrier – Mary, newly pregnant, looking tense but 'putting on a brave face' for the children ('only two weeks after all'), the children, at five and three, holding one of her hands each and observing not altogether comprehendingly and certainly unhappily their father going off; not for a few days lecturing but to be a soldier again. The grouping was repeated when I returned, though this time it broke up into rushings forward. It was as well the authorities had not sent our uniforms to us, or the sense of strangeness on leaving would have been compounded. A fortnight is a very long time in such circumstances, for those left behind.

There was no boyish, on the spree, Territorial Army summer camp atmosphere. Almost all of us looked much as we had when demobbed, but a little fuller in the cheeks and generally softer in our lines and expressions. We also looked and felt – and proved – extremely cack-handed in our gun-drills, both officers and men. 'A bit daft, eh?' summed up the most common attitude, though said dryly; not a funny lark. One sergeant was worrying about how his grocery business would fare with only his wife to look after things; one gunner was worried about a sick child. A major, a randy plump barrister, was irritated by the dislocation not only to his briefs but to his hectic social life. He had resourcefully arranged for his latest girl-friend to come down on the middle weekend, and announced they would tour the countryside on the free Saturday afternoon in his open two-seater, knock back a few swift g-and-t's and then have a good screw or two in the hotel room he had booked.

We were in some ways professionally refreshed in the two weeks, but I doubt if the North Koreans or, later, the Chinese would have noticed. The most astonishing aspect of the whole enterprise was the sight of our guns and gear. In all important respects they were those on which we had trained in the early Forties, and dragged through the war. No magnificent and sophisticated new electronics from the arms industry in the intervening years. Standing on those bleak Welsh coastal hills, shouting the old orders, time was collapsed. This could have been Llandrindod Wells, or any of the sites on which we had perched temporarily in Britain, Algiers, the Tunisian desert, Bizerta, Pantelleria, Naples.

True to form, the officers' mess was established and set about its habitual social life, within the limits of time and physical constraints. The high point was a pre-lunch cocktail party given, with formal invitations, on the middle Sunday by the temporary colonel of our temporary regiment to all his officers, to officers of neighbouring units and to the camp's permanent officer complement. It had to be in a marquee with one side open, that opposite the wind; and there we stood quaffing our g-and-t's – a ritual which always reminds me of my first g-and-t, at the home of Bonamy Dobrée, and my gaucheness there. I couldn't, as it happened, stand chatting with the others in the marquee. I was crouched, almost entirely unseen because of the long tablecloth, under the table with the drinks on it. I had learned that the Third Programme's *Critics* would be discussing *Auden* at just about that time, and a senior officer had found a portable radio. The critics treated me kindly so far as I could tell at the time – the sound surged and ebbed, and voices above said: 'Oh, those boots sticking out? It's the Prof under the table. He's written a book! They're talking about it right now on that Third Programme. Never listen to it myself. But he must be a bright chap if he's up to that sort of thing.'

The second emblematic incident came in the late Fifties, after we had returned from America and after *The Uses of Literacy* had been published; so it was probably in late 1958 or early 1959. I call it emblematic because it brought together important questions about duty to the family and to the stranger outside, especially if that stranger had, though you had not known it, been influenced by you.

An Ibsenite situation. Of the sort which challenges so much of that urge in ourselves and our society which makes us seek to control all situations. The urge for controlled situations is one of the most powerful many of us know. Not to be taken by surprise, off balance, by outside irruptions, booby-traps. It is, oddly, easier to stick your neck out intellectually, especially if you think (as you certainly will) that right is on your side, and no matter how much abuse you attract or what advantages you know you have now forfeited. It is easier to face that than to meet, confidently and with moral assurance, situations forced upon you from outside which involve actual events and real people, in the flesh.

This can be in some ways a fearful attitude, in other ways a proper regard for one's responsibilities to those to whom one is directly responsible. Yet for so many of us it is easy to be comfortable here, compared with many more in this society outside the corral, and many millions more throughout the world. To go from a home as watertight as you can make it, in an enclosing car, to a warm office and a manageable job and so back again in the enclosed car to the enclosing home; not to find yourself carless on a dark night, waiting in a broken-down district at a bus shelter in the rain, aware without any distancing of the miserable, unprotected lives of those you have been on the whole content to ignore.

Many years ago, so long ago that I do not remember why I was there, I was standing at a bus stop and realised that a middle-aged and obviously working-class woman also standing there was weeping quietly. She had lost her purse. Perhaps it was a petty confidence trick she pulled regularly. I didn't think so, but didn't know. Since there was doubt, she had to be allowed the benefit of that doubt. I gave her a five pound note and walked away to avoid her thanks. Five pounds was a reasonable sum in those days and I would have to go to the bank next day. But it was, on a larger view, easily affordable by me and a huge release to her. I did not feel at all generous or virtuous. I knew it had to be done and was glad I could do it. It presented no serious moral dilemma; it was manageable – an instance of an unexpected situation and challenge absorbed into the circle of controlled and no longer challenging situations.

What happened on a Sunday morning in Hull, in the late-1950s, was a much more complex challenge. The doorbell rang quite early. On the doorstep I found a young man, probably in his early twenties, holding a brown paper parcel. 'You are Richard Hoggart? I've come to you. You'll understand' – in a broad but not uneducated Scots accent. I asked him in, Mary came down and we gave him breakfast, the children looked on puzzled. He had just come, he said, from Germany; he wrote poetry and would show me some; he had read *The Uses of Literacy* and decided he must seek me out. From the soft insistence of his speech, the clear intelligence mixed with inconsequence, there emerged the sense that he might be to some degree mentally ill.

He came from Clackmannan and told us a little about his family. They did not know exactly where he was, so I asked if I might phone to put their minds at rest. Of course. There followed a variety cross-talk act of no significance in this story except that – like a moment of mad relief in a sombre play – it highlighted by contrast the troubled nature of the event. There being at that time no direct dialling I had to phone the local area. A voice answered: ''Allo'; I replied ''Allo'; ''Allo' said the voice again and ''Allo' said I once more. And again, so that I wondered when we would break out of the waltz. Then the voice said, slowly and more clearly as to an idiot Sassenach, 'This is Allo-a'. Alloa, the local exchange, and I was through.

In a more serious sense his father was also unsettling. 'Oh good,' he said, 'I'm glad he's with you. He's talked about you a lot.' And that in practical terms, in any suggestion of parental involvement, seemed to be at that point the end of the conversation. But I did learn that the young man had been in a mental home, had discharged himself voluntarily and set off no one knew where. Whether he had been to Germany before calling in at Hull we never knew.

What best to do? How disturbed was he and what forms might that disturbance take? There were children of twelve, ten and six in the house. I doubt if I would have suggested he stay with us but could not do so anyway since Mary's parents were due and the spare bedroom pre-empted. He was clearly my responsibility not just as another human being in need but because he had been moved to seek me out by the effect some writing of mine had had on him; in particular by the chapter 'Scholarship Boy', about intellectual and emotional problems in adolescence, in *The Uses of Literacy*. I realised then more sharply than before that to write about inner problems of personality (to write about a great many other things too) is to issue an invitation on your own charity to those who read you. You are not free to push the writing out on the open water and disown it; it is always registered back to you at your intellectual address, a judgment by and on you.

I went with him to a hotel two hundred yards down the road, on the main avenue, very close to where the Mayfields lived. I signed for the bill in advance and told him he was welcome to have his meals with us. He had only a few, because his father sent to our address a postal order for £10 and that allowed him to eat in town a mile and a bit away, where he could pursue enquiries about the possibility of work. He called on us, though, for the few days he was in Hull. He often ate at the Salvation Army and met strays with ideas for making money quickly; he met others like them in the reading room of the public library. He was most interested in a memory man from the variety stage whom he met in the Kardomah café.

Whether the memory man had his eyes on what was left of the ten pounds or was just lonely I do not know. Certainly, he was short of a 'feed', one who would mingle in the audience and feed questions to him to warm up the show. Once he had a feed he could make a long-planned tour in Iceland. How about it? We talked earnestly with the young man about the proposal but he was set on it, and revealed reserves of shrewdness. The memory man sounded more like a loser than a trickster, so in the end there was no more we could do. Whether they ever reached Iceland we do not know; we had a friendly letter from London and that was the end of the incident. I often think of him and wonder what happened to him.

That incident is a long way in the past, about three decades; and sometimes seems even further away. Sometimes it seems to have happened only yesterday; then whole decades are no more than a long weekend, and all of life even more fragile and temporary than usual. Odd to notice how some young people, and I was much the same in my time, act superior simply because they are younger, have much more time in hand. Which is true but not very important. The moment of moving onto a new mental plateau, for a period, is when you realise fully that you are on the conveyor belt too, the same unstopping conveyor belt.

This week I unearthed a note from the early Sixties, one of the many notes about the passing of the years, in which I wrote how short a time it seemed since Simon was a baby and the two of us still in our twenties; double the time, I wrote to myself, and he'll probably be married and a father. As will the others. The little slip of eight with 'salt-cellar' hollows under her collar bones became a slender young woman and is now mother of three; Paul and Simon are each fathers of two.

'There's no vocabulary.' That phrase in the title of this chapter comes from T. S. Eliot's *The Elder Statesman*: 'There's no vocabulary /For love within a family, love that's lived in /But not looked at . . .' That is less consciously uplifting but no less affecting than Chesterton's 'The family is the test of freedom; because the family is the only thing that the free man makes for himself and by himself.'

We have little language left for love; to try to talk about it without sentimentality or the throw-away is like walking on broken glass in bare emotional feet. Even as we try to write we fear retribution, that to acknowledge this sense in words is to invite punishment for hubris. Yet it is good that our children and their partners and their children are close and loving, to us and to their other parents and grandparents. Whatever the weaknesses and failings, that doesn't seem too bad a thing to put in the other scale. As we, characteristically inhibited by nature and by Englishness, just manage at last to say.

CHAPTER 9

A SHAPE PROPER TO ITSELF? : ON WRITING A 'LIFE AND TIMES'

Time to take stock of what I am trying to do. Here is a pastiche:

'On those high summer Saturday afternoons in Poplar the light, in memory, lies always level across the grey-green roofs. All sounds were low, too, horizontal: a muted murmur just below the level of real awareness. I could go on reading whatever book had then caught my burgeoning imagination (it might be Percy F. Westerman; it might be Tolstoy; it might be anyone between these two poles).

But I was happier simply because the noise was there, this low susurrus of family and neighbourhood sounds – a front door banging down the street, my mother turning on the back-kitchen tap to fill the kettle for tea, the tragic plover's cry of a footballing boy two streets off, the steady warm hum from the shops and traffic of the main road three or four hundred yards away. All this established the ground within which only and from which my spirit could begin to soar. It spoke a subtle, comforting, established language of love and interest and belonging and respecting. That being given, like some first magnetic mark, my heart was freed to explore, with a freedom I have never since known. I would find it hard to over-estimate the value of such rooted assurances at that time in my life.

So as the light sank lower and the air grew chillier I began slowly – very much like someone in the last hour of a night's sleep – to come to the surface, ready to assume my other life (but they were really one, and happily so). I would then, as like as not, hear my father's solid chargehand's tread and decent low voice as he rounded the corner with his workmate, John Armitage. The football match was over; Rangers had lost or won for another week. I heard the unmistakable, sensuous plop of salmon as it left its tin to land on the largest tea-plate; and I could smell the newly-baked oven-cakes.

I went in . . .'

I knocked out very quickly, for a lecture many years ago, that spoof on much modern English autobiographical writing. Hiccupingly anecdotal, full of boozy Uncle Alberts with tobacco-stained waistcoats (against which the little lad or lass loved to lean), they are, again to use their own generously metaphorical language, like an over-sweet rice-pudding stuffed with large raisins. They are the dream-Christmas cakes for a world in which every day is Christmas, in which almost everything – even grief – is seen in a retrospective glow and the predominant time of day and year is the winter gaslight, closely followed by the haze of high summer.

They are folksy, winning, rampantly poeticised, ripely humane, falsely naïve, casual with such give-away soft-shoe'd openings as: 'I suppose we all at some time or other have . . .' They are loosely impressionistic and sprawling, because their only principle of form and order is the simple succession of the years and of the racy events within them.

Epithets are used for their likely effect on the reader, not to catch the nature of what is being described. Their successive stories aren't going anywhere, have no reverberations outside themselves, no suggestions of the meaning of this kind of life in this sort of place at this time.

I

Why bother to write a sort of autobiography anyway, especially if it is not to be a short-term effort but will occupy several years of a working life? I think it is Trilling who says somewhere that there are two kinds of writer, the centrifugal and the centripetal, those who spread their authorial interests widely over space, time and persons, and those who spin on their own axes for years and years. Among great names Shakespeare and Tolstoy would be centrifugal and Joyce centripetal. Allow for the due reduction in scale and I am centripetal, a muller-over of my own experience not an inventor of others', imagined experiences.

On reading *The Uses of Literacy*, of which most of those around him assumed he would disapprove, F. R. Leavis is said to have remarked that it had some value but 'he should have written a novel'. I imagine he was implying that some descriptive parts were not without merit. However, though I would like to create a self-contained world (and in some respects may be doing that even here), my invention and so the interest in plot are thin, as is the interest in creating other characters in motion and development. I enjoy trying to capture people I have known, in thumbnail sketches; I have never shown or been tempted to show a character and that character's relationships with others, changing over the years. I once tried to write a play. One act showed the attempt was doomed. I forgot I had several people in a three-dimensional space, that as their relationships developed so they had to move around, to go out and enter, be joined by others; and that events, irruptions, from the world outside had to come upon them. They simply stayed wherever they were – and talked.

Yet I am not happy to call what I am now engaged on an 'autobiography'. The word brings back all the qualities just criticised. 'Memoirs' is even worse and suggests names being dropped in every chapter. 'Life and Times' is least unsatisfactory. 'Life' to be taken to mean not 'My Life . . .' but 'Life as it has been lived by many of us', and 'Times' as 'In these Times I/we have known'; so 'Life and Times' is meant to suggest both a degree of distancing and a recognition of common experience.

The word 'exemplary' might at first glance seem apt but could suggest the idea of a model, to some extent to be admired. 'Typical' is too general since the story told here is in much untypical. Darwin, Mill, Newman, all of whom wrote autobiographically, were exemplary intelligences; some important strands in the texture of their age were exemplified in their lives. Henry Adams, Edmund Gosse, Edwin Muir were less towering and public eminences, but their life stories also reveal exceptional capacities to exemplify important elements in the intellectual and imaginative history of their times. None of the six was 'typical'.

In so far as my story is to some extent either typical or exemplary this is because it shows the movement of a certain time in provincial England from a poor working-class home to a classless professionalism, which one has also to call in some respects middle-class; it exemplifies some main features of that sort of movement. But it is not exceptional; many thousands have trodden that path, that sort of path. Nor is the story of My Life and Hard – or Soft – Times, or of anyone else's, inherently interesting.

Or at least it may be interesting only in so far as the writer learns how to set about showing it as that. One might have thought that people who lived through great events could not fail to tell interesting stories. Yet they can and do, as in the memoirs of statesmen, which are more often than not so dull and unaccented that one is led to think: amazing that he could have lived through so much, have done so much, and yet hardly have realised what the inner movements of his age were.

The number of 'I's has to be reduced so far as possible; but the 'I' behind it all cannot but be there – as it is in almost any novel, no matter what its aesthetic form and qualities, and no matter how much particular writers may deny this of particular novels. The writer in the personal mode, no matter how much the 'I' has been reduced, is inevitably much more exposed than the novelist; he has chosen to be, and cannot complain of the consequences.

Self-consciousness is essential or there is nothing to say, but can soon slide into self-justification. Even the most restrained writer is in part and at bottom trying to get straighter with himself – but in a reader's presence. Self-flattery can look at first like self-effacement, a decent modesty before others.

Oddly, it is easier, once you begin to think about what you are trying to do, to write about your own weaknesses and failings than about virtues and successes. This too can be merely a device to exhibit your own honesty before yourself and others, a way of mixing a bracing cocktail of those personal qualities you are willing to put on display. So again, unless you take yet further thought, you may end implying, not 'Aren't I an interesting/fascinating chap who has beautiful, sensitive thoughts' but rather 'I admit I'm a sod/ bastard . . . but, you've got to admit, an interesting/fascinating bastard – and at bottom a truthful fellow'. As Dr Johnson inevitably said: 'All censure of a man's self is oblique praise. It is in order to show how much he can spare.'

Those are still the shallows of the sea you have embarked on. In the deeper waters you try to avoid all such self-congratulatory presentation of yourself, whether as hero or villain; whenever relevant, you try, as though talking to yourself, to delineate aspects of your character which you now find unsatisfactory. You must then be prepared for some reviewers to take you at your own valuation, to accept the discounted price you have put on your own character. The cheekier among them will not even say: 'He rightly admits to this or that weakness.' They will appropriate as their own discovery the weakness you have admitted in yourself. 'The predominant weakness of so-and-so is moral cowardice before . . . as is plain from [not "as is admitted in"] the story here'. Still, though it may sometimes be brave to expose your Achilles heel, you – once again – cannot complain if someone uses the knowledge to kick you there.

Finding the right tone, the right stance before your material and – though this is less important – before your readers, is one of the earliest and hardest problems. It is, especially in autobiographical writing which aims to be more publicly 'telling' than personally revealing, a matter of distance and angle, distancing yourself and coming in obliquely rather than talking directly and close-up. That Henry Adams met the problem by talking of himself in the third person is curious and amusing, but no help at all today.

For the writer at least as much as for the reader the biggest initial limitation in autobiographical writing is the one-stringed tonal fiddle, the single channel for tones of voice. You are very soon sick of the parade of self as this is expressed in your favourite locutions, twists, turns, stresses, lifts and drops; you detect your own forms of special pleading as soon as the reader does. Then you wish you were after all writing a novel or a play, something which would allow you to escape from the carapace of the self, to be and to sound like someone other, to use tones your own personality cannot encompass and so to inhabit other personalities. Even the most oblique and dispassionate tone soon seems like a brand-name or signature-tune, something being sold. You become bored also by your own one-angled vision, your often predictable responses; it would be a relief to climb out of the skin of your own assumptions. There are ways, some of them fairly effective, of reducing the monotony of tone, angle and perception; but if they are too much relied on they deny what may be the strength of the record – a particular way of seeing, hearing, naming a world.

I like a French writer's remark, though do not entirely understand it. At least, I understand and very much like the first half of his sentence; and, in the way I interpret it to myself, also like the second half: 'Good autobiography reads as though no one in the world was ever to read it, yet it also feels as though it is meant to be read.'

One of the main compensations for the autobiographical writer, and it is a considerable compensation, is in the revelations about yourself, some shaming, some cheering, which the process of tapping memory gives. Until you begin to do it, you have scarcely any idea of the depth and width of your own memories. We all carry in our heads enormous reserves of incident, of movements in time, of characters; even more exciting, we can have the power to make linkings, through words and images, between all this material from different times, and between it and the present, powers we never suspected before we began memory-divining, linkings which can delight by their often oddly revelatory rightness; an apparently inexhaustible and endless process of discovery, largely but not entirely self-discovery.

All this is as if biologically linked to your writing itself. From which may come uncovenanted gains. You discover, for instance, that you write most strongly about creditable areas of character in which you are yourself weakest; but you only discover those weaknesses, or see them clearly, after the change of pressure in your writing has revealed them to you. The pressure of the writing is greater where you are describing qualities you admire, wish you had, but know you haven't — at least not by nature. I find myself writing with especially warm feeling about people who trust that the long run will iron out irritating attitudes in others, who are not thick-skinned, for if they were they could not respond so charitably; but who are not thin-skinned either — so they remain emotionally open and hospitable beyond clamourings from their own personalities. Conversely, you can find yourself writing with special force against flaws in others which, you now realise, are yours also.

You can learn to some extent — as you dredge in the depths — to recognise the moments when a memory comes up which you know immediately you do not wish to see the light of day. You throw it back before it reaches the surface, that set of metaphorical dirty pictures from some part of your past and personality. But they will

keep bobbing up again; and you will keep pushing them back, or
trying to tear them up by half-acknowledging them, or sliding
quickly and too casually over them if they do surface. Or even, at
the limit, you will recognise them but try to adapt them so that they
become manageable, liveable with. All this is as much a pleasure for
the perceptive reader as for you, though for you it is the taxing
pleasure, the internal gymnastics, of greater self-recognition; which
you may or may not allow to affect your behaviour from then on. If
the process were automatic, the progress towards virtue would be
much easier; but free will – which means nothing if it doesn't
include, doesn't mean also, the freedom to go to hell in your own
way and with your eyes open – would be lost; and so would the
chance to go to whatever heaven may be.

I used to think the self-censorship of memory worked only to
obliterate those memories which are embarrassing, belittling. It
does work in that way even if the memories are of no more than
comical or endearing weaknesses we have forgotten but find,
though only slightly, difficult to accommodate within our present
sense of ourselves. I now know, from being reminded of one
particular event in the North African days (described in Chapter 2),
that praiseworthy incidents can also be stuffed down to the depths
of the pool – perhaps because the memory of even small incidents of
virtue might seem to others like boasting; and might, whatever
others thought of them, embarrass you; it is simply easier to
recognise motes than merit, even your own.

The inability entirely to control what you are writing has much in
common with what many novelists have noted in their own work.
You may think you know what you want to say and for how long
about all the people – real people – who move through your pages;
but some will get away, run off on their own. Aunt Ethel, one of the
aunts who helped bring me up, after the three of us were orphaned
and shared among relatives, was a dominant figure; that I knew. I
did not know what a deep cistern of memories of her lay in my head,
or that I was still fighting within myself battles about our
relationship. I knew these things and much more by the time she had
taken over several pages of the first volume of this sequence and
elbowed out others who seemed to merit just as much attention. By
comparison my grandmother, a much more important figure to my
conscious mind, seemed to get short shrift, being so much less

colourful. Yet in the end the writing did not turn out that way: another part of my mind – it was not a deliberate technical decision – indicated that the best way to present grandmother, after the melodramatic figure of aunt Ethel, was through a couple of understated but especially telling incidents.

You learn also something about your particular, uneven pattern of responses to objects, people and ideas. I did not know until it became clear in the writing how strong was the impulse to bring the different kinds of experience together, the abstract and the sensuous, the public and the private, the large and the small, the big issues and the small habits, the large ideas and the petty smells. I found that in describing individuals my responses to their physical presences are, though sharp, quite limited; teeth are evident because they were in my childhood, being usually false; and ways of walking, especially since flat feet were also common then. In general, I proved more responsive to 'style', 'air' than to height, weight, colour. Tones of voice, yes; and stance, and ways of walking (in addition to the obviously carried-over sensitivity to flat feet), or of sitting, particularly the way in which different manners of sitting are forms of communication (the edge of the chair, I'm-not-stopping manner, most evident in men; the knees-crossed-and-handbag-on-knee style in women visitors who propose to be businesslike). But all in all hearing proved sharper than sight; especially of voices and especially of the way in which manners of speaking, both the music of a voice and the locutions favoured, give clues to character. There seems little responsiveness to touch but much to taste; far more food and meals appearing than I would ever have expected and a great, a very early-acquired, interest not so much in taste as in 'tastiness'. Sharper than any other sense is that of smell; but that, I suspect, is very common indeed.

It is harder to write about the way this kind of exploring may affect not simply your understanding of your own sensuous responses but also your habits of thought. After you have looked for a long time at some set of opinions you have never looked closely at before, which have done service for a very long period, after all sorts of qualifications to them have floated up from those peculiar depths you are now plumbing, you realise with what disconnected and half-considered fragments of thought many of your conversations on these matters have been conducted. You have then, if you are lucky, cut through many of the usual and expected tritenesses about, say, the emotional patterns of working-class life, or the meanings of the pressures experienced when you move from working-class to professional life, or the meanings of family itself. Even though the harvest may still seem small and the changes more a matter of discarding flotsam and jetsam than of taking a solid catch on board, you feel glad to have put yourself in a position to go through that rejecting and rediscovering process, in some matters at least. It is, above all, a process of refining thought (it is tempting to discount the claim by cautiously saying 'views' or even 'opinions', but 'thought' is more accurate) by testing it, probably for the first time in this detail, against the experience the thought has for long purported to assess.

As the weeks pass and the pages pile up, the actual process of writing becomes slower and slower. Take a typical morning. You have a few indicative notes, sketching where you want to go that day and where to end. Quite soon, and almost always, something you had thought a matter of a summary sentence takes on a life of its own and leads you into several paragraphs. Or one apparently small and incidental item breeds others you had entirely forgotten but now cannot ignore. The morning's straight line of narrative has become a winding doodle, with bypasses ballooning from it at intervals before they rejoin the main line; or the main line is entirely superseded. The process is neither casual nor accidental; it has its own internal logic, the logic of memory discovering more sense in apparently disparate experiences than you had suspected. These can be among the better gifts, the happier 'givens', of the often painful and only half-understood labour of recall.

2

The most pressing, recurrent, single problem is that of selection. The memory is so full of images that you could, if you were megalomaniac or insane enough to think they all mattered to some larger purpose, literally spend every day from early maturity to death writing them down. What can be the principles of selection? Can any principle of selection be incontestably justified to a doubter?

There are a few simple and practical principles which each writer must establish for himself, knowing that even here others may not accept them. For example, I have in my time played down some details of sexual behaviour in working-class life, on three grounds: so as not to make my surviving relatives feel shame (even though there was no suggestion that their own behaviour was being described); so as not to feed a prurient, *nostalgie de la boue* instinct in some; and so as not to discourage the emerging sympathetic understanding of others to whom such descriptions might seem extremely shocking. No doubt explicit descriptions of some middle-class habits would be just as shocking if not seen in print before. I made these changes in response to the reactions of two or three otherwise sympathetic and certainly thoughtful readers. Looking back, I think I was mistaken; the writer of such a passage has to find a way of telling the unmodified truth which neither alienates nor nudges.

I feel surer about the justification for the other practical rule of selection. This relates to my own relatives. Except where it would be against sense to do so, since their identities are obvious from the story, I always change their names. Some embarrassment at seeing their lives described cannot be avoided, but false names help far more than people used to reading books would suspect. The embarrassment seems to have two sources. First, it is embarrassing simply to be talked about, even if the references to you are entirely complimentary. You don't thus expose yourself to others, and above all not to the neighbours. You keep yourself to yourself; you don't show yourself up, make an exhibition of yourself. If the references are at all critical, that is terrible; if complimentary, that is showing off, getting above yourself. It is no accident that working-class conventional speech is full of apophthegms running in this direction. It is as though if such things are actually expressed, put on paper, some virtue will depart from you and from the propriety of your life.

The second source of embarrassment is less obvious. It is that almost all working-class people have been used to living as if subject to merely successive events; if the assault has a pattern it is that of birth and growth and death; it is that of the seasons and main dates of the year; and of the weekly wage packet. Working-class life has long been dominated by the thisness of things and events and people; an unordered thisness.

What almost all working-class life – almost all levels of life –

avoids or, better, is unaware of, is intellectual pattern-making, generalising across and about habits in space and time; and so of gathering such generalisations together and hazarding judgments, general statements about, especially, the common elements in our lives – in traditional working-class life about the origin and meaning of the fear of booze, about the sense of family cohesiveness, about the Them and Us nature of the world outside, about a multitude of other such patterned assumptions which make up the elaborate fabric of experience. To generalise about them is strange and can be disconcerting.

It is in keeping that talk in most working-class homes, in factories, in pubs and working-men's clubs, should be almost entirely anecdotal or, where it is not anecdotal, should run on the tramlines of received, unchallenged and untroubling conventional opinion. So for that matter, as I keep saying, does most middle-class conversation. Summarising, reflective habits are rare in most areas of society – and are the greatest single gain for a working-class child, or a child from a conventional middle-class home, who manages to make the break. There are some homes in all parts of society who do not fit this pattern though they are, in the nature of the terms offered there, rarer in working-class homes than in middle-class. That is obvious and to deny it – as do some liberated people who find the recognition worrisome – is to limit understanding which may lead to change.

The above are practical and relatively simple problems when you are thinking about what items to use and how to present them; the important decisions are much harder to make. The overwhelming and ever-present question is: how do I know that this particular anecdote is 'telling', is different from that other which seems no more than an anecdote, amusing or sad though it may be. 'Telling' events have the habit of floating up and presenting themselves as just that; you feel you know them and their worth the moment you see them. But that may indicate something about you and your needs and have no larger meaning to a reader. It is part of your job so to present them that the reader does sense a larger meaning; or says – 'I see what you are trying to show but am not convinced. To me this is only an anecdote. Your duck is a duck and you can't make it into a swan by over-stressing it.'

When similar images begin to cluster so that, for the first time, you see common qualities in them, you feel surer of each one's force for you and of the greater collective force of the group. Writing, again in the first book of this sequence, about my childhood I remembered that the elementary school headmaster, chagrined that I had failed the scholarship examination at eleven, took one of my essays to the offices of the Leeds Education Department and invited the relevant officer to reconsider, to admit that this boy was 'bright'. Obviously this was an important moment, one that helped change the course of a life.

Even though I did well in the 'Matriculation' examination at sixteen I might have left grammar school then and become a clerk, if it had not been for the brilliantly explanatory intervention of the Board of Guardians visitor talking to my grandmother. Another points-switching moment. Later, a remark by the headmaster of the grammar school suddenly opened my mind to both the excitement of abstract thought and the many meanings of the word 'culture' when you are studying a society. Not a physical switch but a mental; yet no less a key moment. Last, in this little bundle, at Leeds University Bonamy Dobrée set off a number of controlled explosions designed to open the minds of those few he had decided were promising in more than the usual ways.

I have listed all these because taken together they make the point about 'clustering'. They occurred at widely different points in my early life, and only quite well on in writing about that life did I realise not simply that they were each interesting in themselves but that, seen together, they made another and more important thematic point. They are all examples of timely leg-ups; they show that much of the progress of my life was decided, stage by stage, by the helpful intervention, the willingness to act beyond the call of duty, of a succession of 'outsiders'. Plainly, they thought there might be something in this boy which if developed might get him out of the narrow life he had been born into. Yet they might not have bothered; or I might not have met them or others like them; so there seems to be an element of luck in it all. Or will there almost always be someone of that sort for young people of that sort?

Such is the larger-scale stuff of this kind of exploration. The smaller-scale material, the individual visual and verbal elements of the tale, also tend to float up so that you can take hold of them, with no advance warning and no 'trigger' you can identify. They too seem simply to be 'given', though I suspect that, further back than we can usually reach, they have been born out of connections, similarities, associations, all working together like yeast. Why did I suddenly 'know' that the image, a sort of snapshot, of an old widower or bachelor with a little dog on a lead, making his choice at Woolworth's pick-and-mix counter, held much of the essence of old, lonely, working-class life?

I had remembered for over half a century my first sight of a girl's breasts, my cousin Winnie's as she washed at the kitchen sink. But only when after all that time I wrote about the incident, in *A Local Habitation*, did I find myself moving out to make a generalisation about the shape of breasts and their likely relation to social class. That was not at all intended until it began to appear on the page. Nor was a paragraph about the realisation, inspired by the memory of a remote aunt, that the ability to make a home look homely or a meal taste tasty seems to depend on a certain kind of *nous* which some women do not have and either cannot or do not wish to pick up.

I wanted to describe our widowed mother's face in all its sick, poverty-stricken greyness. Piling up adjectives is a second-best. Then I remembered one thing which seemed at first slightly shocking; but which very quickly was right, what I had been hoping for. It was that the lines on her face were etched with dirt, the residue of years of snatched washes under a cold tap with cheap soap. This was the very image of that kind of poverty.

There were other such instances: as that shoes – the condition of them, the shapes of them and what those shapes said – loomed much larger in our lives than I had suspected, second only to bare knees; and the haunting, shaming importance of shiny suits for men who are aspiring to get out via white-collar jobs – suits had to be worn but they had to be cheap and went shiny quickly, the uniform of those who know they are trapped. Nor, as I said earlier, had I fully realised before writing this book how strong and varied was the place of Woolworth's in the daily drama of working-class lives; that only became clear as the references accumulated.

Most difficult of all to trace to their sources are individual metaphors. I now understand why I harked back to Woolworth's in the following metaphor; I do not know how the metaphor itself came to be formed. It was about Aunt Ethel, who had a constant urge to start fierce family arguments. I found myself saying that in this she was as driven as a kleptomaniac in Woolworth's; and of Aunt Annie, that in old age her mind flowed and spilled out all over like a busted corset (the initial memory is plain there too; it is of cheap, heavily-boned corsets – but that does not explain how the link came about); and the flat-footed uncle by marriage, Jack Birtle, who when slightly drunk moved about the house with excessive carefulness, as if he was walking over broken Christmas decorations in his stocking feet. Plainly, the decorations would have come from Woollie's. I see I have used a similar image in the previous chapter here, vulnerable feet walking on a nasty surface; that too just appeared. It is easy to invent an alternative – like crossing a ravine on a tightrope, like crossing a flimsy bridge over a torrent, like edging round a shallow ledge above a ravine – but they are willed and don't click in the same way as the images which come up of their own accord, sometimes more than once.

The greatest surprise of all has been the power of some scenes to rise from the recesses of memory as fresh as if they had happened yesterday. Each marked a new page in emotional understanding – seeing the act of sex for the first time in all its violence and receptivity; or being near a pair of southern, middle-class, young women whose whole air and manner breathed a life liberated beyond anything girls in Hunslet were likely to know. These were experiences of the early teens.

Most moving and incomprehensible of all have been two or three moments, no more in a whole life, in which I seemed to move outside myself and see the world, life, time spinning on its axis; not disconcertingly but peacefully. One such apprehension came at about eleven or twelve years old, as I sat alone on my grandmother's front steps; the other was half a century later, at Aunt Annie's deathbed. No discoveries in this many-years-long attempt to recapture memories has been more unexpected or, I now think without knowing why, more worthwhile. Touches of Traherne:

> The corn was orient and immortal wheat, which never should be reaped, nor was ever sown. I thought it had stood from everlasting to everlasting. The dust and the stones of the street were as precious as gold; the gates were the end of the world. The green trees when I saw them first through one of the gates transported and ravished me, their

sweetness and unusual beauty made my heart to leap, and almost mad
with ecstasy, they were such strange and wonderful things . . . Boys and
girls tumbling in the street, and playing, were moving jewels. I knew not
that they were born and should die; but all things abided eternally as
they were in their proper places. Eternity was manifest in the Light of
the Day and something infinite beyond everything appeared . . .

Recovering memories, selecting some, rejecting others, making up
the principles of inclusion or exclusion in a largely *ad hoc* way,
being led on trails you never expected by the insistence of memories
you never expected – the whole business sometimes seems a sort of
confection or concoction, a construction made from the old rope
and orange boxes at the back of your mental garret. Left to itself,
the thing would be like an overfull string bag with objects poking
out on all sides; or like a rickety shed with no evident principle
holding it together, to prevent it from simply falling apart.

Underneath, the procedure is not so casual. When it seems to be
working well, your mind is like a magnet you own but do not
control, and all the memories iron filings. As you work over the
material it sets itself into shapes, patterns, you had not intended or
known; it makes links which do not look forced, because they have
their principles of order. Similarly, particular paragraph openings
often propose themselves as the right links between stories,
anecdotes, elements – thematic links, which show themselves even
as your fingers reach for the keys.

3

Things do not always work well; you are more often beset by the
barrage of material. It is easier to stick tight to the chronological
line: 'I was born in Muswell Hill on a fine June day of 1910, the
14th. My mother, I was told, had a hard labour of it' . . . right
through to the twilight glow. But a Life and Times should have
more shape than that. Not a phoney shape, though there are many
of those, but a shape which emerges from the material as you go
along. A shape proper to itself. I do not claim to have found that,
but I have become aware as the record has unrolled of some
elements of a pattern in the carpet.

Elements such as these help define what it is you are writing about below the level you intend. As usual, readers may see more of the pattern than you do. One reader asked: 'Did you know when you began that a main theme of your story would be language, the way it still carries much of the meaning of your early life; and how today it is increasingly detached from roots like those or any other particular cultural roots, is manipulated for all of us from outside?' I knew this to be true when she said it, having had some sense of it when certain words held me up, made me stay with them until the weight of their meanings had become clearer. Usually they were words which are little used nowadays; they have faded with the culture for which they were markers. Such a word is 'shabby': that spoke of insistent working-class fears of the loss of respectability; you knew your clothes had the built-in certainty of early shabbiness. Happily, the word is much less known to children today and where it is known cannot usually carry all the implications of its old uses, its indications of much in the terms of life for you and most people around you. Two or three days before I wrote this, a faded black and white 'snap' came through the post. Me with two other boys at about twelve years old; they were the nephews of a friend of one of my aunts. They wore the white shirts and grey-flannel shorts of lower middle-class children on holiday. I wore a jacket so indeterminate in colour, so ill put together, so plainly made of 'shoddy', so 'shabby', that for a moment it made me feel twelve again.

About the language of modern consumption – consumption of goods, of fashions, of opinions, of instant politics – it is harder to speak because that ground has been so well-trodden; but to so little effect, with so little increase in comprehension. Yet one goes on, recording the changing fashions and trying to pin down their meanings, what they indicate of changes in our attitudes to each other. Noting that today if you are against 'development' (exploitation of land for profit) you are 'in a time-warp'; and that, though 'senior citizen' is an insensitive invention which no civilised body should use, few people object to it. It's mildly releasing to get such criticisms off your chest, but you know you are spitting against the wind, trying to draw on the currency of a bank which has gone out of business. I find myself reaching too often for words which suggest a still-available range of moral judgments – words such as 'decent', or 'texture' (as against the 'threadbare' and 'thin', or the 'shallow', in habits and attitudes). Language as telltale gesture: this book is scattered, I see on rereading, with words and phrases such as 'exemplary', 'emblematic', 'focus' (so as to find the meaning behind), 'live with', 'accommodate' and their near-synonyms (putting together elements against the collapse of a sense of meaning) and, inevitably, 'losing the language' – for talking about judgments of value. It is a back-door method.

Some years ago, in a grocer's shop in the Scottish Highlands, we heard a salesman for packeted soups making a linguistically and humanly horrendous sales pitch – special offers, discounts, 'promotional' presentations. After a while the grocer, a tall, elder-of-the-kirk build of man, stopped the Glaswegian flow and said, in a manner as measured as his pronouncement demanded, 'Young man, give me no more of your inducements. Show me your goods and I will tell you if I will buy.' Only one word of more than one syllable, to give a judgment of a type and force that salesman had probably never heard before on his rounds, and almost certainly could not understand, could not afford to understand if he was to continue in his trade. The grocer seemed even then a representative of a dying species.

The second main thematic thread in my own writing of this kind has proved to be Time, but specifically not chronological time. I had long had at the back of my mind, without feeling the need to examine it, Eliot's 'If all time is eternally present . . .' As this record has developed, that line has become more relevant. This is by far the most important reason why a chronological procedure simply will not do. You are at all moments the boy, the elderly man, the middle-aged man, the youth just setting out; you constantly shuttle between them all as events stir memory. Yet at the very beginning of the attempt to get on to paper something of all this which had been nagging for many years – it was by now the early Eighties – I knew there would have to be a sort of chronological thread. It would have been perverse to do otherwise, since one main aim is to show how a movement through different parts of society was bound up with the various stages of education; education at different levels was one of the most important levers of change as life moved along. So: chronology to some extent. And also because that principle reinforced the appearance, as proved necessary, of recurrent themes – such as the nature of 'ordinariness' and 'obscurity' – and still allowed the insertion of wholly thematic chapters which owed nothing to chronology; especially the more directly personal chapters.

But not a beginning at day one; that would have been, right at the start, against the sense of all time being eternally present (though I did not then borrow that poetic way of putting it to myself). At the time, my Aunt Annie, the last of her generation, was very ill in Leeds. I was on a London bus and not actually thinking about the proposed first book of this series when one short sentence floated into my mind: 'My Aunt Annie is dying in St James's Hospital.' I knew immediately that would be the opening sentence and that quite soon after, no more than a couple of pages, I would go back more than half a century to the day Aunt Annie saw me at eight years old cross her mother's threshold, newly orphaned; and that the story of the years before, of the three of us with our mother, would find its place in a later chapter. Then I wondered whether such an opening might seem a fanciful way to arrest attention so, characteristically, aimed in the second sentence to head-off that impression. I could not give up the first sentence.

There are smaller ways in which a record of this sort may find its own cohesion, the shape proper to itself. Again, not through conscious planning; echoes offer themselves to you in the very process of writing; repetitions demand to be made; you find yourself harking back more than once to events which have now assumed a more exemplary importance than you had imagined. But those two – the sense of language as the bearer of layers of meanings about the cultures you have moved and are moving through, and the sense of Time, of all the times you have known, being held in the palm of your hand – those two are the strongest of all the sustaining strands of the narrative. From them there may come, if you are lucky, an enhanced sense of the power and importance of language itself to all our doings, and an enhanced sense of our own fragility and temporality. We are not then exactly possessed by death; we are much more aware of it than before, as people fall off one by one from the ranks on what is now seen as a not very Long March.

But we have to come back again, finally, to the question of the relation of such a story to the 'truth'. That relation is at the best only partial. You may try very hard to be 'truthful', to have your eyes as open as possible; but in the end you are creating a scenario you can live with, even if it proves to be a horror story. Dr Johnson was nodding when he said: 'The writer of his own life has at least the first qualification of an historian, the knowledge of truth.' That's a qualification many of those who observe the writer may have, more than he has.

Rémy de Gourmont was nearer the mark when he said: 'The whole effort of a sincere man' – though I am uneasy about that 'sincere' – 'is to erect his personal impressions into universal laws.' Well, to offer them as, yet again, in some ways 'exemplary'. A reader can refuse a larger 'meaning' to any incident, can say, 'It's interesting, amusing, quite nicely described, and I can see why you want to give it that force. But actually – no; it has no further meaning or importance; there is no overall "truth" or "universality" in the tale you have told.' And you have nothing further to say in justification. But you go on writing.

INDEX

Adam, Ronald, 60
Adams, Henry, 206, 208
Administrative Staff College, 77
Advisory Council for Adult and Continuing Education (ACACE), 125-6, 137
Alcott, A. B., (epigraph), 71
Alkit (outfitters), 15
Annie, Aunt, 217, 221
Army Bureau of Current Affairs (ABCA), 59 et seq., 74, 75,
Arnold, Matthew, 79
Arts Council of Great Britain, 10, 59, 104
Auden, W. H., 67, 84, 131, 138-9, 157; *Another Time*, 67,
Auden: An Introductory Essay (book by R. H.), 67, 86-9, 128, 138-9, 198, 199; *see also W. H. Auden*

Bacon, Francis, (epigraph), 173
Bagehot, Walter, (epigraphs), 1, 71
Banff (Alberta, Canada), seminar at, 110-11
Baxter, Major B., 53-6
BBC (British Broadcasting Corporation), 90, 138-40, 155, 158, 199
Bench of Magistrates (essay by R. H.), 86
Bennett, Arnold, 191
Bennett, Joan, 112
Beveridge Report, 60
Birtle, J., 217

Blackmur, R. P., 104
Boyle, Edward, 136
Braine, John, 191
Brett, R. L., 146-7
British Broadcasting Corporation, *see* BBC
British Council, 73, 75, 114, 170, 177
Browning, Robert, 103
Butler Act, 60
Butler, Samuel, 186-7

Cameron, James, 109
Camus, Albert, 117; *The Outsider*, 32
'Cassandra' (Bill Connor), 68
Casson, Lewis, 10
Campaign for Nuclear Disarmament (CND), 196
Chase, James Hadley: *No Orchids for Miss Blandish*, 144-5
Chaucer, Geoffrey, (epigraph), 173
Chesterton, G. K., 203
Childe, Wilfred Rowland, 122-3
Churchill, Winston, 31, 61, 62, 75, 126
Clark, General Mark, 52
Cold War, 195-9
Colette, 185
Connor, Bill, *see* 'Cassandra'
Contemporary Cultural Studies, 95
Cooke, Dorian, 90
Council for the Encouragement of Music and the Arts (CEMA), 10
Crane, Muriel, 75, 116
Croce, Benedetto, 56-7

Daiches, David, 177
Day-Lewis, C., 87
Defence Studies, Royal College of, 158
Dine, Joe, 51-2
Dobrée, Bonamy, 8, 50, 86-7, 88, 137-8, 199, 215
Dostoevsky, Fyodor, 134, (epigraph) 175; *Brothers Karamazov*, 179, 182
Douglas, Keith, 41

Ealing comedies, 91
Eden, Anthony, 154-5
Eliot, T. S., 162, 163; *The Elder Statesman*, 203; *Four Quartets*, 10, 38, 91, (epigraph), 173, 220
ENSA troupe, visit, 39-40
Essays in Criticism, 141
Ethel, Aunt, 210-11, 217

Fairey family, 103
Faulkner, William: *Sanctuary*, 144
Fitzgerald, F. Scott, 191
Flaubert, Gustave: *Madame Bovary*, 131, 145
Fleming, Ian: *From Russia with Love*, 145
Forster, E. M.: *A Passage to India*, 51
Frankel, Charles, 162
Fraser, G. S., 88
Fyvel, T. R., 86, 140-1

Garbett, Cyril, 82
Gielgud, John, 115-16
Gourmont, Rémy de, 222
Grandmother, 210-11
Green, Ernest, 64
Greene, Graham (essay on, by R. H.), 141
Guardians, Board of, (Leeds), 215

Hamlet, see Shakespeare, W.
Hartley, Jean, 98
His Majesty's Inspectors (H. M. I.), 124, 126
Hoggart, Molly, 16
Hoggart, Tom, 16

Holocaust, the, 197
Hudson, Kenneth, 139
Humphreys, A. R., 120
Huxley, Aldous: 'The Farcical History of Richard Greenow', 145

James, Henry, 161, 162
Jarrell, Randall, 157
Jessop, Tom, 73
Johnson, Samuel, 207, 222

Keyes, Sydney (essay on, by R. H.), 67
Kilvert, Francis, 103
Klingender, F. D., 142
Koestler, Arthur, 91
Korean War, 197-9

Labour Government of 1945, 62, 77, 91
Lanyon, Peter, 55
Larkin, Philip, 92, ch. 5, *passim*; (epigraph) ix; *The Less Deceived*, 98
Lawrence, D. H., 91; *Lady Chatterley's Lover*, 112; *Women in Love*, 84
Leavis, F. R., 88, 206; *Scrutiny*, 88
Leavis, Q. D., 134-5, 141; *Fiction and the Reading Public*, 134
Leicester, University of, 119, 120
Lewis, C. S., 135
Lewis, John, Partnership, 74
London School of Economics (LSE), 89

Manchester Guardian, 86
Mansbridge, A., 93-4
Marvell Press, 98
Mayfield, G. E. T., chs. 4, 5, 6, 7 *passim*
Mendelson, Edward, 157
Morgan, A. E., 114
Morris, Charles, 111
Morris, Philip, 61, 111
Mountbatten, Lord, 30-1, 155
Murry, J. Middleton, 91

Nicholson, J. H., ch. 5 *passim*, 147

Open University, 136

Orwell, George, 86, 91, 135, 141

Penguin Books (and its ancillaries), 9, 10, 59, 104, 134
Poetry Review, 67
Pound, Ezra, 135
Princeton University, visit to, 170
Public Library Reading Room (essay by R. H.), 86

Railway Station Bookstalls (essay by R. H.), 86
Raybould, Sydney G., chs. 5 and 6 *passim*
Reckitt and Colman's, 98, 150-1
Richards, I. A.: *Interpretation in Teaching*, 130
Robbins Report, 146
Rochester (N. Y.), University of, ch. 7 *passim*
Roosevelt, Franklin D., 31

San Carlo Opera Company, 52-3
Scarfe, Francis: *W. H. Auden*, 87
Scrutiny, see under Leavis, F. R.
Searls, T. H., 114
Sedgwick, Fred, 113
Seth, James, Lectureship, 111-12
Shakespeare, William, 38, 66, 205; *Hamlet*, 131-2; *King Lear*, 134
Shaw, G. B., 65, 130
Shaw, Roy, 92, 119, 125, 126
Shonfield, Andrew, 50-1, 58, 67, 138
Shute, Nevil: *On the Beach*, 196-7
Suez, invasion of, 154-5, 196

Tawney, R. H., 93 *et seq.*, 126
Temple, William, 93 *et seq.*
Thompson, E. P., 92, 132; *The Making of the English Working Class*, 96
Thompson, George, 113
Thorndike, Sybil, 10
Three Arts Club, 53 *et seq.*, 75

Toynbee, Arnold: *A Study of History*, 91
Traherne, Thomas, 217-18
Tribune, 86, 140-1
Trilling, Diana, 168-9
Trilling, Lionel, 90, 91, 205
Turgenev, Ivan, (epigraph), 175; *Fathers and Sons*, 182
Turnbull, Violet, 128

UNESCO, 165, 180-1
Universities, new, 90, 146
Use of English, 140
Uses of Literacy, The (by R. H.), chs. 4, 5, 6, 8, 9 *passim*, 170

Vines, Sherard, 145-6

Wadsworth, A. P., 86
Waller, Robert, 139
Waugh, Evelyn, 104; *Brideshead Revisited*, 59
W. H. Auden (British Council booklet by R. H.), 170
Williams, Raymond, 92, 126, 135; *Culture and Society*, 96
Williams, W. E., 59 *et seq.*
Wilson, F. P., 65, 66
Winnipeg, (Manitoba, Canada), seminar at, 110
Woolf, Leonard, 143
Woolf, Virginia, 191
Woolworth's, 188-9, 216-17 and *passim*
Wordsworth, William: *The Prelude*, 132
Worker's Educational Association (WEA), 64, chs. 4 and 5 *passim*, 126, 129

Yeats, W. B., 159-60

Z Reserve, 197-9